Negotiating Empire in the Middle East

In the early 1840s, Ottoman rulers launched a new imperial project, partly in order to reassert their authority over their lands and subjects, crucially including the Arab nomads. By examining the evolution of this relationship between the Ottoman Empire and Arab nomads in the modern era, M. Talha Çiçek puts forward a new framework to demonstrate how negotiations between the Ottomans and the Arab nomads played a part in making the modern Middle East. Reflecting on multiple aspects of Ottoman authority and governance across Syria, Iraq, Arabia, Transjordan and along their frontiers, Çiçek reveals how the relationship between the imperial centre and the nomads was not merely a brutal imposition of a strict order, but instead one of constant, complicated, and fluid negotiation. In so doing, he highlights how the responses of the nomads made a considerable impact on the ultimate outcome, transforming the imperial policies accordingly.

M. TALHA ÇIÇEK is Associate Professor of History at Istanbul Medeniyet University. Formerly the British Academy's Newton Fellow at SOAS University of London, and Humboldt Experienced Research Fellow at Leibniz-Zentrum Moderner Orient, he is the author of *War and State Formation in Syria: Cemal Pasha's Governorate during World War I* (2014).

T0372740

Negotiating Empire in the Middle East

Ottomans and Arab Nomads in the Modern Era, 1840–1914

M. TALHA ÇİÇEK
Istanbul Medeniyet University

CAMBRIDGE
UNIVERSITY PRESS

Shaftesbury Road, Cambridge CB2 8EA, United Kingdom

One Liberty Plaza, 20th Floor, New York, NY 10006, USA

477 Williamstown Road, Port Melbourne, VIC 3207, Australia

314–321, 3rd Floor, Plot 3, Splendor Forum, Jasola District Centre, New Delhi – 110025, India

103 Penang Road, #05–06/07, Visioncrest Commercial, Singapore 238467

Cambridge University Press is part of Cambridge University Press & Assessment, a department of the University of Cambridge.

We share the University's mission to contribute to society through the pursuit of education, learning and research at the highest international levels of excellence.

www.cambridge.org
Information on this title: www.cambridge.org/9781108995382

DOI: 10.1017/9781108993852

First published 2021
First paperback edition 2023

A catalogue record for this publication is available from the British Library

ISBN   978-1-316-51808-3   Hardback
ISBN   978-1-108-99538-2   Paperback

To my dear beloved, Öznil

Contents

Figures

Maps

Acknowledgements

A large number of persons and institutions have supported this project over the years. First and foremost, I would like to thank my colleague, friend and teacher, Benjamin Fortna, whose extremely generous support enabled the writing of this book. He also read the whole manuscript and made authoritative comments which I will always appreciate. Eugene Rogan was also kind enough to read previous versions of my text and make constructive comments. I am very indebted to him. My thanks also to William G. Clarence-Smith and Yorgos Dedes, who hosted me at SOAS and shared their experience with me when my initial co-applicant Ben Fortna moved to the University of Arizona. I am also very thankful to M. Şükrü Hanioğlu for his guidance and invaluable advice with his broad knowledge at critical times.

The realization of this project was made possible by the support of two important institutions. I applied to the British Academy for a two-year Newton postdoctoral fellowship. Without the academy's widespread research opportunities, this book would not have been produced. Therefore, I would also like to thank them very much. The Turkish Academy of Science (TÜBA) also supported the project, for which I am indebted to them.

Istanbul Medeniyet University was my professional home during the writing of this book. My superiors M. İhsan Karaman, Gülfettin Çelik, Mustafa Cicekler and Ahmet Cihan deserve special thanks for facilitating the tricky issues of university bureaucracy. My head of department Hayrunnisa Alan and her successor Turhan Kaçar generously tolerated my long-lasting absence from the department for research. I will always remember their kindness. A very special thanks also to my glorious dean, the wonderful İhsan Fazlioglu, whose strong backing always motivated me to complete this study. I am very indebted to my friend İsmail Hakkı Kadı for his friendship. Special thanks are due to Erhan Berat Fındıklı, Fatih

Durgun, Zahit Atçıl Oğuz Yarlıgaş and Selim Karahasanoğlu for their friendship and conversation.

Many friends and colleagues have been kind enough to offer suggestions, material, criticism and support along the way. Y. Hakan Erdem, my lifetime teacher, has read the whole manuscript and pointed out the crucial aspects. My long-suffering friend, Abdurrahman Atçıl, gave invaluable support at various phases of my research and publication process. Zeynep Çelik, Selim Karlıtekin and Alim Arlı read the embryonic version of the book when it was a research proposal and constructively commented on it. Kenan Yıldız and Bilgin Aydın provided material support at critical times. I will always remain indebted to them. Ayhan Aktar, Mehmet Ö. Alkan, Selim Deringil, Tariq Tell, the late Roger Owen, Abdulhamid Kırmızı, Yunus Uğur, Hala Fattah, Faisal Husain, the late Richard Lawless, Feridun Emecen, İbrahim Şirin, David Motadel, Nader Sohrabi, Tufan Buzpınar, Gökhan Çetinsaya, Engin Deniz Akarlı, Gagan Sood, Hasan Kayalı and Stefan Winter listened to my ideas and made thought-provoking comments on them. I am thankful to them for wasting their valuable time for me. I have spent wonderful times in conversation with Sebahaddin Abdurrahman and Cumhur Bekar in the beautiful gardens of London and it is my pleasure to thank them. I have had the opportunity to discuss my arguments with the valuable friends at Leibniz-Zentrum Moderner Orient during my stay as the Humboldt Experienced Researcher. I particularly owe thanks to the wonderful colleagues and friends Ulrike Freitag, Katharina Lange, Steven Serels and the members of the Environment and Justice Research Group. Newcastle University Library was very kind to grant copyrights of photos from Gertrude Bell Collection. I am very indebted to them.

I cannot find an appropriate word to appreciate the contribution of my two beautiful flowers, Ayşe Serra and Fatma Hale, who have grown up with this book and become wonderful colours of our life. They had to sleep in airports and play in the gardens of archive buildings in their father's pursuit of knowledge. My beloved wife, Öznil, had to bear the most painful processes with me. I dedicate this book to her invaluable friendship and being my better half.

Note to the Reader

It is always an issue for the historians of the Middle East to transliterate the Ottoman Turkish and Arabic terms. In this book, with a few minor exceptions, I followed the Modern Turkish transliteration to minimize the problematic distortion of the Ottoman era pronunciation – for example – 'Mehmed', not 'Mehmet' or 'Muhammad'. For the Arabic terms, the *International Journal of Middle East Studies* transliteration system is employed. For well-known place names, I use English and the transliteration from Turkish or Arabic depending on the common language of each place: Istanbul, not İstanbul; Hawran, not Havran; but Deir al-Zor, not Der Zor. The names of the tribes are transliterated with reference to the most common usage in English; Anizah, not Anazeh or Anazee; but Wuld 'Ali, not Walad 'Ali.

Abbreviations

A.AMD	Sadaret Amedi
A.MKT	Sadaret Mektubi
A.MKT.MHM	Sadaret Mektubi Mühimme
A.MKT.MVL	Sadaret Mektubi Meclis-i Vala
A.MKT.UM	Sadaret Mektubi Umumi
BEO	Bab-ı Ali Evrak Odası
C.DH	Cevdet Dahiliye
C.ML	Cevdet Maliyet
DH.EUM.EMN	Dahiliye Emniyet-i Umumiye Emniyet Şubesi
DH.İ.UM	Dahiliye İdare-i Umumiye
DH.İD	Dahiliye İrade Dahiliye
DH.MKT	Dahiliye Mektubi
DH.MUİ	Dahiliye Muhaberat-ı Umumiye
DH.SYS	Dahiliye Siyasi
DH.ŞFR	Dahiliye Şifre
DH.TMIK	Dahiliye Tesri-i Muamelat ve Islahat Komisyonu
HR.TO	Hariciye Tercüme Odası
İ.DH	İrade Dahiliye
İ.ML	İrade Maliye
İ.MMS	İrade Meclis-i Mahsusa
İ.MVL	İrade Meclis-i Vala
İ.ŞD	İrade Şura-yı Devlet
İD	İrade Dahiliye
MF.MKT	Maarif Mektubi
MV	Meclis-i Vükela
MVL	Meclis-i Vala
ŞD	Şura-yı Devlet
Y.MTV	Yıldız Mütenevvi Maruzat
Y.PRK.ASK	Yıldız Perakende Evrakı Askeri Maruzat

Introduction

In 1906, Homer Davenport, an American who had been deeply interested in the Arab horse for many years, planned a journey from the United States to Syria to obtain Arab mares and stallions of absolute purity of blood that he could trace as coming from the Anizah Bedouin, whose pure-bred horses had worldwide recognition. It was not, however, easy to obtain permission from the Ottoman authorities as the imperial government forbade the exportation of Arab horses. He appealed to President Theodore Roosevelt for help and was granted an endorsement letter, with which he applied to the Ottoman embassy and an *İrade* was issued by the Sultan permitting him to export 'six or eight' mares from the Ottoman Empire. Davenport immediately set off on his journey and arrived in Istanbul, from where he took the road for Syria. In Antioch, the vice-consulate assigned an interpreter to him and they departed for Aleppo where they were to meet Ahmed Hafız, an Anizah sheikh and the political and commercial agent of the tribe settled in the city for thirty years who was described by the governor of Aleppo 'as the smartest and shrewdest Bedouin that the Ottoman Empire had ever known'.[1] Davenport's intention was to finish his trip in Deir al-Zor on the Euphrates where he might be sure of purchasing horses from the Anizah themselves. Firstly, they visited the bazaar in Aleppo to buy 'saddles and bridles, and horse trimmings which were used in the desert'. Hundreds of Bedouin were available in the town market for shopping. They also came across an Anizah tribesman in the bazaar who informed them that the Anizah were within ten hours' ride of Aleppo. Shortly after that they fell in with another Anizah, who told them that Hajim Bey Ibn Mheid, the paramount sheikh of all Anizah tribes, was then in Aleppo paying a visit to Ahmed Hafız. The Bedouin offered to take them to Ahmed Hafız, which meant that they could buy

---

[1] Davenport, *My Quest*, 185.

1

their horses directly from the Anizah tribe itself. 'It was no longer a question of going to Deyr [sic].'[2]

Ahmed Hafız told them that Hajim Bey 'had been his guest for ten days, but had gone the night before, back to his tribe, which was encamped at a distance of ten or twelve hours' ride'. Prior to Davenport's visit, Hafız had been informed about the *İrade* 'from the Sultan of Turkey, and letters from the one Great Sheikh of all the Americ[a] tribes', meaning President Roosevelt.[3] Then, Ahmed Hafız took them to the governor Nazım Pasha and, on their way, they came across the Anizah tribesmen who showed respect to Hafız and kissed his hand in joy. The pasha presented Davenport with the best horse in the desert called 'the Pride of the Desert' gifted to him by Hajim Bey and the latter, in return, sent a cheque as a 'present' for 100 French pounds. Following that, Davenport and his translator started their trip in the desert to find the purest-bred of the Anizah horses accompanied by Ahmed Hafız whose presence, according to Davenport, 'was more than an army' in terms of protection.[4] It seems that it was possible for them to buy horses from the bazaar in Aleppo as the Anizah horses were also sold there, but the desert presumably contained the best quality, which might attract the traveller. They peacefully visited many Bedouin encampments between the vicinity of Aleppo and Deir al-Zor including the Seb'a, Gomussa and Fid'an, met their sheikhs, visited the *mutasarrıf* of Deir al-Zor and the members of his administrative council together with some of the Anizah sheikhs and bought the best horses of different kinds from the Anizah sheikhs themselves. Hafız bargained with all the sheikhs on behalf of his guests and persuaded them to consent to a reasonable price, which most likely comprised part of his mission. The sheikhs, including the paramount sheikh Hajim, put their seals on the pedigree of the horses they sold, which was very important as proof of the horses' purity. When they reached the limits set by the Sultan, they returned to Aleppo and Davenport returned to the United States together with the horses he had bought.

* * *

Davenport's account sheds light on many aspects of the empire-nomads' relations in the Arab lands during the modern era and challenges many theories produced about them. A senior Anizah

---

[2] Ibid., 79.   [3] Ibid., 81.   [4] Ibid., 94.

representative living in Aleppo and mediating the political and commercial deals of the tribe and tribesmen walking on the streets of the city may even be surprising for those scholars with an expertise in the Ottoman Arab Middle East. It is also striking that the Anizah's paramount sheikh visited Aleppo and stayed there for ten days because he was usually supposed not to have such sophisticated relations with the Ottoman officials. This account shows the strength of the nomadic ties with imperial authorities and the high-level interactions between the urban and the desert spaces, which undermine the prevailing theories that assume an eternal 'state-tribe' conflict and subordination of the tribal communities by the government during the Ottoman modernization. The story may also be interesting as it challenges the 'civilized-nomad' contrast which is supposed to shape the empire-city-tribe relations in the nineteenth century.

This account, however, is only a partial manifestation of the empire-tribe partnership that was established and ripened during the nineteenth century, which the present book analyses. Focusing on the making of this partnership together with its influence on tribal governance, this book analyses the emergence and evolution of the specific strategies and policies employed by the Ottoman Empire to govern, shape and control the Shammar and Anizah confederations in the nineteenth century dispersed across Anatolia, Syria, Mesopotamia, Hijaz and Najd, which resulted in their integration into the regional, imperial and global networks by protecting their tribal structures and the lands they used in the desert and the imperial domains. The key questions it explores are how the empire treated Bedouin tribes under its sovereignty during the imperial modernization initiative, how these tribes reacted to Ottoman policies throughout the Tanzimat, Hamidian and Young Turk periods and how they came to a point of compromise, which defined the empire-tribe relations in many regions for a long time and determined the ultimate outcome.

In the early 1840s, the Ottoman rulers launched a new imperial project – the Tanzimat reforms – to reassert their authority over their lands and subjects which by all accounts produced new socio-political conditions. Their primary purpose was to establish a harmonious centralized bureaucracy to circumscribe the influence wielded by local, secondary and autonomous actors. Collecting taxes regularly and providing security to the imperial lands were considered an indispensable precondition of the maintenance of a centralized state. The nomads constituted a serious problem for the realization of these aims in many parts of the Arab countryside as they adopted a mobile lifestyle which made their control very difficult. In addition, they collected *khuwwa* taxes (the protection money paid to a tribal chief to shelter the peasants and caravans against other nomads and members of the protecting party) from the peasants of the empire and created a security problem due to their attacks on the caravans and settled regions, as well as fighting between themselves.

The Anizah and Shammar groups maintained a dominance in the great majority of the Syrian and Iraqi countryside and desert, and played an influential role in the social life and governance in the region from the end of the eighteenth century. According to one scholar, 'until the 1920s about two-thirds of what was to become the Syrian Republic was controlled by Bedouin, with the camel herders of the 'Anaza [sic] confederation as a hegemonic force among them'.[5] The nomadic domination over the Iraqi countryside and desert regions was no less in Syria.[6] Studying their relations with the Ottoman Empire in the modern age will therefore fill an important gap in the socio-political history of the Middle East, and will make a meaningful contribution to the social history of the region as well as the history of the nineteenth century.

This book argues that the late Ottoman period witnessed an unprecedented interaction of state and nomadic groups which evolved from conflict to reconciliation, with a focus on the Anizah and Shammar, the two largest nomadic confederations of the Arab east. The more the empire modernized, consolidated and expanded itself, the further both parties had to interact and negotiate for a cooperated co-existence. During the Tanzimat period the degree of cooperation was lower and not systematized, and state-tribe rivalry, tribal resistance and the imperial ambitions to dominate, subjugate and pacify the nomadic communities determined the nature of relations between the state and tribes in many places. With respect to their relatively late arrival in the region from the Najd and removing many peasants from their lands and villages to use these areas as pastures to their animals, the imperial authorities saw them as 'alien' to the region, considering the nomadic groups violators of regional order and obstacles to the proper taxation

---

[5] Büssow, 'Bedouin Historiography', 163.
[6] For a detailed description of the Shammar and Anizah branches in the Ottoman Iraqi provinces, see: Mehmed Hurşid Paşa, *Seyahatname*.

of the eligible subjects living in the regions due to their exaction of *khuwwa* and occasional raids. The nomads' domination itself constituted a question for the determined Ottoman modernizers. The nomads, on the other hand, considered the imperial expansion as detrimental to their interests as they grazed their animals in many areas in the Syrian and Iraqi countryside, and *khuwwa* that they collected from the peasants, agricultural tribes and caravans was a substantial source of income for them. Conflict between the two parties thus maintained itself for about three decades although short-term compromises were reached and tribes came with their flocks to the vicinity of the towns under the imperial control. The frequent violation of the compromise by both sides, however, prevented a final solution to the question. By the 1870s, contributed to by the increase of the Ottoman deployments in the desert frontier and the expansionist policies towards the desert, the systemic change was completed and collaboration between tribal chiefs and state authorities minimized the hostilities. Both sides had gradually reconciled on their rights, responsibilities and duties regarding grazing lands, city markets, *khuwwa*, tax collection, justice and regional security.

This should not, however, be considered as a unidirectional process which resulted in the extension and reinforcement of government authority against the tribal domination in the desert and other areas where the nomads frequented. The process was more complicated than a mere extension of state authority into the tribal areas and frontier regions. In the long run, the tribes also benefited from the process by at least making their temporary achievements – that stemmed from a regional power vacuum from late eighteenth to mid-nineteenth century – an established and compromised situation. First of all, only a small, and perhaps negligible, amount of the pasture lands could be colonized by the empire as agricultural lands: besides recognizing the tribal hierarchy and sheikhly authority in the desert and among the tribal societies of their fellow tribesmen in the regions such as Deir al-Zor and Hawran where the imperial bureaucratic rule was extended, the Ottoman government had to acknowledge and guarantee many of the nomadic privileges in the imperially dominated regions such as Aleppo, Hama, Damascus, Urfa, Mosul and Baghdad where a more or less uninterrupted Ottoman rule had continued for more than three centuries. The great majority of the 'agricultural lands' abandoned due to the Anizah and Shammar migrations at the end of the eighteenth and

early nineteenth century had to be presented to the tribesmen to be used
as grazing lands by their animals. For the sake of imperial recognition
and protection, in some regions, the allocated tribal pastures were also
secured from attacks and occupation by rival tribes.

In addition, the tribes were not exposed to the social engineering
projects of the modern state formation: while skilfully negotiated and
reconciled with the Ottoman government, sheikhs successfully protected the tribal structure, maintained the tribal hierarchy and solidarity, and did not open the way for the conversion of their fellow
tribesmen into ordinary imperial subjects as initially envisaged by the
Tanzimat statesmen which would supposedly enable the empire to
control tribesmen and desert space in a stricter and 'more effective'
way. As a newly emerging modern state, the Ottomans gave concessions to the tribes from their statehood by exempting them from their
duties against the state such as soldiering, and by being flexible about
the duties that the tribes had theoretically to perform as the subjects of
the sultan. Similarly, they did not conduct a census among the tribes
and did not know the number of tribal animals. However, some
Ottoman bureaucrats believed that, as in the example of the Cossacks
of the Russian Empire, putting all these policies into practice and
transforming the nomads into Ottomans would obviously increase
the imperial human and material resources in the process of modernization and would make the modernization project more effective.[7]

An important question here is whether not conscripting the nomads
or taking censuses of human and animal populations, and not levying
all the taxes they normally would have was worth the effort and
expense as long as the tribes remained mobile and hard to pin down
in those expanses of desert. To put it differently, the question that arises
here is about the authenticity of the concessions given by the empire.
Given the problems of the Ottoman modernization and post-Ottoman
experiences, it seems that the proper taxation of the nomads, their
education in the Ottoman institutions and conscription to the
Ottoman army would definitely be worth it if the imperial authorities
could do it. The increase in number of the Ottoman soldiers by the
addition of the nomads – as achieved by Glubb Pasha during the

---

[7] For some thoughts by Subhi Pasha, a prominent Tanzimat statesman, on how the
nomads' contribution would increase Ottoman power as in the example of the
Russian Cossacks, see: FO 195/995, Damascus, 24 June 1872.

creation of modern Jordan – would not only multiply the effectiveness of the Ottoman army in the region, but also expotentially increase the tax amount collected from the whole region as it would enhance the capability of control for the government and minimize tax evasion. During the 1930s, Glubb Pasha both respected the tribal structure and established the strongest army in the region by conscripting the tribesmen into the Jordanian Army.[8]

It was such 'mutually concessive' attitudes that determined the state-tribe relations in the Arab Middle East, with both sides having to give concessions as well as taking advantage of them. Therefore, the present study identifies the state-tribe relations as a 'partnership' and argues that it became possible due to a constant 'politics of negotiation' by both sides over tribal responsibilities to the state and the government's concessions to be given to the tribes. The domination of one side over another (the state's subjugation, for instance, of the Anizah and Shammar) could not be possible. A sense of practical equality – although it was not an official and absolute equality – frequently determined the relations as tribal consent usually remained a precondition of successful government policies regarding the desert and its frontier. Government approval, on the other hand, enabled the nomads to sustain their mobility within the areas practically controlled by the imperial authority. A certain trust had been established between the two parties after the early 1870s as the tribes did not fear government troops' attacks and local officials were usually confident about tribal raids. The Ottoman government could not act against the nomads as they did against the other urban and peasant societies due to the tribal resistance. Therefore, the relations between the two parties were like 'mutual recognition'. The two parties respected each other's interests and, in this way, a reconciliation was arrived at. They also cooperated with each other for the establishment of regional peace which constituted an important aspect of the partnership. The key role here was played by the sheikhs and this is why I describe them as partners of the empire.

To sum up, the Ottomans were compelled to adopt a conciliatory attitude to 'solve the tribal question' and to incorporate them into the imperial system of governance as much as possible. There were further

---

[8] For an analysis on the creation of the Arab legion, see: Glubb, *The Story of the Arab Legion.*

local, imperial and global reasons for the empire to shift from 'coercion' to 'negotiation'. Locally, the new settlement undertakings (Chapter 2) and newly established administrations in the desert frontier such as Deir al-Zor, Karak, Ma'an and Hawran (Chapters 3 and 4) increased the necessity of developing good relations with the nomads. Imperially and globally, the Tanzimat ideology was abandoned and a more pragmatic policy was adopted due to changes in the global realm during the reign of Abdulhamid II: the Ottomans no longer had friendly relations with Great Britain due to the latter's occupation of Egypt and its increasing presence in the Persian Gulf which were interpreted by the Ottoman policymakers as a direct threat to their existence in the Arab lands. Therefore, during the Hamidian era, it became a necessity to please the autonomous power-holders in the region such as the nomads, not to cause their rapprochement with other imperial powers. A new notion of solidarity around the image of the caliph based on the idea of Muslim unity was developed and served the state-tribe rapprochement.

The tribes also found the reconciliation beneficial as it would guarantee a secure access for them to the imperial lands, which was crucial for the maintenance of a mobile livelihood, and would protect the pastures allocated to them from being occupied by their rivals. The expansion of the Ottoman rule into Deir al-Zor and the southernmost area of the province of Syria, and fortification of the desert frontier and caravan routes by the imperial army made reconciliation the most reasonable option for the tribes as raiding the villages was no longer a gainful and unrisky method. The maintenance of chaos would presumably have compelled the imperial authorities to make further military investments in the desert and its frontiers which would make their approach to the settled areas almost impossible.

In this regard, the present study examines the changes made to the initial imperial project to forcibly control the Bedouin, and the subsequent shift in imperial tribal policy from the 'coercive' ideal to a more 'conciliatory' practice by questioning state-centric paradigms regarding the nature of the Ottoman modernization, challenging the theses on state-society/tribe relations and discussing the results of the expansion of state authority in the desert and countryside. As such, it examines the negotiated compromise that emerged from the empire-tribe relationship, and the impact of such an accommodation on government measures such as taxation, settlement, justice, security and appointment of the tribal sheikhs. The state-tribe interaction not only affected government policies in the desert and countryside but shaped the whole Ottoman modernization enterprise and order of things in the Arab lands. The failure of the imperial attempts to colonize the desert space by either including or excluding the Shammar and Anizah from the Syrian and Iraqi pastures changed the direction of the Ottoman reforms as the imperial treasury was deprived of a substantial revenue source and human resource. This book therefore makes a very meaningful contribution to extend the scholarly perspectives trying to understand the nature of the Middle Eastern social and political transformations from the Ottoman times to the contemporary era by focusing on the negotiating aspect of the imperial policies due to the very existence of the Bedouin nomads.

Empires and Nomads: A Comparative Global-Imperial Perspective

The Ottomans were not the only imperial power in the modern age to attempt to impose its will on nomadic peoples. Other empires with significant nomadic populations embraced a *mission civilisatrice* ideology, forcibly displacing these groups through expansion and settlement policies. In the early nineteenth century, nomadic communities subsisted by breeding and farming animal flocks that stretched thousands of miles from 'the southern boundary of the Scandinavian-Siberian-Manchurian forest belt to the Himalayas, the highlands of Iran and Anatolia, and the Arabian Peninsula'. Nomads also occupied lands from the Volga, across swathes of Russia, almost as far as the gates to Beijing.[9] The bureaucratization of empires and improvements in the techniques of coercion opened the way to more effective control over nomads and their lifestyle. Mobile populations with tribal structures, living in rural and desert areas with a strong sense of group solidarity, showed stiff opposition to the imperial consolidation of power, and often compelled imperial authorities to rethink their methods. The tribes supported resistance movements and resisted the centralization efforts of colonial and traditional empires as well as imperial expansion into 'waste lands' to solve critical issues of burgeoning populations and bureaucratic expansion. Both these posed a fundamental threat to

[9] Osterhammel, *Transformation*, 356.

nomadic lifestyle as they co-opted land used by nomads for pasture of their animals. Force was the primary tool used by empires and enabled them to penetrate the tribal regions, but the tribes maximized the advantage of their mobility, easily escaping from the imperial offensives into the desert and mountainous areas and thereby resisting subjugation. The empires reacted by employing more effective methods. Some developed sophisticated techniques of inclusion and compromise such as negotiation, bargaining and mediation. As such, a 'middle ground' was established, 'in which negotiated compromises, temporary equilibria, and intertwined economic interests – sometimes also cultural or biological "hybridity" – developed between "natives" and "newcomers".'[10] Through these, the authorities sought to prevent tribal groups from violating the imperial order and to integrate them into the imperial system.

The British and Ottoman rulers conformed to this type as they usually adopted a policy of 'negotiated conciliation' towards the tribal groups. The British Empire's policies towards Indian tribes exemplify such an approach; colonial authorities respected tribal autonomy and attempted to win them over. As a result, tribes along India's north-west frontier did not feel threatened for a long time after the conquest of Punjab by the British troops. The imperial authorities adopted a policy of 'Masterly Inactivity', founded on respect for tribal lifestyle and autonomy. The colonial government forbade their civil and military officers to travel beyond the foothills into the mountains or passes where the tribal zones began, so as not to threaten the tribesmen. The concerns of the Pathans – the name given to the tribal society of the region – were always carefully addressed, and the British adopted a conciliatory stance in their dealings with them. They even offered a subsidy to some of the tribes in return for their cooperation.

The British-Russian struggle in the Great Game, however, compelled the British to embrace a forward policy in the 1890s that required the Indian government to move into the Pathans' territory. The Indian government signed an agreement with the amir of Afghanistan in 1897, determining their respective spheres of influence along a line that cut through the lands inhabited by the Pathans and neighbouring Balochistan. The two parties neglected to include the tribes in discussions, provoking a large-scale tribal revolt. Although the motivation

---

[10] Ibid., 323.

for the agreement was to counter Russian expansion towards India, the tribal communities felt seriously threatened by the British encroachment on their land. The imperial troops eventually emerged victorious, but at a substantial human cost and the mission certainly brought little peace. The Indian government adopted a friendly approach towards the rebels in a bid to appease the unrest. The tribal zones in the northwestern frontier were organized as a separate province under the rule of a chief commissioner who was directly accountable to the Indian colonial government. In addition, British and Indian troops deployed to the region were withdrawn to mollify the tribes. Additionally, as in the Ottoman case, local tribesmen were recruited to the police force to protect the more remote areas along the frontier. As such, the tribes were incorporated into the imperial system of security and governance.[11] As will be detailed in this book, the Ottomans adopted a similar method to incorporate the Bedouin into their imperial endeavour.

The second tactic employed by imperial authorities was excluding, which aimed to isolate the tribes as much as possible. The Russian and French empires both eliminated the tribal question by deliberately leaving nomads out of the imperial system and cutting them off from settled areas. As they were unable to completely disarm the nomadic groups, the Russians were initially forced to recognize the rights of the nomadic peoples of the steppe. Following their conquests, the Russian authorities did not impose new agricultural settlement projects on the tribal areas until the 1890s when several hundred thousand Russians emigrated from European Russia to Siberia. Subsequently, native Siberians were either forced to settle or were driven deeper into the forest. Despite this, they adhered to their nomadic traditions and the Russians did not force them to abandon them, perhaps an implicit acceptance of the tribes' way of life. The nomadic tribes of the Kazakh steppe had a similar experience: the region was still largely controlled by Kazakh nomads and, thus, deemed insecure by the imperial authorities as late as 1829 when Alexander von Humboldt travelled there. A substantial Cossack escort was provided for his journey between Orenburg and Orsk, a potentially treacherous route. The steppe was slowly incorporated into the Russian Empire in

---

[11] Simner, *Pathan Rising*; Mills, *The Pathan Revolt*; Barthorp and Anderson, *The Frontier Ablaze*.

the second half of the nineteenth century out of a desire not only to secure the region but also to convert the nomadic horsemen into farmers. The Kazakhs were also employed in the newly created administrative units. Subsequently, Ukrainian and Russian peasants migrated to the Kazakh steppe to cultivate the most fertile pastures in the northern part of the steppe. The indigenous nomads were meanwhile stopped from owning land by the Steppe Statute of 1891. A combination of the territorial administrative order, taxes and new land laws impeded the Kazakhs' mobility and compromised their economic system based on barter and pasture. As a result, a number of Kazakhs chose to settle. However, the majority remained loyal to the nomadic lifestyle and resisted the surveyors, administrators, soldiers and peasants. The Russian imperial enterprise failed to convert the Kazakh nomads into Russian subjects during the period covered by this study. Only in 1930 were they brutally coerced by Stalin into abandoning nomadism and settling.[12]

The French experience with the *Kabyles*, the Berbers and Bedouin of Algeria, was also comparable although the colonial authorities invested heavily to keep the nomads in check. Nomadic tribes constituted a significant proportion of Algeria's population and, in the early years of the French occupation, tribes from across the country provided considerable support to the tribally based and religiously legitimated revolt of Abd al-Qadir, who organized a systematic resistance against France and established a separate state that endured until the 1870s. Some others, who refused to join with Abd al-Qadir, sought protection from the French commanders during Abd al-Qadir's uprising. Abd al-Qadir's popularity among the tribes enabled him to conduct protracted negotiations and sign treaties with the French authorities. Tribal regions put up the stiffest resistance to the expansion of French colonial rule in Algeria. 'The most serious of all revolts in the period of "pacification" broke out in Kabylia in 1871' and spread to eastern and central Algeria. The distant corners of the Sahara Algérien were only incorporated into the colonial administration in the 1890s. The Berber-speaking Tuareg people of central Sahara maintained their resistance until 1902. Coincidentally, perhaps, this was also the period that the Russian and British empires expanded towards the nomadic areas. The

---

[12] For a detailed description, see: Kappeler, *The Russian Empire*, 188–191; see, also: Osterhammel, *Transformation*, 363–366.

French government had to maintain its military government in the Sahara until the very end of colonial rule due to the potential risk of tribal uprising. As with the Russian experience in Siberia and the Kazakh steppe, nomadic supremacy came to an end in the Sahara as the tribal trade networks from Sudan to Tunisia were compromised and ties with the villages and towns were cut by the colonial army. The nomads were increasingly isolated. The French empire used the most coercive means against nomads, rarely resorting to negotiation in its tribal administration. This led to sustained violent resistance by the tribal groups, forcing the French to spend enormous amounts of money on military solutions to keep the tribes in check.[13]

Ottomans and the Bedouin Nomads

In the Ottoman case which this study analyses, the situation was the opposite of what other empires experienced. Vast areas of pasture in the Arab, Turcoman and Kurdish imperial heartlands of southern Anatolia, Syria and Iraq were gradually invaded throughout the eighteenth century – and especially during its last quarter – by the large nomadic groups of the Shammar and Anizah from Najd, in search of fertile pasture for their herds due to drought there. At that time, these two large tribal confederations consisting of several sub-confederations such as al-Jarba, Ruwalla, Fid'an, Seb'a and Wuld 'Ali, annually invaded the principal pasture and agricultural lands, and desert regions in Syria and Iraq, from Diarbekir to the frontiers of Hijaz and northern Najd. As the newcomers were bellicose migrant societies, they posed a serious challenge to the imperial order on several fronts; regional trade was disrupted as road security was compromised; the incomes of the provincial treasuries dropped severely as a result of Bedouin-orchestrated raids of local villages whose inhabitants ultimately had to abandon their lands; and, for similar reasons, navigation routes were threatened. As the empire was weakened at that time for various reasons, their domination in the Arab countryside and the desert could not be effectively challenged.[14]

---

[13] McDougall, *A History of Algeria*, 58–80, 121; see, also: Zurcher, *La pacification*; Lieutenant-Colonel Daumas, *Le Sahara Algerien*; Tandoğan, *Tevarikler*, 306–398.

[14] For a document expressing the imperial inability to counter the tribal threat dated in 1827, see: BOA, C.DH 3874, Lef 1, 22 Cemaziyelahir 1242

A Sociological Overview: Geography, Society and the Sheikh

Arab tribes of the Middle East are named 'Bedouin'. The term is used in contemporaneous documents and the majority of the secondary literature for all the tribal groups including purely migrant nomads, mixed nomads/semi-settled tribes and settled tribes. Yet these societies somewhat differ from each other in terms of their lifestyle, mode of subsistence and their relations with the state although all of them were the products of the same ecology.

The 'migrant nomads' – or pure nomads – constituted the firmest form of nomadism. They enjoyed the highest degree of mobility among others and could rapidly move between the settled regions and the desert. This lifestyle complemented the pure nomads' lack of reliance on agriculture, strengthened their hand in resistance to the designs of imperial power and conferred on them the most privileged position vis-à-vis the empire among other tribal groups. During the nineteenth century, although the empire approached them with an expansionist policy, they could maintain considerable autonomy in various sectors of their life which the government would normally have wanted to contain and control. 'Mixed nomads' – or 'semi-settled' tribes – represent an intermediate form: they maintained migrant life because they possessed camel and sheep herds and thus had to wander to graze their animals. On the other hand, they were engaged in agriculture which remarkably restricted their mobility in comparison to the pure nomads. Dependence on agriculture and land also influenced their relations with the Ottoman government which facilitated their control and containment by the latter. As demonstrated by Rogan, Barakat and Amara, in Transjordan, in Salt and in Beersheba, respectively, it was comparatively easier for the Ottoman Empire to extend its authority to the lands of mixed nomads who could not escape into desert leaving their lands and agricultural products behind them.[15] The third type of Bedouin tribe is the settled groups. These agricultural transhumants, who were also called Bedouin by the Ottomans, could not easily be differentiated from the sedentary society in terms of their relations with the state: they dutifully paid their taxes without objection. They were willingly subject to the sharia courts to resolve intra- and inter-tribal disputes, to

[21 January 1827] quoted in Saydam, 'Aşiretlerin Yol Açtıkları Asayiş Problemleri', 245.

[15] Rogan, *Frontiers*; Barakat, 'An Empty Land?'; Amara, 'Governing Property'.

approve sales contracts and authorize marriages. They tended to form small independent tribes rather than large, unwieldy confederations, which meant that the government could easily keep them in check.[16]

This book analyses the relations between the pure nomads and the Ottoman Empire and thus, a detailed analysis of the pure nomads' social structure is necessary to understand the tribal action and position, and evolution of the state-nomad relations in the late Ottoman Empire. However, prior to that, an analysis of why the migrant lifestyle was vital for nomadic existence must be made in order to understand the persistence of tribal lifestyle for centuries and the tribal insistence on nomadism during the Ottoman age of reformation. In this regard, the desert environment can be seen as the main factor, out of which the nomadic societies emerged. The geography that the Anizah and Shammar used as summer pastures spreads in the south from the desert that lies above Basra in Iraq to that above Aqaba in Transjordan. In the middle and north, it lies west of Palmyra and east of Aleppo in Syria, south of Urfa and Mardin in Turkey and west of Mosul and Baghdad in Iraq in the Jazira region. Although these deserts contained broad expanses of sand here and there, unlike the other deserts of the region, they were not a sand-desert. It was like 'a paradise for the Bedouin seeking a place to stop and graze his animals' as many parts of it had the best pasturages where plentiful quantities of herbage grew. Part of them were formerly the agricultural lands abandoned by their owners following the migration of the Shammar and Anizah from Najd.[17] Owing to the beneficial climate in these deserts the herds of the tribes frequenting this area prospered.[18] Significant decrease in heat during the winter and the inability of the nomadic animals to survive the cold weather forced the nomads to move in winter towards the southern parts of these deserts, Wadi Sirhan and the Hamad contained by Arabia. The herbage in these territories was also important for the immunity system of the tribal animals. The intense heat meant that only particular trees and plants could grow, the consumption of which enabled the desert animals to be resistant to thirst for longer.[19]

The obvious result of this ecology was the Bedouin, people of the desert engaged in animal husbandry and nomadism, *badawa*, which means a mobile desert life based on raising and tending livestock. Herds

---

[16] Jabbur, *The Bedouin and the Desert*, 31–32. [17] Ibid., 49.
[18] De Gaury, *The 'Anizah Tribe*, 16. [19] Ibid., 47.

of camels and flocks of sheep, goats and horses constituted the Bedouin nomads' principal wealth. The desert conditions described imposed a migrant lifestyle on the Bedouin and unlike urban and village societies, one which required long-lasting seasonal migrations from one region to another in search of water and pasturage for their huge number of animals. 'The optimum living and reproduction conditions for the livestock of the camel-tending nomads are provided only through long-ranging searches for food and sojourns in the grazing lands of the desert.'[20] The camel, which the Bedouin called *safinat al-barr* [ship of the land], was also the vessel for crossing the barren deserts of the region and comprised a crucial pillar of nomadic life.[21] For centuries, if not millennia, they had existed as societies constantly on the move together with their herds in search of water and pasture.

The conditions of this mobile life and threat from other tribes, the government and settled societies to the grazing lands and animals required a high-level unity, solidarity and coherence of the tribal society to survive, which resulted in a hierarchical and solid warlike society. Several

Figure 0.1 Anizah tribesmen in an encampment near Aleppo. Davenport, *My Quest*, 113.

---

[20] Jabbur, *The Bedouins and the Desert*, 29.   [21] Ibid., 197.

instruments served that purpose. In this regard, articulation of a common history and genealogy laid the foundations for the imagination of tribal commonness. The real and fictive blood ties going back to an apical ancestor – Adnan or Qahtan – united the tribesmen and gave the tribe 'a pyramid-like structure with real, living units as its base and the mythical ancestor at the top'.[22] The acknowledgement of a common ancestor is, however, a political preference 'as part of a shared foundation myth and history' which created a mainstay of the tribal 'imagined community' and also identified the 'other'.[23] The Adnan-Qahtan difference legitimized the long-lasting rivalry between the Shammar and Anizah, which significantly contributed to the reinforcement of the tribal camps and consolidation of tribal identity.[24]

Imagination of a common ancestor and believing in the superiority of one's descendants to others contributed to enhance the level of integration and solidarity in the tribal society. Tribes could easily determine the social environment of tribesmen and absorbed tribal individuals by producing close physical relationships within the members of a tribe, such as marrying within their own tribe as their kin was superior and thus more preferable.[25]

The existence of such imagined and real kinship ties among the tribesmen and the influence of ecology and the wider world also forced the tribesmen to communalize and mutualize their lives. They influenced Bedouin society so crucially that if a tribesman was murdered, all his kin were responsible for avenging him. 'If, on the other hand, he killed someone else, every member of his kin bore the responsibility for the shedding of blood and might be killed in revenge. A man's honour could be stained by an act of one of his kin; the honour of the whole group could be forfeited by one of its members.'[26] Although this 'common fate principle' caused everlasting feuds between the rival tribes, such strong ties both increased the loyalty of the tribesman to their tribe as they felt themselves safe under the tribal protection and consolidated the tribal society which can be interpreted as the outcome of the desert geography. To put it another way, long-lasting feuds among the various tribes enhanced the unity of individual tribes and consolidated the tribal order. However, it required the tight control of the tribesmen to avoid unnecessary hostility with rival tribes.

---

[22] Chatty, 'The Bedouin in Contemporary Syria', 29.   [23] Rogan, *Frontiers*, 7.
[24] Kay, *The Bedouin*, 75.   [25] Ibid., 73.   [26] Ibid., 79.

The hierarchical organization of tribes emerged out of these eco-
logical and socio-political conditions. The maintenance of the migrant
life with a large number of animals against the external threat would be
impossible without a strict hierarchy. The tribal hierarchy was also
their political order. 'According to this system, peoples divide into
tribes, the tribes into clans, the clan into sub-tribes, the sub-tribe into
sections, and the section into extended families, until we reach the
nuclear family and its single head – the foundation of the tribal
order.'[27] The unification of the tribes carved out the great tribal confederations such as the Shammar and the Anizah. The organization of
these large confederations was loose and did not necessarily mean
hierarchy, solidarity and cooperation. For instance, different sub-
groups which belonged to the Anizah such as the Ruwalla and Wuld
'Ali waged long-lasting feuds against each other and they were not
subject to a higher paramount sheikh.

As the Bedouin communities were hierarchical, sheikhs played crucial roles in leading the tribe, commanding raids, defending the tribal
pastures and flocks, and establishing and maintaining peaceful

Figure 0.2 Shepherd of the Seb'a tribe and his flock in Muhaywir. Gertrude
Bell Archives, Newcastle University, Y_108.

[27] Jabbur, *The Bedouin and the Desert*, 287.

relations with other tribes, townspeople and government authorities. Successful conduct of these duties gave an undisputed legitimacy to the sheikh and strengthened his position among his fellow tribesmen while his failure might threaten his position as the leader of the community. He was expected to rule the tribal affairs successfully and strengthen the tribal position against the other tribes, cities and the government. As the tribes needed to approach to the settled areas and as raids constituted a major income for themselves, the sheikhs were expected to be both good politicians, diplomats and warriors. Nomads needed to develop peaceful relations with villages and cities to be able to use their markets for selling their products and buying their needs. In addition, the sheikh must be a skilful commander to lead raids against rival tribes, caravans and villages, and defend the tribal property against raids by other tribes and attacks by the government.[28] Furthermore, the Bedouin sheikh was expected to exercise 'a species of surveillance' over the sub-sheikhs, and intervene in every case of injustice and misgovernment among his fellow tribesmen.[29] 'The sheikh could not rule the tribe without counselling the tribal elders, and those who were consulted could have opposed the will of the sheikh.'[30] Wellsted calls these elders 'a divan of old men' and adds that 'without their sanction little of moment is undertaken'.[31] All these are sources of tribal legitimacy from which the sheikh derived his authority.

The paramount sheikh was principally elected by the tribal council from the leading family of the tribe such as the Sha'lan family of the Ruwalla and the Faris family of the Shammar. When the sheikh died, a brother of the sheikh, or the best of his sons, replaced him. He owed his power to his personal character, wisdom, natural powers of leadership and his record as a warrior.[32] In practice, however, intra-tribal hostilities and government support influenced the maintenance of the sheikh's leadership. As will be detailed in Chapter 1 and Chapter 5, more charismatic and more skilful alternative candidates who gained support of the tribal majority – and the Ottoman government in some cases – could challenge the sheikh's authority and replace him by defeat.

---

[28] Ibid., 301–302.   [29] FO 195/800, Aleppo, 30 September 1864.
[30] Bostan, 'Zor Sancağı', 199.   [31] Wellsted, *Travels*, 197.
[32] Kay, *The Bedouin*, 80.

It is finally worth noting that nomads did not live isolated only in the desert. They often interacted with settled populations when they approached the environs of towns. They visited town markets to sell their products and animals, and buy goods they needed. The deficiencies of desert life and commercial reasons made them dependent on the settled life. The situation was similar for the settled people's relations with the nomads. They also visited the nomads' camps as merchants and other professionals and stayed there for months to make money.[33]

To sum up, nomadism was an amalgam of the desert environment, constant mobility, exploitation of fresh pastures and intertwined relations with agricultural and urban spaces. Restrictions on any of these pillars would make the maintenance of the nomadic lifestyle impossible. Therefore, the tribes vehemently resisted the Ottoman designs to expel them from the pastures in the desert frontier and imperial plans to expand into the depths of the desert. The empire ultimately had to abandon its plans to expulse the nomads into the desert and reconcile with the sheikhs by negotiations to make the imperial expansion into the desert frontier possible.

The politics of negotiation was systematized with the Anizah and Shammar groups in the early 1870s and sheikhs became the intermediaries between the tribal society and the Ottoman government. Support for and recognition of the government consolidated the sheikh's authority over his subjects; in many cases, sheikhs were assisted by government troops when some disloyal branches breached their orders. Such obvious shows of support only increased the sheikhs' power and charisma within tribal hierarchies.[34] They strove to gain *robes d'honneur* and medals from the government, and provoked unrest when the authorities refused to reward them for services they had rendered.[35] Government recognition and appointment of a sheikh benefited his subjects, endowing them with the right to engage in trade with local settled populations, purchasing the latter's cereals and general merchandize, and to sell them Bedouin animal products.[36] As will be fully explored in the following chapters,

---

[33] See p. 178.
[34] For an example, see: BOA, BEO 338/25348, 25 Kanun-ı Evvel 1309 [7 January 1894].
[35] The government authorities abstained from their attacks and advised the central government not to refuse the tribal demands for reward. For an example, see: BOA, İ.DH 961/76778, from the governor of Baghdad, 24 Eylül 1301 [7 October 1885].
[36] FO 195/675, Aleppo, 4 February 1861.

Bedouin sheikhs thus became the principal partners of the official authorities, and fulfilled numerous governmental functions including the arrest of criminals from their own tribes and others, taxation and ensuring the security of roads, rivers and cities.

A Historical and Geographical Overview: The Shammar and Anizah Migrations in the Regional Context

The Shammar and Anizah were the major and dominant nomadic confederations in Syria and Iraq (and Northern Arabia) where Ottoman direct rule existed or expanded. Other confederations such as the Rashidis and Saudis of the Central Arabia basically remained immune to Ottoman direct rule as the imperial attempts to absorb these regions failed. The Shammar tribes migrated from Najd in the late eighteenth century for a number of reasons including internal dissent, seeking a secure location away from the Wahhabi-Saudi expansion towards Hijaz and Iraq and lack of pastures in Arabia.[37] They were among the early adherents of the Wahhabi movement and according to a local historian's estimation, 20,000 Shammar tribesmen swelled the ranks of the first Saudi state that existed in Najd between 1744 and 1818. When the Shammar conflicted with the Saudis, sections of the confederation left for Iraq in 1791.[38] They spread across the regions of Diarbekir, Aleppo (Deir al-Zor), Mosul and Baghdad. The Shammar confederation had three major branches, al-Jarba, al-Zaidan and al-Umar, and many sub-branches loyal to them including al-Harisah, al-Sayih, al-Najm, al-Sabit, al-Amud, al-Fadagha, al-Abdallah and al-Katiyan.[39] They occupied the fertile pastures in the Jazira region and the Middle Euphrates within the boundaries of Mosul, Baghdad and Aleppo provinces. The most influential major branch was the al-Jarba branch, which would later dominate the others. This tribe was named in honour of their first sheikh, Faris al-Jarba, who was succeeded by Safuq, probably in the late 1810s. Safuq significantly extended the Shammar's influence in Iraq and Syria, taking advantage of the power vacuum created by the empire's ongoing war with Iran.[40] According to Shammar law, the sheikhship was a hereditary title. As such, only the

---

[37] Tooth, 'The Transformation of a Pastoral Economy'.
[38] Fattah, *Politics of Regional Trade*, 30.
[39] *Diyarbekir Vilayet Salnamesi*, 123–128.
[40] Zakariyya, *Asha'ir al-Sham*; Fattah, *Politics of Regional Trade*, 30.

descendants of the first sheikh Faris were eligible. Although the Ottoman government never managed a census of the Shammar territories, in around 1850 Hurşid Pasha estimated the total number of men for the Shammar al-Jarba as 11,600.[41] In 1857 Ömer Lütfi Pasha, the governor of Baghdad, estimated their numbers to be 4,000–5,000 warriors within the boundaries of the province.[42] In 1868, the British consul in Aleppo suggested the Shammar numbered 25,000 tribesmen in Iraq and Syria which consisted of numerous sub-divisions.[43] They were 'the greatest mobile society' east of the Euphrates, but unlike the Kurdish tribes in Iraq, the Shammar did not follow a particular seasonal migration route.[44] This made it very difficult for the state to monitor them, and authorities were forced to rely on the sheikh, or sheikhs, to keep their tribesmen in check.

The great majority of the Anizah also migrated from Najd to Syria and Iraq for the same reasons that had forced the Shammar's move.[45] In 1858, the Anizah population in Syria and Iraq is estimated in an Ottoman document to have been 800,000 tents.[46] One of the largest moves of the Anizah towards Syria and Iraq took place in the late eighteenth century when the aggressive expansionism of the Wahhabis threatened to oppress them.[47] The branches migrated to the plains east of Aleppo, Hama, Homs, Damascus and the west bank of the central Euphrates valley (Fid'an, Khrissa and Seb'a).[48] The Wuld 'Ali branch of the Anizah tribe moved to Southern Syria (Transjordan) around the early eighteenth century while the Ruwalla seem to have begun their regular migrations at the end of the century.[49] The overwhelming majority of the Anizah groups maintained a migrant lifestyle and regularly migrated in winter to the desert in Najd for their camels. The Anizah moved north to the neighbourhood of Hawran, Aleppo, Urfa, Hama and Homs, and Deir al-Zor 'to find water and grazing for the summer, to sell their

---

[41] Mehmed Hurşid Paşa, *Seyahatname*, 166; The book includes a detailed account of all the branches of al-Jarba.

[42] Marufoğlu, *Kuzey Irak*, 128; The same document claims that the Shammar's population consisted of 80–100 tents when they came to Iraq. But the number is too low when considering that they had great influence in Iraq as soon as they arrived.

[43] FO 195/902, Aleppo, 2 April 1868.   [44] Marufoğlu, *Kuzey Irak*, 127.

[45] Zakariyya, *Asha'ir al-Sham*, 593; Hathaway, *The Arab Lands*, 183.

[46] BOA, İ.DH 399/26448, 1274 [1858].   [47] Hathaway, *Arab Lands*, 184.

[48] Lewis, *Nomads and Settlers*, 1, see also: Zakariyya, *Asha'ir al-Sham*, 594–595.

[49] Hathaway, *Arab Lands,* 183–184 ; Lewis, 'Hawran and Palmyrena', 35.

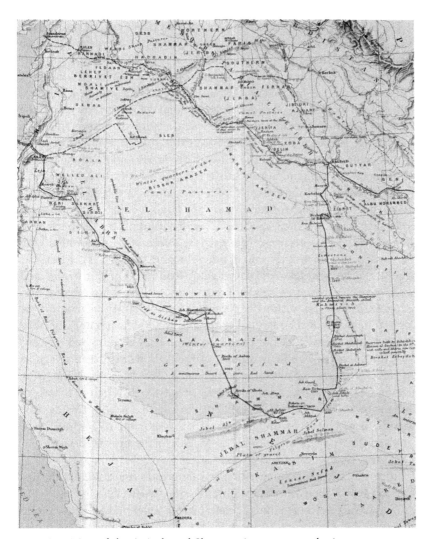

Map 0.1 Map of the Anizah and Shammar's summer and winter pasturages. Blunt, *A Pilgrimage to Nejd*.

produce and to buy what they needed for the coming winter'.[50] They had a reputation for their pure-bred [*asil*] Arabian mares.[51]

[50] Lewis, 'Hawran and Palmyrena', 34.
[51] Fattah, *Politics of Regional Trade*, 162.

The Syrian and Iraqi countryside contained tribal groups prior to the Anizah and Shammar migrations which even preceded the Ottoman domination of the region. Following the conquest, the Ottomans divided the tribal regions which would later be dominated by the Shammar and Anizah such as Jazira, the Khabur valley, and the middle Euphrates valley into several quasi-independent sanjaks rather than annexing them to direct Ottoman rule and a relationship of partnership was established between the tribal leaders and the imperial rulers. For instance, the governorate of the tribes in the Jazira and Palmyra regions was granted to the semi-autonomous Abu Rish amirs who were called in the Ottoman documents *çöl beyi* [the amir of the desert], *emir-i urban* [the amir of the Bedouin] or *çöl hakimi* [king of the desert]. Following them, the sheikhs of the Mawali tribe replaced them towards the end of the seventeenth century whose domination was ended with the Anizah invasions at the end of the eighteenth century. At around the same time the Shammar displaced the Ubaid and Djebbur tribes and occupied their pastures in the Jazira region. The Mawali properly recognized imperial authority, performed a fundamental mission for the maintenance of the regional order and road security, and supplied the imperial army in its campaigns to Iran. They also helped officials with the successful implementation of the settlement projects such as the *Rakka iskanı* [the Raqqa settlement]. The Mawali chiefs were gratified by the sultan with the title of pasha.[52] When the Anizah endeavoured 'to effect a lodgement' in Aleppo's countryside, the Mawali firmly resisted under their chief, Muhammad Hufran, who repulsed the first two attempts. The Anizah finally prevailed and dominated the Syrian desert and countryside.[53]

From the very beginning of their migrations the nomadic groups interacted with the rulers of the empire and city-dwellers. In 1803 and 1805, the Anizah and Shammar chieftaincies cooperated with the empire by providing significant support to the Ottoman army. The tribes' military contribution enabled the Ottomans to counter the potentially destabilizing Wahhabi attacks on Baghdad, to repress the uprising of the slaves and to reimpose imperial sovereignty in the Jazira region.[54] At around the same time, the southern branches of

---

[52] For a detailed description of the *çöl beyliği* post, see: Winter, 'Alep et l'émirat du désert (*çöl beyliği*)', 86–108.
[53] FO 195/416, British Consulate Aleppo, 19 July 1857.
[54] Barout, 'La renaissance', 107.

Figure 0.3 The southern Syrian desert. İstanbul Üniversitesi Nadir Eserler Kütüphanesi, 90605/60.

Anizah regularly supplied horses and provisions to pilgrims 'while protecting the caravan from attacks by other Bedouin tribes in return for a payment from the Ottoman treasury'.[55]

The Bedouin meanwhile sought a market in the environs of towns for their young camels, horses and wool and to purchase dates, coffee, tobacco and manufactured goods.[56] The city markets were of such importance to Bedouin subsistence that a fair amount of their raids during the Tanzimat era were in response to their restricted access by the government to towns and cities. The city-dwellers equally benefited from the tribes. They bought the purest breed of horses from tribesmen,[57] entrusted their animals to the tribesmen for better grazing and made a great profit; the Bedouin guaranteed their caravans safe passage through the desert, and even provided the camels and horses necessary to transport the caravans although they could not fulfil such promises in full capacity and the main caravan routes remained closed until the 1870s due to the difficulty of controlling all the branches of a tribal confederation by the orders of a sheikh and insufficient security measures by the government.

In spite of such friendly relations with some segments of the urban society and the imperial rulers, the nomadic migrations, however, meant a great disaster for the Arab countryside whose inhabitants suffered greatly from the tribal invasions. The damage they imparted was so great that the Shammar's arrival in Mardin was 'regarded as the punishment of God', like plague and locusts.[58] In the northern Syrian

---

[55] Hathaway, *Arab Lands*, 184.   [56] Blunt, *Bedouin Tribes I*, 62.
[57] Mehmed Hurşid Paşa, *Seyahatname*, 43.
[58] Dolbee, 'The Locust and the Starling', 105.

districts such as Hama, Homs and Aleppo, a substantial number of agricultural lands and villages were abandoned by the peasants for safer areas such as Maraş, Adana, Ayıntab, Trablussham and Damascus, which also meant a sizable loss for the imperial revenues. Those who still kept cultivating their lands and living in their villages were either forced to pay heavy duties by the tribes or raided heavily.[59] All their villages and crops were either burnt or stolen by the tribesmen.[60] In 1829, according to the governor of Aleppo, the vast agricultural areas extending from the banks of the Euphrates to Arabia had been almost completely depopulated due to the security problems caused by the Anizah tribesmen. Their inhabitants preferred to migrate to safer zones while the other tribal groups in the regions of Baghdad, Mosul, Raqqa, Aleppo and Damascus joined them to be immune to their attacks.[61] The influx of the Anizah and Shammar caused havoc in the Iraqi countryside 'as the newcomers vied for control of pasture-lands and raided riparian towns and villages'.[62] The Anizah and Shammar used the banks of the Euphrates on the eastern and western sides of the river, which left all the villages around entirely abandoned.[63] The weakness of the Ottoman state at that time pre-vented the officials from protecting the Arab countryside whose disorder continued up to the 1860s and 1870s when the imperial authorities developed new strategies to deal with the tribes and reconciled with them on a 'mutually concessive' basis.

Existing Literature, Outline and Argument of the Book, and Sources

There are three main approaches to state-nomad relations in the available scholarship. The first group adopted the centralization approach and its scholars assume that the Ottoman officials were practitioners of centralization policies decided by the state, aiming to eliminate the influence and resistance of the local powerbrokers. The overriding concern of these scholars is to examine government structures and

[59] Öğüt, 'Birecik Sancağı', 129.
[60] For some details and statistics on the impact of the tribal migrations, see: Saydam, 'Aşiretlerin Yol Açtıkları Asayiş Problemleri'.
[61] BOA, HAT 48/006-I, 1245 [1829], quoted in Öğüt, 'Birecik Sancağı', 128.
[62] Faisal Husain, 'The Tigris-Euphrates Basin', 200.
[63] Öğüt, 'Birecik Sancağı', 129.

they thus focus on administrative divisions, the limits of governors' authority and other instruments of administration, and paid less attention to the Bedouin and their role in the evolution of the Ottoman administrative reforms in the Arab lands.[64] According to Ma'oz, for instance, 'the major cause of the Ottomans' failure to accomplish during the 1840s and the 1850s what the Egyptians had succeeded in achieving in the 1830s, lay in their ambivalent and unsystematic Bedouin policy'. This argument attributes what he describes as 'success' or 'failure' to the imperial actions while disregarding the nomadic reactions and resistance which reconfigured many decisions of the central government. The present study aims at analysing the Ottoman Bedouin policy taking into consideration the nomadic response which made a constructive impact not only on the Ottoman strategies but the modern history of the Arab east.

The second group are scholars who have been influenced by frontier theories and draw a distinction between 'indigenous tribes' and 'outsider imperial rulers'.[65] The term is used to convey the distance between the frontier regions and the imperial heartland, and the autonomy of the local population given the absence or weakness of the state authority. The frontier 'represented socio-political orders apart from the institutions of the Empire at large'.[66] 'The three main factors that determined the characteristic of a frontier region and in turn the Ottoman government's approach to it were: the power of the local elites, the level of European intervention in that region, and the local attitude towards Ottoman rule.'[67] The problem of the frontier theory, with specific reference to the Shammar and Anizah, is that many of these groups lived not only in the frontier regions or the desert, or 'tribally dominated areas', where the influence of the state was minimized, but also visited the very outskirts of the imperial heartlands such as Aleppo, Damascus, Mosul, Diarbekir and Baghdad, and spent at least one season in these regions. It is therefore difficult to determine spatial divisions between the so-called frontier and heartland. In addition, as detailed previously, the migrations of the many Anizah and

---

[64] For some studies in this sense, see: Lewis, *Nomads and Settlers*; Moshe Ma'oz, *Ottoman Reform*; Çetinsaya, *Ottoman Administration of Iraq*; Ceylan, *Ottoman Origins of Modern Iraq*; al-Amr, *The Hijaz*.

[65] For a distinguished study on Transjordan with this perspective, see: Rogan, *Frontiers*.

[66] Rogan, *Frontiers*, 6.   [67] Minawi, 'Beyond Rhetoric', 78.

Shammar groups from Najd to the 'frontier regions' and 'imperial
lands' were also recent and these tribes may also be called 'outsiders'.
Therefore, classifications based on 'divided spaces' and 'authenticity'
may not be appropriate to understand the Ottoman governance of the
Shammar and Anizah groups. As the present study attempts to do, the
state-tribe relations can better be understood by treating them as
a process evolving from conflict to affirmation, negotiation and collaboration in which the parties had to give considerable concessions and
obtained significant gains in terms of socio-spatial dominance.

The final group of scholars concentrate on the Ottoman rhetoric of
the Bedouin societies, influenced by postcolonial approaches. They give
attention to the derogatory 'colonial attitude' of the Ottoman officials
towards the tribes and demonstrate the 'orientalist' remarks used by
the Ottomans when they reported about the Bedouin. According to
these scholars, 'the Ottomans adopted a colonial stance toward the
peoples of the periphery of their empire. Colonialism came to be seen as
a modern way of being'.[68] They describe the ideology of empire as 'a
socially elitist, politically centralist, and culturally modernist project'
aimed at civilizing an identified backward other.[69] It is right that the
'civilizing mission' was never far from their minds and, as will be
indicated through the chapters of the present study, the Ottoman
policymakers targeted from time to time the nomadic lifestyle with
a *mission civilisatrice*. As in Abdulhamid II's 'correctionist' project
aiming at putting right tribal religious beliefs, these ideas occasionally
came up as possible alternatives to 'the politics of negotiation'.
However, they had to be abandoned shortly due to tribal unwillingness
and resistance and due to the prevalence of the Ottoman officials who
defended negotiation as the basis of the imperial tribal policies. Such
failures and retreats make it difficult to identify a 'racialized' imperial
practice towards the Bedouin.

Another important problem with colonialist approaches is that they
frequently confuse the sedentary communities' perception of the

---

[68] Deringil, 'They Live in a State of Nomadism and Savagery', 313; for other
      studies with similar approach, see: Makdisi, 'Ottoman Orientalism'; Kühn,
      Empire, Islam and Politics of Difference.
[69] Minawi, 'Beyond Rhetoric', 80; see, also, Minawi, *Ottoman Scramble*, chapter
      6; For critical assessments of such approaches, see: Emrence, *Remapping the
      Ottoman Middle East*; Gölbaşı, '19. Yüzyıl Osmanlı emperyal siyaseti',
      199–222.

nomadic people with what they identify as 'orientalist and colonialist attitudes'. As we know from Ibn Khaldun's book *Mukaddimah*, even before the emergence of Orientalism and as a reflection of the Roman, Islamic and Persian imperial political cultures, the sedentary [*hadari*] peoples despised the nomadic groups, describing them as 'savages' and 'nomads', and considered them to be of separate and inferior ethnic origins. Long before, as well as during the modern period, Ottoman officials described the tribal groups, who were of an Arab, Kurdish and Turkish origin, with similarly derogatory remarks, making it difficult to call it a version of colonial 'racialization'.[70] However, policymaking and creation of 'racial hierarchies' are 'practical' activities affecting social life rather than becoming a 'mental' category experienced by words alone. The 'ideal society' in the minds of some Ottoman officials should not be considered as part of the imperial practice. In addition, such approaches compound the personal views of officials with state policy and ideology.[71] It is consequently difficult to consider the Bedouin in a racialized hierarchy produced by the Ottoman practices.

As Minawi demonstrates convincingly, local authorities deliberately portrayed the Bedouin 'as an unreasonable and superstitious people', to justify their inability to control the local population rather than producing new social conditions based on a racial hierarchy between the Bedouin and the settled communities.[72] As the following chapters demonstrate, such prejudices did not have a decisive influence on the determination of the Ottoman policies particularly after the adoption of the politics of negotiation which made 'pragmatism' the major principle of tribal governance. The imperial space could not be organized in a way which would reflect the difference between the state and sedentary communities on the one hand, and nomads on the other. The Ottoman concerns on the protection of crops and tax revenues merely directed them to allocate certain pasture lands located in the neighbourhoods of the cities and the vicinity of the agricultural lands to the Bedouin.

This book adopts an 'equalized perspective' on empire-tribe relations during the Tanzimat, Hamidian and Young Turk eras by

---

[70] Kırmızı, 'Going Round the Province', 387–401.
[71] Many examples can be found in the writings of the Ottomans and the official documents insulting the Bedouin lifestyle. But it is not easy to relate them with the imperial policies. For an example, see: Ali Suad, *Seyahatlerim*, 76.
[72] Minawi, 'Beyond Rhetoric', 93.

acknowledging and highlighting tribal agency in late Ottoman history. This equalized perspective interprets the Ottoman-Bedouin relations in the modern era as an amalgam of the imperial policies towards the nomads and the tribal strategies in response to them and vice versa. It will take into account the tribal and imperial agencies as independent – but also interdependent – and interacting phenomena which mutually shaped the late Ottoman history of the Arab countryside. To put it differently, such a perspective qualifies the historical roles played by both the tribal and imperial actors in the making of the Arab east. This perspective also carefully avoids such definitions as bottom-up and top-down due to their implicit inclinations to perpetuate hierarchy by assuming one party as 'top' or 'up' while characterizing the other of being 'bottom' or 'down'. Neither the nomads nor the Ottomans are eligible to be described in such a way.

This book agrees with the available scholarship that things began to change with the Tanzimat period, when the visibility and efficiency of the government gradually increased. However, it disagrees with the above-mentioned theories regarding the nature of the change that took place in the state-tribe relations in the late Ottoman Empire. The book addresses the nomads – particularly their sheikhs – as the active agents of the transformation that took place in the nineteenth century. What happened in the period of Ottoman reform was that the reform projects decided by the imperial authorities were not put into practice. The initial imperial plans to increase government control among the tribal groups became remarkably transmuted and their direction changed during the implementation due to the opposition raised by the nomads. Therefore, this book rather handles the leaders of nomadic groups as negotiating partners, mediators and collaborators of empire than approaching them categorically as the opponents of the imperial reorganization and expansion. Although they could not resist imperial expansion to the frontier regions and had to accept the imperial author-ities as their superiors, the tribesmen restructured the imperial state formation in such a way that their social and political organization and their interests in the Arab countryside would not be damaged. This restructuring made an impact on the region-wide order of the things as the Ottoman reform found another direction and had to ascribe more importance to the local voices. It can better be seen when we adopt an objectified equalized perspective which also demonstrates the repro-duction of the imperial projects at the local level.

In this regard, Chapter 1 is dedicated to demonstrating the failed imperial attempts to subjugate, pacify and 'deport' the Anizah and Shammar groups by force. During the 1840s and 1850s, and early 1860s, the authorities made several attempts to reach to that end. However, the Anizah and Shammar successfully resisted the imperial project and remained in the lands they occupied as pasturages mostly since the late eighteenth century in spite of official objection. Their achievements stemmed from the lack of sufficient troops, which compelled the officials to consent to tribal existence. Again, for to the same reason, particularly in the 1850s, the tribal sheikhs occasionally helped the local governments to suppress the local rebels to expand their influence in the Arab countryside, which gradually constructed a long-term compromise. In this way, they both forced the government to recognize their privileges and give them new privileges. This occasional cooperation and 'forced consent' to tribal existence, however, did not transform into a systematized partnership as the imperial officers occasionally endeavoured to exile them into the desert and the tribes maintained their plundering and raids against the villages and caravans. The state of hostility continued to dominate state-tribe relations until the early 1870s although its intensity gradually decreased.

Other concurrent projects were put into practice to limit the nomadic access to the sedentary areas for the security of the countryside. These were to reinforce the desert frontier with new settlements and collaborate with the chiefs of the settled tribes and local notables to have their support in the form of irregular soldiers. As Chapter 2 examines, the new settlements could only make limited contributions to the imperial project of 'cordoning the desert' and the necessity emerged to compromise with the Shammar and Anizah even for the protection of the new settlements. In a similar way, the irregular troops under the command of the sheikhs of the settled tribes and the local notables, who were occasionally supported by regular troops, organized military campaigns in the desert and its frontiers to defeat the tribes, which, in spite of temporary achievements, ultimately failed. Their failure to eliminate the 'nomadic question' caused a revolutionary change in the structure of the desert troops: the replacement of the irregulars with regular troops. In the early 1860s, this change caused the evolution of the Ottoman approach to secure the desert from organizing 'exclusionist attacks' into 'regulatory security providing' which composed a fundamental aspect of the reconciliation with the nomads and consented to the existence of the tribes in the lands that they had occupied since the end of the eighteenth century as pasturage.

Another process which brought about the empire-tribe reconciliation was the policy of expansion towards Deir al-Zor and the southernmost area of Syria, although it aimed at realizing the reverse. The forward imperial policy was successful in expanding government authority in the frontier regions and the desert notwithstanding that it did not take place in a way its planners envisaged and brought about the consolidation of the state-tribe partnership while it 'provincialized'[73] the Anizah and Shammar. The expansion of Ottoman direct rule towards Deir al-Zor and Transjordan, which Chapters 3 and 4 examine, created important reasons for the reconciliation. The reinforcement of Ottoman rule in these territories could not limit the tribal movement in these areas, but made the new administrative units dependent on nomadic collaboration. Now the Ottomans were in the tribal regions while the tribes still maintained their supremacy in the imperial countryside. This signified that the Ottoman strategy towards the nomads evolved from 'expulsion' into 'containment' in these regions as the regular troops served only as security providers and the nomadic 'goodwill' was required for the maintenance of the new settlements. Following the consolidation of the administrative units, in Deir al-Zor, Hawran and Balqa', the Anizah branches like the Fid'an, Seb'a, Ruwalla, Wuld 'Ali and the Shammar under Faris al-Jarba's sheikhship became partners of the empire, with which many of whom had already compromised. The expansions increased mutual dependence and systematized the state-tribe partnership.

The tribes paid a moderate amount of taxes on the basis of the declaration, of which the sheikh had a quarter of its share, and gave assurance that they would stop collecting *khuwwa* from the villagers, most of whose lands were located in the imperially dominated areas. In return, they could use the imperial pasture lands in the Jazira, Middle Euphrates, Palmyra and Hawran within the boundaries of the Aleppo, Mosul, Kürdistan, Baghdad and Damascus provinces. The allocation of certain pastures to the tribes did not limit their movement as these lands had already been occupied by them for decades. It was only the recognition by the government, which secured these lands against rival

---

[73] I borrow this term from Samuel Dolbee, see: Dolbee, 'The Locust and the Starling', 108.

tribes. The threat by Ibn Rashid to the Anizah pastures in Ma'an could be prevented by government protection. Similarly, the expansion of Ibrahim Pasha al-Milli could be limited by the opposition of the Deir al-Zor government. The tribes also found an opportunity to reach the imperial and global markets and sell their animals in the markets established in such places as Aleppo, Deir al-Zor and Hama. In addition, predesigned social engineering projects targeting the nomadic social structure could not be put into practice. Following the reinforcement of Ottoman rule in the frontier regions, an implicit 'social contract' mediated by the sheikhs between the nomads and the empire was reached, which required tribes and state to respect each other's interests in their areas of domination and the tribesmen's acceptance of Ottoman rule. That mutual dependence rendered a reconciled governance of the desert and its people possible although it was not perfectly implemented at all times.

There were certainly places where the politics of negotiation failed and produced crises as in the Mosul province in the 1890s and early 1900s. Bargaining with the sheikhs was interpreted by the Mosuli officials as an opportunity to maximize their interest by exploiting the Shammar nomads. In this regard, Chapter 5 studies how the relationship of partnership with the Shammar of Baghdad and Mosul worked from the early 1870s onward. After Farhan's death, good examples of partnerships and provincializations were experienced in Deir al-Zor and Baghdad, while the plots of the Mosuli authorities disregarding the tribal requests in the appointment of the sheikh could wreak havoc with the politics of negotiation. The incidents in Mosul demonstrate how it could be disastrous for imperial policies to ignore tribal concerns and use the negotiation process for their own benefits.

In a similar way, Bedouin taxes could be collected with the consent and cooperation of their sheikhs as examined in Chapter 6. Sheikhs persuaded their followers of the necessity of paying a moderate tax to the government, which demonstrates the role of the sheikh as the agent of the empire. Although the tax was moderate, the great quantity of tribal livestock made the amount a remarkable contribution for the provincial treasuries. The sheikly collaboration was in return for a quarter share of the collected taxes.

Finally, Chapter 7 deals with the practice of justice for the tribal societies, which demonstrates the fields of tribal autonomy and sheds light on the role of the empire in the solution of the tribal disputes.

While the imperial authorities carefully abstained from intervening in intra-tribal disputes and entirely left them to the tribal judicial system, they played a significant part in the solution of many inter-tribal conflicts due to their influence in the imperial order. Again, negotiation was the principal method to solve the Bedouin disputes. It can be concluded in light of the chapters outlined here that the state could function in the desert and countryside of Ottoman Syria and Iraq by virtue of reconciliation with the tribes and due to their support.

The book draws on documents from many sources including the national archives of several countries. The documents in the *Prime Ministry Ottoman Archive* (BOA) are of major importance to this work. Telegrams sent by Ottoman officials in Syria and Iraq to the Ottoman central government (only recently made available to researchers) have been used in the book for the first time to explore the tribal context. These documents are critical to an understanding of desert policies and the dealings between state officials, local elites and tribal peoples. This book also employs *Sharia court records* of Hama and Mardin (in Arabic), and Urfa (in Turkish). These records reveal the dealings between tribes and merchants, peasants, landowners and bureaucrats, as well as highlighting the Bedouin perspective, since the latter regularly visited courts to express their concerns and seek justice.

Additionally, I have consulted European diplomatic archives to source valuable correspondence and documents concerning Ottoman-Bedouin relations. Due to their close personal, political and commercial relations with the Bedouin during the period under examination, the reports and memoranda of British and French diplomats often present alternative versions of events, revealing the concerns of non-state local actors and tribal figures, deliberately or unintentionally ignored in Ottoman state documents. Consequently, I consulted a large number of British and French archival sources at *The National Archives, Centre des archives diplomatiques de Nantes* and *Centre des Archives diplomatiques de La Courneuve*.

I have also reviewed the private papers of *Mirza Wasfi*, the commander of the Ottoman gendarmerie in Amman in Jordan (in Arabic). These include correspondence between the state authorities and the Bedouin sheikhs, which present the Bedouin view, as well as dealings between the empire and the Bedouin. Other valuable sources such as memoirs, diaries, travel books and newspapers provide context to the archival research.

1 | *Conflict*

Imperial Attempts to Terminate Nomadic Domination in the Arab Countryside and the Tribal Response

Were the military authorities to prevent them for two or three consecutive years from acquiring strength by opposing their entrance into pashalick, they would be less inclined to cross so vast a desert on the chance of being repulsed, and would probably refrain from coming altogether, as they did during the latter period of the Egyptian rule in Syria.[1]

It is obvious that these tribes will starve and remain without any clothes [*aç ve üryan*] in the deserts, if their commerce [*ahz ve ita*] is curtailed and they were restricted from purchasing cereals and other goods. If the Fid'an and Shammar refuse to comply and settle, they should be compelled to do so by commandeering their goods and property [*emval ve eşya*] . . . when they are thus thoroughly coerced from all sides, all of them would have to accept the sedentary life as a last resort (despairingly).[2]

[Subhi Pasha] expressed the conviction that if the Sultan's government would abandon all attempts to enforce the payment of tribute by these tribes, allot them lands to cultivate, and apportion districts for the pasture of their camels, a very valuable auxiliary force, superior to the cossaks of Russia, might be added to the Turkish army.[3]

These remarks more or less reflect the mindset of the Ottoman authorities during the Tanzimat period which defined the framework of Ottoman tribal policy at that time. They wanted either to properly benefit from the human and material resources of the imperial subjects including the nomads or to prevent their periodic migrations into the imperial lands. Inspired by the Western models of state formation and to survive against the Western powers in the inter-imperial world of the nineteenth century, the Tanzimat statesmen like Subhi Pasha envisaged

---

[1] FO 195/226, Damascus, 31 May 1845.
[2] BOA, MVL 772/41, Urfa, 24 Zilhijja 1280 [31 May 1864].
[3] FO 195/994, Damascus, 24 June 1872.

a strict control over the imperial subjects.[4] Such an effective state could have been founded by properly taxing the Ottoman subjects, conscripting them to the army and reasserting security through the imperial realm. In sum, the Ottoman government had to be the principal authority 'conducting the conduct of the subjects' in the Foucauldian sense.[5]

In the Arab lands, one of the greatest challenges to the Tanzimat project came from the Bedouin tribes. When the Ottoman modernization reforms began in the early 1840s, the majority of the imperial countryside in Syria and Iraq was practically under the control of the Anizah and Shammar during the summer months. Beginning with their first move towards Syria and Iraq in the late eighteenth century, the tribal raids and plunder created a major security crisis and triggered great economic troubles for both the local society and the imperial treasury; the peasants abandoned their lands and migrated to the safer zones which meant a significant revenue loss for the imperial treasury while merchants' caravan trade was seriously halted.[6]

The 'tribal question' thus emerged as a vital problem for the imperial authorities in the early 1840s when the modern Ottoman state began to function. This chapter examines the imperial strategies adopted during the Tanzimat era to terminate the problems which stemmed from the Anizah and Shammar nomads, and the tribal reactions to it. The struggle between the empire and these nomads was over the pastures and the permission to the tribesmen to visit the towns and cities for shopping and trade. The government authorities were not willing to allow the tribal groups to approach the settled areas, as they were difficult to keep under control and it was difficult to impede their plundering and raiding due to the lack of sufficient troops. In addition, much of the pasture lands were previously cultivated as agricultural lands, which the Tanzimat officials wanted to 'reconquer' and re-cultivate by expelling the nomads to increase the taxes and finance their modernization expenses. Furthermore, the nomads exacted

---

[4] For some details on the Tanzimat reforms in the Iraqi provinces and Syria, see: Ceylan, *Ottoman Origins of Modern Iraq*; Çetinsaya, *Ottoman Administration of Iraq*; Ma'oz, *Ottoman Reform*.

[5] For studies analysing Foucault's concept of 'the conduct of the conduct', see: Foucault, *Security, Territory, Population*; Dean, *Governmentality*; Gordon, 'Governmental Rationality'.

[6] See, Chapter 2.

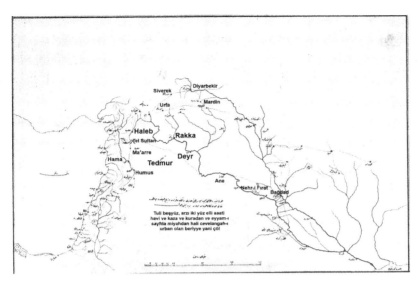

Map 1.1 An Ottoman map of 1849 showing the towns and cities the tribes frequented and the desert area the Anizah and Shammar tribes controlled. BOA, İ.MVL 167/4938.

khuwwa on the available agricultural lands closer to the desert area to the detriment of the imperial treasury. At the same time, it was vital and existential for the tribes to come to the sedentary areas and the pastures around them for grazing their animals, selling their products and animals, and shopping. Leaving these areas to the control of the Ottoman state would mean significant impoverishment as it would be disastrous to the tribal economy by decreasing the size of the flocks due to malnutrition, as well as the loss of control of the caravan routes and minus a considerable *khuwwa* income.

This chapter argues that during the Tanzimat era, due to their inadequate means of coercion the imperial authorities mainly embraced a policy of 'exclusionist struggle' to regulate the movement of tribes and keep them in check, and played off one sheikh against the other. Exclusion would automatically solve the 'tribal question' by completely 'getting rid of them'. As is clear in the map drawn in 1849, the tribal areas were displayed as the desert in the unreachable and impenetrable regions 'devoid of water in the summer and township and villages' [*kaza ve kuradan ve eyyam-ı sayfta miyahdan hali cevelangah-ı urban olan beriyye yani çöl*]. This remark may be interpreted to mean that the Anizah and Shammar were regarded by the imperial authorities as alien to the areas directly controlled by the empire.

These conditions of armed confrontation and projects aiming at the transformation of the nomadic lifestyle, however, could not be sustained due to the strength and resistance of the tribes, and the inadequacy of the imperial army. It was ultimately replaced with a reconciliatory and 'diplomatic' attitude after 1870 when the empire consolidated its position in the desert frontier and understood the impossibility of pushing the nomads into the depth of the desert or transforming their lifestyle into a more controllable and profitable one. The following sections will analyse the emergence and evolution of the Ottoman-nomad conflict focusing on the two major nomadic confederations in Syria, Iraq and Northern Arabia.

The Shammar

The branches of the Shammar had dispersed through Urfa, Mardin, Deir al-Zor, Mosul and Baghdad and they frequented the countryside of these cities from spring to autumn. The relationship between the Ottoman bureaucrats and the Shammar sheikhship was usually turbulent and antagonistic, beginning with the reinstatement of the Ottoman state in the 1830s up to the 1860s when Sheikh Farhan united the tribal groups around Mosul and Baghdad under his sheikhship and his brother, Abd al-Qarim reinforced his authority among the tribesmen around Deir al-Zor and Urfa. This indicated to government authorities that they could not be successful in implementing their plans regarding the exclusion of the Shammar from the imperial heartland and that they had to collaborate with them for the establishment of a peaceful coexistence. As will be detailed in Chapter 2, the simultaneous consolidation of the Ottoman position on the districts and routes that the Shammar used for grazing and migration made such a cooperation possible. Otherwise, there would be no reason for the tribes to be prevented from raiding villages and caravans and collecting *khuwwa*.

Sheikh Safuq and the Tribal Rejection of Imperial Authority

The restoration of the Ottoman rule in the Baghdad region (including Mosul) as part of the Tanzimat reforms set off the local authorities on a quest to find new sources of revenue for the provincial treasury and to expand imperial control over the territories of the province. The fertile lands occupied by the Shammar as pasturage became the target of the officials as they could be recultivated and taxed; this initiated a long-lasting struggle between the Shammar and the Baghdad and Mosul governments. In this regard, Ali Pasha, the governor of Baghdad, his successor Necib Pasha and the *mutasarrıf* [sub-governor] of Mosul argued with Safuq, the paramount sheikh of the Shammar, about the regions used as pasturage by the Shammar's flocks. Initially, in 1841, government troops attacked the Anah pastures which had been cultivated until the 1820s but had to be abandoned by the peasants due to the tribal invasions.[7] The scope of operations widened to the whole province in the following year to expel the Shammar from the provincial boundaries and expand government control in the countryside. After the failure of the sheikh's attempts to solve the issue diplomatically and use the region as grazing land, in 1842, Safuq fought back and rebuffed all attacks by the Ottoman army.[8] Due to the deficiency of the troops and absence of Ottoman fortification in the strategic points of the desert frontier, the Shammar and various other tribes dominated the provincial countryside, expanded their supremacy and plundered both on land and by river (Tigris) up to the very walls of the city. The government authorities had to accept the authority of Safuq and the Shammar sheikh entered into an agreement with the Pasha of Baghdad to prevent his tribesmen from attacking the settled areas and boats sailing on the Euphrates and to support his government in Baghdad.[9]

It was difficult, however, to sustain peace and stop the nomads with such agreements which were not supported by sufficient security measures at the desert frontiers. The Shammar, who established superiority against the empire due to the fragility of the government position and the weakness of the Ottoman troops in the field, were inclined to reject

---

[7] Mehmed Hurşid Paşa, *Seyahatname*, 126; as shown in Map 0.1 the region remained as camel pasturage at least until the mid-1870s. It is clear in the Ottoman documents that no settlement undertaking took place after that period which meant that Anah could not be colonized by the empire until the end of Ottoman rule.

[8] FO 195/228, Mosul, 10 August 1841; FO 195/204, Baghdad, 22 June 1842; for some correspondence between Necib Pasha and Safuq, see: BOA, İ.DH 61/3006, 1258 [1842]; the reports sent by the governor to the central government do not specifically mention the problem between Safuq and the Baghdad government, but describe his actions as 'discrepancy' [*uygunsuzluk*].

[9] FO 195/207, Aleppo, 16 July 1842.

imperial authority and organized new attacks in the following year such as seizing a considerable number of the British merchants' goods.[10] Being incapable of responding to the Shammar with force, the Ottoman authorities applied another most convenient tactic and tried to find a new sheikh to weaken Safuq's authority among his fellow tribesmen. In 1844, the governor of Baghdad attempted to replace him with his cousin Najris.[11] The governor rewarded the sheikh with pastures of the fertile Jazira region, presumably to encourage tribal loyalty to Najris.[12]

The Shammar's division would obviously weaken Safuq's position and strengthen the Baghdad government's hand. Therefore, the sheikh fought against the new candidate and the latter was killed in conflict between the rival groups. Hostilities among the Shammar groups due to the feud caused by the death of Najris and ongoing conflicts between them and the government troops completely ruined regional order in the countryside around Mosul and Baghdad, and made peace between the fighting sides an urgent necessity. Immediately after the conflict Safuq, with his son Farhan, were invited by the Pasha of Baghdad to put an end to the period of disorder.[13] However, both Shammar raids and government operations continued until 1847 when Safuq was killed in battle by Ottoman troops.[14] His death, however, did not mean a victory for the Ottoman government as the Shammar, motivated by the oath of revenge for their paramount sheikh, laid waste to the countryside between Diarbekir, Mosul and Baghdad. Consequently, regional security in general, and the security of the roads and rural countryside in particular, was seriously compromised due to the conflicts between the government troops and the tribes, and among the tribes themselves.[15]

Hostilities between the Baghdad government and the Shammar demonstrated the limits of Ottoman power to the officials. They realized that they should not challenge the tribe's position in the provincial countryside while the empire was in a militarily vulnerable position.

---

[10] FO 195/204, Mosul, 23 November 1843.
[11] FO 195/228, Baghdad, 14 June 1845.
[12] FO 195/237, Baghdad, 17 September 1845.
[13] FO 195/272, Baghdad, 29 September 1847.
[14] BOA, İ. MSM 51/1313, Lef 1, 17 Zilka'de 1263 [27 October 1847] quoted in: Akyüz, 'Irak ve Hicaz Ordusu', 93.
[15] FO 195/301, Mosul, 11 December 1847.

The only policy option in such conditions was to develop peaceful relations with the tribe. On the other hand, the tribe was aware of its strength and used every opportunity to widen their influence over the provincial countryside.

Supremacy via Recognition: The Shammar's Policy of Collaboration, 1850–1870

Safuq's son, Farhan, succeeded him as the Shammar's paramount sheikh and controlled the majority of the tribe. Unlike his father, the new sheikh was a good politician, disposed to agree with the imperial authorities and reassured all the local bureaucrats of their fellow tribesmen's loyalty.[16] Farhan appeared a more conciliatory figure, worthy of the favour of officials in Baghdad, and provided support to the government at critical times when requested.[17] However, the Shammar's loyalty and collaboration was not a mere recognition of the Ottoman authority, but a well-calculated policy aiming to improve the tribal position against the government, increase their fellow tribesmen's wealth and spread the tribe's influence into the new areas. The sheikh simultaneously eliminated the imperial plots to weaken – or end – the paramount sheikhship of the Shammar. On the other hand, the empire-Shammar collaboration did not mean that the Ottoman purpose of ultimately expelling the nomads from the imperial lands was abandoned. The collaboration existed due to the urgent imperial need for help against the imperial authority. The frequent plots against Farhan by the imperial officials prove the maintenance of the Ottoman strategy to weaken the Shammar and push them outside the imperial territories.

Rewarding Collaboration with the Government in Baghdad and Mosul

Farhan skilfully benefited from the empire's vulnerable position in the Baghdad province (including Mosul) in the 1850s and early 1860s to increase the legitimacy of the Shammar in the eyes of the imperial authorities and consolidate the tribal position in the provincial

[16] See, for example, BOA, A.MKT 222/33, 17 Ramazan 1265 [7 August 1849].
[17] FO 195/301, Mosul, 30 October 1848.

countryside and the desert frontier. The sheikh both lent a hand to the officials when they needed urgent help and strengthened his authority over his fellow tribes by transforming the collaboration into a profitable business for the Shammar.

A notable cooperation in this regard happened in November 1850 when many Shammar migrated to southern Iraq, answering the urgent call of Abdulkerim Nadir Pasha, the governor of Baghdad. He intended to halt 'the deplorable state of anarchy' that existed in southern Mesopotamia, as a result of conflicts between the tribes in the region. Farhan was drawn to the idea as it would provide an opportunity to extend his influence in the south, where the Shammar had failed to penetrate in the past, unable to overcome the Muntafiq tribe. However, the arrival of the Shammar increased the unrest. They began by raiding the grain stores of the villages around Hillah given a lack of government granaries. The pasha proved unable to stop them. Aware of the weakness of their employer, the Shammar extended their attacks across the region, and very soon succeeded in laying waste to the entire area between the two rivers from Baghdad to below Kut. As reported by the British consul in perhaps an exaggerated way, the Shammar robbed the settled arable farmers of everything they owned and forced them to abandon their lands in the sowing season, thereby ruining the next harvest.[18]

The Shammar's raids considerably damaged the local prestige of the state, which was seen by the people as 'the demander for help by the bandits' due to its weakness. As a result, within a month of their arrival, the pasha had to ask Farhan to withdraw his troops from southern Mesopotamia, and Namık Pasha replaced Abdulkerim Pasha, given the latter's failure to establish order in the region.[19] In this case, the Shammar benefited from his cooperation with the Baghdad government while the latter obviously lost prestige and authority, which indirectly strengthened the tribal position against the empire in the region. It is obvious that the Shammar's aim was not to restore the imperial order in the region but maximize their benefits by raids as much as possible. The governor intended to benefit from the tribal

---

[18] FO 195/334, Baghdad, 16 November 1850 and 20 November 1850.
[19] FO 195/334, Baghdad, 18 December 1850; For the Ottoman reports summarizing the incidents in a similar fashion, see: Akyüz, 'Irak ve Hicaz Ordusu', 158.

human resources, but the latter reversely exploited the material resources available in the imperial lands.

Another large-scale cooperation between the Baghdad government and Farhan took place in 1858, from which the Shammar again benefited politically and financially. The sheikh helped Ömer Pasha, the governor of Baghdad, to halt attacks by the Dulaim and Anizah around Karbala and suppress the rebellion of the Khaza'il and Ma'adin tribes at Hindiyah, who had comprehensively defeated Ömer's force with substantial fatalities, forcing him to retreat. The tribes were rebelling against the Pasha's plan to conscript them into the army and disarm the region.[20] With the Shammar's move down from Mosul and their plundering the Khaza'il encampments and stealing 1,000 of their camels, which was a huge booty by all accounts, the rebel troops of Hindiyah were suppressed in a short time.[21] The only ones to gain from the Ottoman-tribe conflict in the southern districts of the Baghdad province were ironically the Shammar who were almost entirely alien to the region.

In a similar vein, a collaboration took place in 1861 when the Ubaid tribe of Kirkuk rebelled. At the call of Takiyuddin Pasha, the governor of Shahrizor, most of the Shammar tribes were mobilized by their paramount sheikh. As usual, the tribes inflicted suffering and loss on the lesser tribes and settled local inhabitants as well as blocking or halting traffic along the main road.[22] The uncontrolled Bedouin groups attacked the Yazidis, who had come together in an attempt to protect and aid the villages. The Jabbur tribe whose flocks were plundered was another victim of the Shammar's help for the government.[23] Immediately after the Shammar's arrival, however, the Ubaid made peace with the governor of Kirkuk, rendering the role of the Shammar obsolete and Farhan began to withdraw his subjects from the territory with a considerable amount of loot equal to a profitable raid.

From the government's perspective, although they suppressed the rebels at any cost, these collaborations obviously reflected the weakness of the government which disturbed the officials at all levels of the Ottoman bureaucracy. From the tribal perspective, however, helping the government proved very profitable, as they obtained many goods

---

[20] FO 195/577, Baghdad, 15 September 1858.
[21] FO 195/577, Baghdad, 29 September 1858.
[22] FO 195/676, Baghdad, 31 July 1861.
[23] FO 195/676, Mosul, 28 October 1861.

and animals by way of plunder and raids. The government's lack of sufficient troops in the region and Farhan's diplomatic skills thus allowed the Shammar to increase their domination in the region by reversing the imperial attempts to restrict their fellow tribesmen from the settled areas.

Farhan was quite careful in his collaboration with the government and did not make any commitment which would restrict the tribal mobility and weaken them against the empire. Government attempts to integrate the Shammar into the imperial system were skilfully invalidated by the sheikh without conflict as part of his policy of gainful – but preserving the distance – cooperation. Ömer Pasha, the governor of Baghdad, attempted in 1859 to recruit a body of 300 horsemen from the Shammar and Farhan himself was appointed as commander of the troops with the rank of colonel [*miralay*]. As this contingent would be manned by elders of the tribe with rank and pay corresponding to the same grades in the regular army, the government's aim was to detain the tribal leaders in areas close to Baghdad, facilitate their control and prevent them from organizing raids.[24] But this enterprise did not last long, due to the tribal unwillingness to be disciplined and Farhan's political skills.

The sheikh also did not fulfil his promise regarding the abolition of the tribal exactions, an important tribal revenue item, although the government paid him generously for that purpose. Fattah provides evidence, for instance, that at least the practice of taxing the sale of horses was maintained into the early twentieth century.[25] A consular report dated 1857 indicates that, for many years, the merchants had agreed to pay a certain amount to the sheikh for the safe passage of the caravans. The extortion was so widespread that a recognized agent of the Shammar sheikh had been permitted to reside in Baghdad and to levy *khuwwa* at a fixed rate 'on every load leaving the gates of the town on its way through his territory'.[26]

Government Plots to Weaken Farhan's Authority and the Shammar's Response

While benefiting from the Shammar's power, officials maintained the imperial attitude of weaking the tribe and expulsing them from the

---

[24] FO 195/577, Baghdad, 13 April 1858; BOA, A.MKT.MHM 171/61, 1859 [?].
[25] Fattah, *Politics of Regional Trade*, 178.
[26] FO 195/521, Baghdad, 5 August 1857.

imperial territories on the desert frontier and elsewhere, and undertook plots against Sheikh Farhan to undermine his authority, divide the tribe and create more dependent Shammar sheikhs, which would facilitate their limitation in the desert territories – or enable the government to localize the nomads – and give the government an advantage in its struggle with the Shammar. In this regard, after Farhan's sheikhship, another Shammar sheikh, 'Iyadeh, was recognized in 1850 as sheikh of the north-eastern Shammar, with a salary of 1,500 gurush by the Kürdistan governorate. He was charged with the protection of the desert district stretching from Cizre to Siverek. Indeed, he would prevent the Shammar, his own tribesmen, from attacking these districts as the imperial forces were too limited for such an action. In a short time, however, this action was overruled by the central government as it would cause disorder among the Shammar.[27]

Following that, similar attempts were made by the provinces to prevent Farhan from penetrating into the region's countryside.[28] With a similar motivation, only a year later, the governor of Mosul appointed Farhan's uncle Hijr as the sheikh of the Shammar in Mosul. He was provided with a 2,000-piaster salary for his protection of the villages of Mosul, which would motivate the sheikh to resist Farhan's authority.[29] Shortly after that, in 1852, presumably due to his failure to prevent the Shammar attacks on the villages and caravans which might be instigated by Farhan, Hijr was deposed[30] and the Farhan had to be reappointed as the Shammar's sheikh of sheikhs [şeyhulmeşayih] in Baghdad and Mosul.[31]

Consequently, Farhan again controlled the Shammar territories in Mosul. The failure of such attempts stemmed from the tribal support for Farhan who satisfied his fellow tribesmen with the profitable collaborations with the government as explained in the previous section. The Ottoman documents indicate that the authorities of the Kürdistan province and Mosul were particularly concerned by the expansion of Farhan's authority into their region since they perceived him as the man

[27] BOA, A.MKT.MVL 33/108, 21 Zilhicce 1266 [28 September 1850]; BOA, A. MKT.UM 43/86, 26 Safer 1267 [1 January 1851]; BOA, A.MKT.UM 22 Rebiulahir 1267 [25 February 1851].
[28] See, for example, BOA, İ.DH 256/15760, 23 Ramazan 1268 [12 July 1852].
[29] BOA, A.MKT.UM 70/96, 22 Şevval 1267 [20 August 1851].
[30] FO 195/394, Mosul, 8 November 1852.
[31] BOA, BEO.AYN.d. No.174, 20 Ramazan 1268 [8 July 1852], 98.

of the Baghdad province and interpreted the extension of his sheikhship as a plot by the Baghdad province.

Such failures, however, did not persuade the Ottoman authorities in the short run to relinquish their designs against the Shammar. In 1860, anxious about Farhan's spreading influence over the Mosul country-side, Veysi Pasha, the governor of Mosul, dismissed the Shammar sheikh[32] and tried to exclude the Shammar from Mosul in cooperation with Sheikh Dahham of the Anizah.[33] When Dahham rejected his proposal, most likely due to his endeavours to gain a position in the Urfa region, the governor offered the post of protector of the province's desert frontier to Sumair, one of the lesser Shammar sheikhs related to Farhan.[34] This challenge to Farhan's authority caused major unrest among the Shammar in the Iraqi, Syrian and neighbouring Anatolian provinces, significantly impacting regional security. In order to compel the governor to accept his authority and demonstrate his power, Farhan instructed his cousin Nazif to attack flocks belonging to the people of Mosul. They seized 30,000 to 35,000 sheep, as well as a large number of camels, horses and donkeys.[35] The pro-Farhan Shammar launched other offensives in the neighbourhood of Baghdad and ren-dered the roads between the Syrian, Anatolian and Iraqi provinces utterly unsafe.[36] Meanwhile, the central government ordered the gov-ernor of Baghdad to reappoint Farhan as sheikh and insist on his agreement to return property seized.[37] In a short time, the governor of Baghdad intervened in the conflict and despatched both Sumair and the pasha of Mosul.[38] The sheikh of the Shammar once again expanded his sphere of influence within the Mosul region by agreeing with the governor of Mosul to maintain the security of the line between the Khabur and the Great Zab in exchange for a salary of 3,600 piasters per month, equivalent to the pay of thirty irregular horsemen.[39]

---

[32] BOA, BEO.AYN.d. No. 182, 23 Cemaziyelahir 1276 [17 January 1860], 163.
[33] FO 195/603, Mosul, 14 November 1859; an Ottoman document says that Farhan's salary was equal to that of a governor: BOA, DH.ŞFR 145/85, 5 Eylül 1306 [18 September 1890].
[34] FO 195/603, Mosul, 12 December 1859.
[35] FO 195/603, Mosul, 6 February 1860.
[36] FO 195/624, Baghdad, 29 February 1860; FO 195/676, Mardin, 5 August 1861.
[37] BOA, BEO.AYN.d. No. 182, 23 Cemaziyelahir 1276 [17 January 1860], 163.
[38] FO 195/603, Mosul, 19 March 1860; FO 195/624, Baghdad, 11 April 1860.
[39] FO 195/676, Baghdad, 8 April 1861.

The spread of the Shammar's influence in such an extensive area made the government anxious and new policies were again put into practice to restrict and pacify the tribe. Namık Pasha, the governor general of Baghdad with wide-ranging support from the central government to resolve disorders in the province, endeavoured 'to restore order among the [tribal] Arabs in Mesopotamia'. To that end, the governor was supported by considerable number of troops which encouraged him to restore government's 'honour' against the Shammar, which is demonstrative of the Ottoman intention regarding the nomads when imperial strength was sufficiently improved. The Pasha dismissed Farhan and installed his uncle Sumair in his place.[40] Similar to Veysi Pasha's undertaking, the aim was to coerce the Shammar to leave Mesopotamia[41] and 'to annihilate them', as exaggeratedly reported by the British consul in Mosul.[42] Cooperation between the different governorates such as Diarbekir, Kirkuk, Mosul, Aleppo, Urfa and Baghdad saw them surrounded.[43] The number of troops called up from these districts was, according to the British vice-consul in Mosul, between 12,000 and 15,000.[44] Shammar from several provinces united against the government, plundered villages and merchants from Diarbekir to Baghdad and Aleppo.[45] In spite of the mobilization of significant numbers of both regular and irregular troops, the Shammar could not be defeated, and their sustained attacks on villages, caravans and the troops themselves put the Ottoman army in an awkward position.[46]

However, Farhan acted diplomatically and returned to negotiation as the heat of the summer and the lack of wheat put the Shammar in a difficult position.[47] After some negotiation, and an attempt to replace Farhan with another Shammar sheikh, Namık was forced to accept the sheikh's authority and reappointed him as the paramount sheikh.[48] In

---

[40] For a summary of incidents, see: FO 195/717, Diarbekir, 14 October 1862; FO 195/717, Copy of a letter addressed to Sheikh Farhan, Baghdad, 16 June 1862.

[41] FO 195/717, Baghdad, 18 June 1862.

[42] FO 195/717, Mosul, 3 March 1862, quoted in Dolbee, 'The Locust and the Starling', 119.

[43] FO 195/717, Mosul, 3 March 1862.

[44] FO 195/717, Mosul, 31 March 1862.

[45] FO 195/717, Mosul, 14 April 1862.   [46] FO 195/717, Mosul, 17 April 1862.

[47] Dolbee, 'The Locust and the Starling', 120.

[48] FO 195/717, Mosul, 1 September 1862; FO 195/717, Diarbekir, 14 October 1862.

return, Farhan consented 'to accept the surrender of 50,000 sheep, 5,000 camels and 200 remount horses as an atonement for the depredations committed by the tribe last year'.[49] But only a small amount of the promised number (3,350 sheep and 1,391 camels) was delivered to the government.[50] That was the last major imperial attempt to weaken and expel the Shammar from the territories of the Baghdad province. It seems that the Ottoman officials accepted and recognized the tribal reality, and sought for policies in the following years to accommodate the Shammar within the imperial framework. No large-scale conflict happened between the sides until 1871 when Midhat Pasha undertook to transform the Shammar's nomadic lifestyle into a settled one.

Farhan turned the imperial plots against his leadership back on the empire by using these opportunities for widespread plundering of the countryside. This meant a great financial benefit for his fellow tribesmen, which made the legitimacy of his sheikhship undisputed in the tribal society and caused the Ottoman plots to fail. In addition, similar to his collaboration with the government analysed in the previous section, the sheikh increased the political agency of the tribe and consolidated its position in the grazing lands of the desert frontier and elsewhere. The plots against the Shammar, on the other hand, demonstrate the 'non-harmonic' situation of Ottoman bureaucracy in the region. Disputes and competition between the neighbouring governorates caused the government plots to come to naught; an action by a certain governorate, such as Mosul and Kürdistan, was not recognized by another one, for example the governor of Baghdad, while sometimes the central government annulled a local decision as in the appointment of 'Iyadeh. Such contradictions and disorganization help us to understand the complexities of the Ottoman administration.

Midhat Pasha and the Enterprises of Settlement in Iraq

The early years of the 1870s witnessed large-scale imperial projects under the governorship of the prominent Tanzimat statesman, Midhat Pasha, to consolidate imperial power and solve long-lasting problems in the Iraqi territories. The Pasha was supported by a great number of troops and money to prevent him failing as had happened many times

---

[49] FO 195/717, Baghdad, 22 October 1862.
[50] Dolbee, 'The Locust and the Starling', 121.

in the past. During his governorship of Baghdad from February 1869 to April 1872, Midhat Pasha extended Ottoman control into al-Hasa of the Najd, and complemented the Muntafiq tribes' land registration and settlement process. Localization of the Shammar and their conversion from nomads to settled tribes was one of his major projects and manifested a radical change in imperial policies from 'expulsive' struggle to policies designated to contain the Shammar. The nomads would be settled in the lands they used as pasturage which would make them controllable and the lands they used cultivable. In this way, the colonization of the space in the desert frontier would be achieved and imperial rule would be both extended and consolidated. This was one of the most serious Ottoman attempts to benefit from the tribal material and human resources. But the tribal resistance caused the imperial plans to fail and thus gave a new direction to imperial policies in the Arab lands.

Midhat Pasha acted against the Shammar with a *mission civilisatrice*. According to the pasha, effective control over these tribes might have been achieved if they could be compelled to settle and embrace agricultural farming.[51] As a convinced modernist who believed in the existence of a hierarchy among lifestyles, he mistakenly assumed that it would be easy to settle the Shammar: once a branch of the nomads 'tasted the agriculture' [*ziraatin lezzetini aldıkta*], the others would quickly follow suit. Midhat went one step further and associated 'religiousity' with being 'settled' in a similar fashion to Western Christian missionaries preaching to proselytize indigenous peoples in the colonies. In his viewpoint, the settlement was a requirement of being Muslim and following Islamic law [*al-shar'iyya al-Muhammadiyya*] as it would result in the tribes' foregoing 'raiding and robbery' and necessitate their practising agriculture and commerce.[52]

The Settlement Project of Farhan Pasha with His Tribe in the Shirgat of the Jazira Region

Following his achievements in southern Iraq of the settlement of the Muntafiq tribes, and extension of Ottoman rule into al-Hasa, Midhat

---

[51] BOA, İ.DH 630/43847, 1 Mart 1287 [14 March 1871].
[52] BOA, SD 1453/25, 23 Zilhicce 1287 [15 March 1871], quoted in Dolbee, 'The Locust and the Starling', 145.

Figure 1.1 Shirgat of the Jazira from the north. Gertrude Bell Archives, Newcastle University, L_176.

shifted his interest to the settlement of the Shammar tribes, the largest migrant society of the region and, in the view of many Ottoman officials, the most difficult one to control. He invited Farhan Pasha to Baghdad and declared his decision. Upon the decisiveness of Midhat Pasha and becoming aware of the Ottoman military and financial strength at that time, Farhan unwillingly agreed to convince his fellow tribesmen to settle in return for a noticeable increase in salary, signing a contract with the government of Baghdad to this effect.[53] Farhan Pasha was to cultivate the land called Shirgat, on the right bank of the Shat River stretching from Tikrit to Mosul. Farhan's men would pay only the tithe tax and these lands would be registered to the tribesmen with a title deed, which was a crucial step towards individualization of property rights in the tribal society and weakening of tribal ties of solidarity. The district would be referred to as the *sanjak* of the Shammar and Farhan would be appointed as *mutasarrıf* of the new administrative unit.[54] His salary was increased to 25,000 piasters 'as

[53]   BOA, İ.DH 630/43847, 19 Zilhicce 1287 [11 March 1871].
[54]   BOA, ŞD 2149/9, 13 Safer 1289 [23 April 1872].

a reward for introducing his tribe to civilized rule and to compensate for the cost of the buildings that he would construct for tribal members'.[55] The new *mutasarrıfate* would also house a number of the Ottoman soldiers, presumably to prevent the escape of the tribesmen and not to leave everything to their will.

Shortly after the agreement, Farhan established his own quarters at Shirgat, and the government began to build barracks for the troops, a suitable residence for the governor and a market. The Bedouin, however, resented their new lifestyle, and, thus, shortly after Farhan's taking up residence,[56] nearly all those Bedouin with him at Shirgat left as they had to move on for the well-being of their camel herds that required specific pasture in different seasons. Many of them went south, while others followed relatives who had moved on to Najd.[57] The nomads were requested to engage in a new mode of subsistence which was completely alien to them and thus they reacted to their sheikh. This was the most serious bottom-up challenge to Farhan's leadership and severely undermined the legitimacy of his sheikhship, which constituted a major reason for the failure of this enterprise. Following that, the Ottoman government soon abandoned the project and adopted other strategies which facilitated control of the Shammar and contributed to the maintenance of good relations between the two sides.

The Settlement Attempt in Deir al-Zor and the Shammar Revolt

The branches dispersed between Deir al-Zor and Mardin did not respond as peaceful as the southern ones when Midhat Pasha requested them to settle on the banks of the Khabur River. In response to the government order, the tribes organized under the leadership of sheikh Abd al-Qarim, Farhan's brother, and moved towards Mardin in revolt winning significant support among the Shammar, the majority of whom resented the settlement projects. Together with his brother

---

[55] BOA, İ.ŞD 24/1057, 10 Ağustos 1288 [23 August 1872].

[56] For a later Ottoman document that refers to Farhan's willingness to materialize Midhat's project, see: BOA, İ.MMS 130/5577, 2 Ağustos 1887 [15 August 1887].

[57] FO 195/949, Mosul, 4 January 1872.

Abd al-Razzaq, the sheikh wrote letters to the chiefs of the different tribes, inviting them to oppose the pasha's attack on their liberty, 'complaining that Midhat Pasha desired to destroy the Arab tents, to make them renounce their independent roving life, and to oblige them to settle in villages and become cultivators'.[58] These were the nightmares of the tribes as – similar to Midhat Pasha's conviction about the sedentary lifestyle – they saw nomadism as superior to the sedentary lifestyle. Supported by the majority of the Shammar, who objected to Farhan's acceptance of Midhat's plan, as well as a number of other tribes like al-Dufair of the Muntafiq, another tribe that Midhat intended to settle, Abd al-Qarim launched a huge rebellion. It devastated the countryside of Baghdad, Mosul, Deir and Diarbekir and rendered caravan routes crossing the desert completely impassable.[59]

The government recognized their best course of action was to persuade Abd al-Qarim to renounce his claims and accept the pasha's plan to settle the Shammar. In spite of considerable efforts by both the governors of Baghdad and Kürdistan, and Farhan, Abd al-Qarim could not alter his stance. His rebellion was suppressed by the joint expeditions of the Diarbekir, Mosul, Deir al-Zor and Baghdad governments as well as those Shammar and Muntafiq groups loyal to Farhan and Nasır Pashas. Shortly after his defeat, Abd al-Qarim was captured by the Muntafiq tribes and sent to Baghdad.[60] Finally, in 1871 on the way as a prisoner to Constantinople, he was executed in Mosul on the order of Midhat Pasha, the governor of Baghdad.[61] However, the settlement plan was ultimately abandoned following Midhat Pasha's departure from Baghdad, and the Shammar were able to sustain their nomadic lifestyle. Abd al-Qarim paid the price for the Shammar's freedom with his life.

The biggest deficiency of Midhat Pasha's projects was that he did not ascribe sufficient importance to the tribal insistence on their lifestyle. The pasha was of the belief that he could force the nomads to change

---

[58] FO 195/949, Baghdad, 2 August 1871 and 30 August 1871; CADN, Serie A, 18PO/Mosul 1872–1877, 14 August 1871.
[59] See, for example, FO 195/949, Baghdad, 17 July 1871; CADN, Serie A, 18PO/Mosul 1872–1877, 29 July 1871.
[60] FO 195/949, Baghdad, 26 September 1871.
[61] For some details, see: BOA, İ.DH 642/44656, 13 Teşrin-i Evvel 1287 [10 November 1871].

their migratory lifestyle by 'bribing' their sheikhs and limiting their actions by force. The Shammar were different from the Muntafiq – Midhat's successful undertaking in Iraq – as they were not mixed nomads and not tied to land. They could easily move from one place to another with their animals and tents and waste all the government attempts. As a result, his successors understood the impossibility of realizing the project without the consent of the tribesmen and completely abandoned it. That was the first and the last serious attempt to localize the biggest nomadic confederation of Iraq. As will be detailed in the following sections, all the later undertakings to settle the Shammar did not go beyond the level of project.

The Fid'an

Similar to the Shammar confederation, hostility, conflict, coercive operations, temporary agreements and the state's failure to eliminate them determined the empire's relations with the Fid'an federation of the Anizah frequenting the districts of Urfa, Aleppo, Hama, Homs and Deir al-Zor during the Tanzimat era. As in the case of the Shammar, the major Ottoman ambition was to keep the nomads as far away as possible from the settled areas, limit their movement in the uncultivable areas and thus provide security in the areas practically controlled by the empire. Contrary to the Shammar, the Ottoman officials in Aleppo produced their own candidate for the Fid'an's paramount sheikhship although this did not solve the tribal question on the part of the empire and bring about the tranquillity of the region. The hostilities between and among the government troops, Jed'an's supporters, the progovernment sheikh and resistant Fid'an groups frequently disrupted the provincial security in Aleppo. From the tribal viewpoint, similar to the Shammar, the imperial weakness provided them an important opportunity to economically prosper and politically expand. In spite of the internecine conflict, the Fid'an were able to expand the areas they controlled as pastures up to the early 1870s when the Ottoman administration in Deir al-Zor was consolidated. The establishment of the Deir al-Zor *mutasarrıfate* and the death of Dahham, the resistant sheikh, in 1871 laid the foundations for the empire-Fid'an compromise, which made the parties more or less equal and mutually dependent.

Figure 1.2 The prominent Anizah sheikhs around Aleppo with Homer Davenport, 1906. Davenport, *My Quest*, 161.

Initial Attempts against the Fid'an's Domination and Tribal Resistance to the Imperial Designs, 1840–1851

The Fid'an emerged as a serious threat to Ottoman rule in Aleppo when the region was returned to the empire from Egyptian rule in 1840. They controlled major pastures in the east of the province and expanded their domination in the countryside by way of raids, which meant a crucial security problem on the part of the empire. The Ottoman efforts to find a solution to the tribal question thus started as soon as the reinstatement of Ottoman rule in the region. As stated previously, the Ottoman policy was to weaken the tribes and limit their movement as much as possible. To that end, immediately after the restoration of Ottoman rule in Syria, the government of Aleppo tried to control the tribal sheikhs by playing off one sheikh against another. Esad Pasha, the governor, undertook an intrigue against the paramount sheikh Dahham in collaboration with some other Fid'an sheikhs by nominating Horan, the sheikh of a lesser tribe consisting of 200 tents, as the paramount sheikh.[62] Dahham reacted to this project by attacking the tax-paying sedentary tribes in the neighbourhood of Aleppo and plundered many of their herds, which meant a serious security problem for the province and a considerable loss of tax revenue for the imperial

---

[62] CADN, Serie D, 166PO/D1/47, Aleppo, 1 June 1841; FO 195/170, Aleppo, 15 May 1841; Barker, Syria and Egypt, 21.

treasury. Similar to Safuq, Dahham refused to recognize the government as the supreme authority and refused to visit Aleppo for negotiations for fear of being conspired against. He openly declared to the local authorities that he was already the sheikh of the Fid'an and did not need government recognition to maintain this office.[63]

Various unsuccessful attempts were made during 1841 by influential persons including the British consul, the Mufti and local notables to reconcile the sides, put an end to the state of chaos and provide peace in the desert frontier of the province, which was essential for the maintenance of trade and agriculture in certain parts of the country. All these efforts, however, failed mainly due to government plots – and sometimes due to tribal fear of official intrigue – and the Fid'an's attacks on trade caravans and the tax-paying settled tribes continued the next year, seriously destroying the imperial treasury's sources of taxation. During these conflicts, Dahham's party always held supremacy in the field and did not allow the government side to have authority over the Fid'an's pasturages.[64]

As the imperial army in Aleppo was extremely weak at that time,[65] the Fid'an's undisputed supremacy continued until 1851 when Sheikh Jed'an emerged as an alternative to Dahham; he seriously challenged the latter's leadership and preferred to cooperate with the government to prevail over his rival. The Fid'an had become the de facto owner of Aleppo's eastern and northern countryside between 1842 and 1851 and deliberately did not try to reconcile with Aleppo officials in order to maximize their profit by raiding villages and caravans. On the other hand, the government was still hopeful about the subjugation of the nomads and, to that end, continued to organize occasional large-scale operations, many of which failed due to the lack of imperial fortifications in the desert frontier which would have more or less prevented the tribesmen from escaping into the desert when pushed by the government troops. Esad Pasha, the governor of Aleppo, also made an effort to find

---

[63] For details, see: Barker, *Syria and Egypt*, 22.

[64] CADN, Serie D, 166PO/D1/47, Aleppo, 10 September 1841; FO 195/170, Aleppo, 25 June 1841; CADN, Serie D, 166PO/D1/47, Aleppo, 1 June 1841; CADN, Serie D, 166PO/D1/47, Aleppo, 31 July 1841; CADN, Serie D, 166PO/D1/47, Aleppo, 15 June 1841; FO 195/170, Aleppo, 2 August 184; FO 195/170, Aleppo, 2 August 1841; FO 195/170, Aleppo, 17 September 1841; CADN, Serie D, 166PO/D1/47, Aleppo, 17 November 1841.

[65] Barker claims that Esad Pasha had only 'two light guns and ... small number of troops'. Barker, *Syria and Egypt*, 22.

allies among the Anizah such as the sheikh of the Seb'a, another branch of the Anizah, to expel the Fid'an. However, these efforts were largely unsuccessful as the Fid'an did not waste the vulnerable situation of the government and consolidated their power for the sake of the abundant booty captured from the villages and caravans. The governor's attempts to reconcile mostly failed – or lasted too little time – for similar reasons. The result for the imperial lands was by all accounts the devastation of the villages in the province's northern and eastern countryside and significant loss of the local merchant's goods due to the tribal attacks on the caravans crossing the desert.[66] In 1846 alone, the Sad'an township[67] [nahiye] of Siverek lost 20,000 sheep, 200 oxen and cows, 50 camels, 25 horses, 40 donkeys, 50 black tents and household goods valued 50,000 piasters to the Anizah. The tribes burned 500 houses and 600 tents in the nahiye. The other villages of Aleppo province suffered similar losses.[68] Similarly, in 1847, the Karacadağ township [nahiye] lost 2,500 sheep, 180 oxen and cows, 60 camels and 15 horses to the Anizah and 100 houses were burnt by the tribesmen as the numerous other villages suffered similar losses.[69] The roads connecting the major cities of the region to each other such as Aleppo, Diarbekir, Damascus, Mosul and Baghdad were utterly unsafe and became unpassable due to the hostilities between the government and the Fid'an.

The Rise of Jed'an and Empire-Fid'an Relations

In the early 1850s, Dahham's authority was challenged by another Fid'an sheikh, Jed'an, who gave the government the opportunity to

---

[66] For details, see: FO 195/207, Aleppo, 27 January 1842; FO 195/207, Aleppo, 10 September 1842 and 27 October 1842; CADN, Serie D, 166PO/D1/47, Aleppo, 31 March 1842; FO 195/207, Aleppo, 4 May 1844; FO 195/207, Aleppo, 15 June 1844; FO 195/207, Aleppo, 24 May 1845; FO 195/207, Aleppo, 7 June 1845; FO 195/207, Aleppo, 4 April 1846; FO 195/207, Aleppo, 8 August 1846; FO 195/302, Aleppo, 29 April 1847; 8 May 1847 and 22 May 1847; BOA, A.MKT 169/7, 19 Safer 1265 [13 January 1849]; BOA, İ. DH 223/ 13281, 1 Zilkade 1266 [9 September 1850]; SCR-Urfa 204, 1265 [1849/1850], Document 64; Karal, 'Zarif Paşa'nın Hatıratı', 470.

[67] This nahiye consisted of 30 villages, 700 households and 600 tents. Saydam, 'Aşiretlerin Yol Açtıkları Asayiş Problemleri', 247.

[68] For similar losses in other villages in the region, see: Saydam, 'Aşiretlerin Yol Açtıkları Asayiş Problemleri', 247–252.

[69] For details, see: Saydam, 'Aşiretlerin Yol Açtıkları Asayiş Problemleri', 248.

Figure 1.3 The Mawali sheikhs. İstanbul Üniversitesi Nadir Eserler Kütüphanesi, 90567/52.

play him off against Dahham and make the Fid'an sheikhs more dependent on imperial decision-making. In addition to the support of a significant number of his fellow tribesmen, Jed'an enjoyed substantial backing from the provincial authorities and local elites as a result of his diplomatic skills. He was accommodated by and collaborated closely with troops paid by the government.[70] Jed'an also fostered good relations with the Hannadi and Mawali sheikhs, whose subjects worked as irregular troops for the government. For himself, alliance with the government and people closer to it was a strategic step to weaken Dahham's power and capture the paramount sheikhship. However, it is difficult to claim that he was a puppet leader made by the government given the level of support by the tribal people and the absence of any

[70] FO 195/302, Aleppo, 17 April 1852.

documentary evidence. The government only allied with him after his rise due to his conciliatory attitude.

There were rational reasons for the Fid'an to support Jed'an against Dahham as they needed to reconcile with the government due to the developments taking place in Aleppo from 1850 onward. The Ottoman military power in the province of Aleppo increased from 1850 as a result of rebellions against the government's decision to recruit soldiers to the imperial army from the region, which caused the Fid'an to lose ground against the Ottoman troops. In addition, as will be detailed in Chapter 2, a series of fortresses had been erected in the desert frontier by that time which somewhat weakened the tribal position. Therefore, for the Fid'an, a more conciliatory and diplomatic figure like Jed'an might be more ideal as the sheikh of the tribe than a warrior chief like Dahham to negotiate with the officials for access to the pastures around Aleppo. Consequently, by 1851, he enjoyed both government backing and substantial support among his fellow tribesmen.[71] He promised to the governor 'by contract' that he would 'from now serve and act loyally and faithfully as the subject of the sublime state' [*bundan böyle teb'a-i devlet-i aliyye'den olarak sadıkane ve rızacuyane hizmet ve hareket edeceğine taraf-ı çakeriye sened vermiş*].[72]

Jed'an's appointment as the paramount sheikh and the granting of privileges of plentiful pastures for their animals as well as trade with the peasants and townspeople increased his popularity among the Fid'an[73] and facilitated Dahham's exclusion to Deir al-Zor.[74] Losing his former superior position vis-à-vis the government, Dahham began to lobby in Aleppo in hope of recovering the sheikhship. However, the governor, Muhammed Pasha, refused to grant his request with lame excuses referring to his previous plunder.[75] The government's military success prevented the dissatisfied Anizahs from drawing the government into their line of action by raids and plunder. They were also prevented from approaching the Urfa district, where they spent summer, grazed their animals and traded with the local people.[76] The roads in and around Aleppo and the desert border were safer, since no incursion could be

---

[71] FO 195/302, Aleppo, 29 March 1851.
[72] BOA, A.MKT.UM 198/98, 11 Ramazan 1271 [28 May 1855].
[73] For the remarks by the governor of Aleppo, confirming this argument, see: BOA, A.MKT.UM 198/98, 11 Ramazan 1271 [28 May 1855].
[74] FO 195/302, Aleppo, 10 April 1852.   [75] FO 195/302, Aleppo, 3 April 1852.
[76] BOA, BEO.AYN.d. No 173, 19 Şevval 1267 [17 August 1851], 19.

made by the Fid'an over the desert frontier, thanks to the governor's measures and reconciliation with Jed'an.[77] Dahham maintained his hostile attitude the next year by attacking Jed'an's party and the settled regions. But, with the help of some regular troops, the government ended the hostilities by forcing Dahham to retreat to the desert and 'bringing peace'.[78]

The government continued to harvest the fruits of dividing the Anizah as good relations with the tribes continued in the following years: reports from Aleppo attest to the peace on the desert frontier, and the tribesmen caused no further disturbance in 1853 and 1854.[79] While that might be interpreted as a partial success for the government as Jed'an's fellow tribesmen were recognized and allowed to enter into the settled areas, he also continued to exact *khuwwa* taxes from the villages on his behalf, as had Dahham. According to the governor of Aleppo in 1861, in addition to the 4,000 *gurush* salary he received from the provincial treasury,[80] Jed'an collected 5–6,000 purses [*akche*] annually in duties from the villages of Aleppo.[81] It was thus by no means a government victory for its preconceived plans against the Fid'an, instead, as in case of Farhan Pasha, it resulted in domination of the tribe under the leadership of a different and more conciliatory sheikh. Following Jed'an's appointment, the imperial policy against the Fid'an increasingly transformed from total war into a partial alliance with more reconcilable branches against the unwanted elements, who were organized under Dahham's leadership.

Another period of hostilities began between 1854 and 1856 with a different character, due to the first Ottoman expedition against Deir al-Zor.[82] In the hope of benefiting from Dahham's influence in the region, the Aleppo government invested in Dahham and salaried him as the paramount sheikh. The new situation, however, frustrated

---

[77] FO 195/302, Aleppo, 29 September 1851.
[78] FO 195/302, Aleppo, 26 June 1852; FO 195/302, Aleppo, 30 June 1852; FO 195/302, Aleppo, 3 July 1852.
[79] BOA, BEO.AYN.d. No. 176, 27 Zilhicce 1269 [25 September 1853], 58; FO 195/416, Aleppo, 20 July and 22 July 1854.
[80] BOA, MVL 754/53, 11 Cemaziyelevvel 1276 [6 December 1859].
[81] BOA, MVL 762/62, 18 Safer 1278 [26 August 1861]; the same amount is repeated one year later in another document: BOA, MVL. 762/91, 11 Zilhicce 1278 [10 June 1862].
[82] For details on the first Ottoman expedition to Deir al-Zor, see: Chapter 3.

Jed'an and his supporters and the sheikh attacked the villages and made a number of incursions around Aleppo. In addition, the Mawali Bedouin, another ally of Jed'an, broke the truce, attacked the settled tribes and wrecked the rural stability.[83] After much dissent, the hostile tribes could be pacified through the involvement of the newly appointed sheikh, Dahham.[84] Due to the sensitive situation in Deir al-Zor and the need for support from the Fid'an, the sheikhship was changed several times between the two sheikhs during 1854–1856. The decision makers were torn between having Jed'an's active support for the expedition and Dahham's good behaviour in Deir al-Zor. In 1855, for instance, Jed'an was actively supported by the government troops against Dahham and the latter was expelled from the Aleppo region and forced to migrate to the province of Damascus. The next year, however, the government's decision changed and Dahham was appointed as paramount sheikh.[85] Dahham was paid as the Fid'an's paramount sheikh up to 1858 when he was deposed by the Aleppo administrative council.[86] The Ottoman failure to dominate Deir al-Zor and the decreasing necessity for his cooperation and increasing popularity of Jed'an among the Fid'an might be the reason for his dismissal. Ottoman reports reveal that an agreement was reached with Jed'an in the late 1850s and early 1860s that excluded Dahham's followers from the Aleppo region and established peace throughout the province, including Urfa and Jazira.[87]

The government's role in the exclusion of Dahham should not be exaggerated given the increasing popularity of Jed'an among the Fid'an and his aim to get rid of his rival. It was in fact the latter – not the Ottoman troops – who defeated and expelled Dahham and his fellow tribesmen from the region in cooperation with the government irregulars. What happened was a change in the power balance within the Fid'an. Otherwise, the position of the tribe did not

---

[83] FO 195/416, Aleppo, 9 October 1855.

[84] BOA, MVL 290/40, 15 Şevval 1271 [1 July 1855].

[85] BOA, A.MKT.UM 198/98, 11 Ramazan 1271 [28 May 1855].

[86] BOA, MVL 772/28, 22 Zilhicce 1280 [29 May 1864]; this document informs us that in 1864 Jed'an was appointed as the Fid'an sheikh for six years, which means that Dahham was dismissed three years after this appointment.

[87] See, for example, BOA, MVL 764/42, 7 Rebiulahir 1279 [2 October 1862]; for another document reporting the Anizah's tranquillity in Aleppo in 1856, see: BOA, BEO.AYN.d. No. 180, 25 Cemaziyelevvel 1272 [9 January 1856], 13; see also, the document in the next footnote.

fundamentally change by the exclusion of Dahham as one group replaced the other. It is also sensible to think that many Fid'an changed their loyalty from Dahham to Jed'an when the latter won against his rival.

Dahham's Exclusion and His Search for New Pastures in the North and East

Jed'an's alliance with the Aleppo authorities and the creation of a partnership with them compelled Dahham to find new pastures for the animals of his fellow tribesmen. In this regard, he shifted his interest from the northern districts of Aleppo province to the south of Kürdistan province from which he had been expelled when the Shammar sheikh Abd al-Qarim replaced him. Raids by those loyal to Abd al-Qarim's on some of the Fid'an tribesmen on three separate occasions and their carrying off thousands of their sheep and camels gave him a golden opportunity to expel the Shammar sheikh from the region and replace him. In response, the entire Fid'an tribe, motivated by a desire for revenge and tempted by the superior pasture lands on the north-east of the Jazira desert, attacked Abd al-Qarim's followers.[88] Hostilities continued into the following year, and resulted in the expulsion of Abd al-Qarim to Mosul. The Fid'an attacked and plundered a great deal of property in the vicinity of the town (Urfa). As a result, Dahham had to be appointed as the 'protector' of the town's desert frontier, whose real mission was not to attack the tax-paying villages. The pasha of Urfa rewarded him with a robe of honour and the salary formerly allocated to Abd al-Qarim. All the property previously taken by the Anizah was restored to its owners, which rarely happened in such instances.[89] Dahham's desire to approach the officials and have a permanent position in the Urfa district might be the reason behind the nomads' return of the plundered property.

The following developments also prove this argument. The governor of Kürdistan reported that the Anizah under Dahham, who was appointed as the protector of the Urfa region and thus his territorial rights were recognized, did not even create a small incident in the

---

[88] BOA, HR.TO 228/26, 1 October 1857.
[89] BOA, MVL 318/24, 26 Receb 1274 [12 March 1858]; FO 195/603, Mosul, 6 September 1858.

Siverek region while they stayed there for three months in the summers of 1857 and 1858. On the other hand, the local officials adopted a more peaceful approach towards them and refrained from using their weapons [*hiçbir taraftan teşhir-i silah olunmamak*] unnecessarily.[90] It was almost impossible, however, for the government to dissociate itself from Abd al-Qarim, who had many tribesmen frequenting the district and the potential to wreck the regional security entirely. The Shammar sheikh had presumably better relations with the Urfa authorities compared to Dahham which made him preferable. Thus, before long, he was re-employed and charged with once again protecting the region.[91] The Fid'an, in turn, renewed their attacks on the villages of Mardin given their hostility towards Abd al-Qarim and his government-protected status.[92] In response, the sub-governor intensified the efforts to remove Dahham and expel the Fid'an completely from the region. In 1859, the governor allied with the Shammar sheikh Abd al-Qarim and eliminated Dahham.

This time, the Fid'an sheikh altered his course towards Mosul and invaded the province's countryside with a great number of tribesmen. Jed'an supported his rival, most likely to get rid of him in Aleppo.[93] The usual protector of the region, Farhan of the Shammar, had been invited by the governor of Baghdad to the southern districts of the province to help the imperial troops against the other tribes, which made Mosul an open country for Dahham. The sheikh migrated there with his fellow tribesmen and organized large-scale raids in the Mosuli countryside defeating all the attempts on the part of the government to stop him.[94] Given the discontinuity of the migrations by Dahham's fellow tribesmen in the following years, it may be inferred that Farhan's return secured the Mosul region from the invasion of a new 'tribal conqueror'. Furthermore, Dahham's permanent occupation of a region in the east of the Euphrates would have destroyed the implicit long-term tribal agreement on division of the pastures between the Shammar and Anizah and would have caused great tribal wars, which would most likely have put the sheikh under a heavy burden difficult to overcome. For these reasons,

---

[90]   BOA, A.MKT.UM 363/57, Diarbekir 3 Safer 1276 [2 September 1859].
[91]   BOA, BEO.AYN.d. No. 181, 28 Şevval 1275 [31 May 1859], 103.
[92]   BOA, A.MKT.UM 379/61, 23 Rebiulahir 1276 [20 November 1859].
[93]   BOA, A.MKT.UM 402/48, 14 Ramazan 1276 [6 Nisan 1860].
[94]   FO 195/603, Mosul, 17 October 1859.

Dahham's undertaking to find a new region for his fellow tribesmen in the east failed.

Finally, in 1862, Ismet Pasha, the governor of Aleppo, adopted a more conciliatory approach, attempting to integrate Dahham's followers into Aleppo's financial network by extending their trade access to villages and towns.[95] The second Deir al-Zor expedition launched in 1864, however, was harmful to tribal finance, as it would limit their pastures and *khuwwa* incomes as well as their authority over the semi-settled tribes of Deir al-Zor. Dahham relaunched his attacks on Aleppo's villages in response to the Ottoman expansion to Deir al-Zor. As will be detailed in Chapter 3, protracted hostilities continued between the government troops and Jed'an's followers, on one side, and Dahham's tribes on the other, until Dahham's death in 1871.

Proving the vulnerability of the imperial position and the tribal strength in the countryside during the period under analysis, it is interesting to note that, in all these engagements, the government could never respond to Dahham unsupported. The officials always had to cooperate with one or more tribal allies to put their plans into practice, none of whom were considered at that time as ideal partners. The expulsion of a group did not mean their replacement by imperial troops, but by another tribal community. This dependence became a major concern for the Ottoman authorities and, as explained above, they tried to weaken the tribes using all the available means. The local governments organized expulsive operations against the nomads when they gathered sufficient strength or found eligible allies.

Following Dahham's elimination, the governor of Aleppo, Kamil Pasha, appointed Jed'an as the paramount sheikh.[96] It seems that Jed'an's undisputed authority made the government anxious that the Fid'an's unity would strengthen the tribal position against the government. Therefore, soon after, the new governor, Derviş Pasha, tried to replace Jed'an with another candidate. Similar to Farhan, Jed'an fought this, and defeated Ottoman troops on a number of occasions, forcing the government to accept his authority by killing his rival and becoming the unrivalled sheikh of the Fid'an until his death in 1882.[97] Jed'an's consolidation of power prevented the

[95] FO 195/716, Aleppo, 14 April 1862.   [96] FO 195/976, Aleppo, 31 May 1871.
[97] Zakariyya, *Asha'ir al-Sham*, 595; Blunt, *Bedouin Tribes* I, 41.

provincial governments from intervening in Fid'an matters. As will be detailed in the following chapters, Jed'an's good relations with the government and consolidation of the Ottoman position in Deir al-Zor, a Fid'an stronghold, did not mean a retreat for the tribal position.

Conclusion

The techniques and strategies used in the Tanzimat era were not successful in establishing a sustainable and peaceful governance of the tribal societies on which both sides consented. When the Ottoman Empire reinstated itself in the Arab provinces, the dominant power of the Arab countryside closer to the desert was absolutely the Anizah and Shammar nomads and the imperial position was apparently vulnerable. The tribal raids and the practice of *khuwwa* constituted a major problem for the expansion of Ottoman rule in the Arab countryside where the nomads frequented. The modernizers of the Tanzimat period tried to assert imperial authority over the nomadic territories and 'solve the nomad question' from the early 1840s onward with several techniques including expulsion by military operation and containment by settlement, which was not accepted by the tribal leaders such as Dahham and Safuq, who considered the restoration of empire a threat to their interests and tribal existence. Their obvious supremacy gave them a free hand to oppose the imperial demands.

As this chapter has demonstrated, however, their resistance was eliminated by either killing them or finding alternative moderate sheikhs from within the tribe. Although these methods resulted in tribal recognition of imperial authority and somewhat smoothed relations, none of them resulted in retreat of the tribal position in the Arab countryside. The eliminated sheikhs were replaced by more conciliatory figures like Farhan and Jed'an, whose cooperation with the imperial troops usually resulted in the expansion of tribal areas of domination and consolidation of the tribal leaders as their support to the government provided profit for the tribal society. It was possible that the Ottoman position could be improved after considerable infrastructural investment in the desert and adoption of a more flexible and conciliatory policy towards the nomads, which the following chapters examine. The infrastructural investments persuaded the nomads not to violate the regional order arbitrarily, while the adoption of a new strategy transformed the imperial attitude in the direction of consenting to tribal existence and recognizing tribal privileges in the Arab countryside. Both sides arranged their positions according to the new circumstances.

2 | Reinforcement

Land Settlements and Military Fortification in the Desert and Its Frontiers, 1840–1870

This chapter examines another aspect of the Ottoman efforts designed to keep the Bedouin outside the settled areas and subjugate them. To that end, the empire established new villages in the desert frontiers and created military fortifications, which was very convenient to the new imperial policy aimed at minimizing the autonomy of the local forces and increasing government authority in the Ottoman domains. In this way, in line with the ideals of the Tanzimat reforms and the general Ottoman policy, the efficiency of the state would increase and the imperial subjects would be productively benefited if modernization was put into practice, such as through the expansion of Ottoman bureaucracy, the collection of taxes and enlargement of the imperial army.

The aims and results, however, somewhat differed: from 1840 to 1870, the policies of colonization and 'militarization' in the desert frontiers of the Ottoman Arab provinces were transformed in line with the moderation of the state-tribe relations. The original aim was to reinforce the imperial existence in the desert frontiers during the Tanzimat era by creating new villages in the agricultural lands abandoned due to the tribal invasions and their excessive demands of *khuwwa*, and by deploying regular troops along the newly established villages and the strategic positions of the desert. But the Ottoman efforts to reinforce the desert frontiers against the nomads could only obtain partial success since the Ottoman military investments and land colonization in the desert frontier during the Tanzimat era served as 'the infrastructural investments' for the regularization of the tribal migrations, reduction of tribal raids and warding off the rival groups fighting each other. To put it differently, the Ottomans began to reinforce the Arab countryside closer to the desert areas to eliminate the nomads in one way or another, but they ended with acknowledgement of the tribal authority in the areas strategic for the tribes. The benefit of the reinforcements for the Ottomans was to obtain nomadic respect for imperial rules and regulations, but not to expel, subjugate or 'Ottomanize' them.

Land settlement was deemed crucial for both security reasons and economic crisis brought about by the huge area of abandoned lands, which seriously shook the regional economy and threatened agricultural production. However, the newly created villages were potentially exposed to the attacks of the nomads. Thus, the formerly settled tribes who had to abandon their lands due to the Shammar and Anizah attacks were negotiated with and persuaded to cultivate the desert frontier, contrary to Lewis's claim that they were forced by the Ottomans to become sedentary.[1] The government authorities assumed that the newly settled tribes would resist the nomads when the government adequately supported them. In addition, in the early decades of the Tanzimat, the new villages were protected by irregular troops made up from the settled tribes. However, as the second section of this chapter attempts to demonstrate, the increase of the settlements in the desert frontier and the simultaneous corruption of the irregular system forced officials to 'regularize' the desert troops for the protection of the new settlements. In many places, the regular troops both protected the new re-settlements and regularized tribal migrations by preventing their plundering of the villages, but allowing them to visit the surrounding pastures. The release of the irregular troops from military service and regularization of the desert troops thus transformed the Ottoman troops from attacking forces into security providers, which to a large extent meant the abandonment of the 'offensive' and 'intriguing' policies adopted in the 1840s and 1850s to defeat, subjugate and pacify the tribes or expel them from the imperial lands. By these improvements, another precondition of reconciliation was to be fulfilled although a full partnership had to wait until the finalization of the administrative expansionism in Deir al-Zor and southern Syria, the focus of Chapters 3 and 4.

Before analysing the land settlements of the Tanzimat, this chapter will examine the question of the abandoned lands which produced a crucial economic crisis and forced the authorities to invest in the desert frontier. It will give us a general picture of the Arab countryside in the 1840s and enable us to better situate the land colonization

---

[1] Lewis, *Nomads and Settlers*.

undertaken in Syria and Iraq as a countermeasure against the improvement of the nomadic domination in the countryside.

The Arab Countryside in the Early 1840s: The Question of the Abandoned Villages

The migration of the large Bedouin population from Najd in the last quarter of the eighteenth century and the 'tribalization' of Syrian and Iraqi provinces made the security of the villages and the peasants' productivity an intractable problem in the region. The Bedouin encroached on arable lands in a search for secure pastures for their increasing number of flocks, leaving villages abandoned.[2] In the absence of effective state protection, the peasants and settled tribes, whose lands were either occupied by the Bedouin for grazing or raided in demand for *khuwwa*, were obliged to retreat and to base themselves near the cities for their own safety.[3] As this coincided with the weakest moment of Ottoman rule, the peasants who continued cultivating their lands were forced to seek protection from powerful tribal leaders in return for their payment of *khuwwa*, which became a major source of income for the tribal economy. The attitude of the imperial authorities suggested that they had to overlook *khuwwa* demands up to the 1860s: in 1822, for instance, a man from the Hasana Bedouin of the Anizah had gone to the village of Tel Sikkin to collect the *khuwwa* due to him and was killed by an officer during his visit. When his uncle, as his sole heir, appealed to the court, the judge ruled that he should receive a compensation payment for the death of his nephew.[4] As explained in Chapter 1, up to the early 1870s, the collection of *khuwwa* had to be recognized as the right of the sheikhs by the state authorities in return for their good behaviour.

By the early 1840s, however, *khuwwa* incomes had become a very attractive financial source for the tribal economy and became a matter of struggle among various Bedouin groups, which caused large-scale plundering of numerous villages in the Syrian and Iraqi provinces.[5] *Khuwwa* had thus turned into a struggle among rival tribes to expand

---

[2] FO 195/902, Aleppo, 2 April 1868.
[3] See, for example, FO 195/ 207, Aleppo, 27 January 1842.
[4] Douwes, *Ottomans in Syria*, 32.
[5] For an example from Aleppo, see: AMAE, CPC, Turquie, Aleppo-1, 31 March 1843.

their sphere of influence and improve their financial situation in the absence of effective government control. As a result, many of the semi-settled agricultural tribes preferred a mobile existence, while other villagers moved away to safer areas to escape Bedouin attacks and their demands for *khuwwa*. A later report by the British consul in Damascus clarifies some reasons behind abandoning the villages:

The sheikh of a tribe takes a town or village under his protection and levies an annual sum of money and grain in recognition of the favour, and in case of this blackmail being refused or delayed, the village is plundered by its so-called protector. Most villages pay to several tribes, and in some cases the aggregate annual payment amounts to five times more than the government demands.[6]

There are many instances mentioned in Ottoman, British and French documents that substantiate the consul's description and demonstrate both the impact of the tribal conflicts for expanding their area of influence on the local life in the Arab countryside and the inability of the Ottoman government to punish the Bedouin: in 1849, they attacked to the villages in the north and south of Damascus and forcibly collected levies.[7] The British consul in Damascus in 1854 reported that the towns of Homs and Hama were besieged by Bedouin, demanding *khuwwa* from the peasants.[8] When the peasants refused the extortion demands, the Bedouin kidnapped their children to force payment.[9] By 1859, the very fertile countryside around Ra's al-Ayn in the Jazira region, once well-populated by peasants, had been deserted as the cultivators of the soil abandoned villages in the face of inadequate protection from the Ottoman authorities against the encroaching nomads.[10] Some of these attacks were made to capture the 'protection' rights of the villages from rival tribes while the reason behind others was the unwillingness of the peasants to pay the *khuwwa* due to their

---

[6] FO 195/677, Damascus, 20 August 1861; for a French report highlighting that *khuwwa* was a greater burden than the government taxes, see: AMAE, CPC, Turquie, Damascus-7, 18 October 1862.

[7] FO 195/291, Damascus, 3 September 1849.

[8] FO 195/458, Damascus, 27 July 1854; for another report by the French consul of Aleppo describing the sufferings of the peasants that stemmed from the Bedouin demands for *khuwwa*, see: CADN, Serie D, 166PO/D1/53, Aleppo, 25 August 1855.

[9] BOA, BEO.AYN.d. No. 177, 9 Zilkade 1270 [3 August 1854], 105.

[10] BOA, MVL 754/53, 11 Cemaziyelevvel 1276 [6 December 1859].

protectors. Nomads were quite intolerant about the payments as *khuwwa* constituted a major income for them and did not abstain from conflicting with the government for it.

The cruciality of *khuwwa* as a source of income caused long-lasting struggles between rival tribes to protect more peasants and have their *khuwwa* revenues, which meant the villages were left either insufficiently populated or completely abandoned. This resulted in a considerable loss of taxation income for the imperial treasury. The tribal pursuit of more *khuwwa* both caused the new agricultural lands to be abandoned and prevented re-cultivation of already abandoned fertile regions which were not used by the nomads as pasture lands for their flocks: the Anizah and Shammar attacks, for instance, caused the settled Karakechili tribe of Urfa, who were one of the most prominent agricultural producers and tax-payers in the region, to leave their lands.[11] The British consul in Damascus reported in 1855 that Hama, Homs and Ma'arre had 'extensively and exceedingly fertile lands'. But they had been laid waste by the Bedouin who ravaged them, and ruled supreme over the territory and its inhabitants.[12] The situation was also comparable in the villages of Kirkuk and Sulaimanya, where peasants endured attack by Kurdish and Arab tribes.[13]

The abandoned and scarcely populated villages had a serious impact on the local economy, too, as it reduced the grain supply in the Arab provinces. A British report of 1859 on the increase in prices of agricultural produce in Aleppo attributed the rise to the decline of agricultural power due to the government's failure to prevent the Bedouin from 'stealing' their crops.[14] In 1861, the deserted villages in Damascus numbered more than 2,000, of which about 1,000 were cultivated and had only been deserted 'within the memory of a man'. These villages were situated in the most fertile districts, but their inhabitants, 'unable to meet the demands of the encroaching tribes of the desert, and equally unable [to] resist them', had either joined the Bedouin or settled in districts beyond the reach of the extortionist tribes. Owing to the devastation of such a significant number of villages, the local grain

---

11 BOA, A.MKT.UM 108/62, 19 Şevval 1268 [6 August 1852].
12 FO 195/458, Damascus, 1855 [the exact date is not available].
13 BOA, A.MKT.MHM 171/61, 1 Cemaziyelevvel 1276 [26 November 1859].
14 FO 195/595, Aleppo, 30 June 1859.

supply faced a serious crisis which compelled the authorities to contemplate an ultimate solution.[15]

The increase of the imperial efforts to effectively tax the agricultural produce and inconsiderate policies adopted by some local officials constituted another important reason for the peasants to leave their lands. In other words, having government protection did not automatically signify the end of the villagers' miseries. By 1850, the numerous tribes of Brazzeries settled on the Chay, Obulce[?] and Boghaz at Urfa, whose villages had been devastated by the Shammar and Anizah had been forced to emigrate over the preceding years to Aleppo, Ayntab, Kilis and Siverek. Another reason for their flight, according to the *kaymakam* of Urfa, was the introduction of the Tanzimat reforms in 1848 with its land registration, signifying double taxation for the villagers as the government would know the extent of their lands and thus estimate their produce, which would signify higher taxes in addition to the sum they paid to the nomads as *khuwwa*. Furthermore, some villagers complained to the Sublime Porte [*Bab-ı Ali*] that harassment [*teaddiyat*] carried out by Urfa's elites compelled them to emigrate.[16] The elites most likely bought the tax collection rights of these villages and firmly pressed the peasants to pay as much as possible in order to maximize their profits, which caused the villagers to abandon their lands. As they enjoyed very close relations with the officials of the town, the bureaucrats at least knew about their misbehaviour. It is equally presumable that the Anizah and Shammar attacks were used as a pretext to overshadow the atrocities of the officials and the elites. Given the absence of further complaint it can be inferred that such problems were solved by the central authorities who ascribed great importance to land cultivation.

A similar situation existed in the Mosul region: a tenth of the population, unable to meet the heavy government demands, abandoned their villages. When the governor asked the *kahias* of the villages 'why people were deserting', they boldly answered that 'he had not only taken everything from them, but had not even left them bread, and passionately added that even were he to cut them into pieces, they could not pay any more'.[17] To prevent those remaining from leaving the

[15] FO 195/677, Damascus, 20 August 1861, emphasis added.
[16] BOA, İ.MVL 203/6479, 1 Safer 1267 [7 December 1850].
[17] FO 195/228, Mosul, 25 September 1845.

region, the governor sent Sherif Bey, a native officer, with the instruction to use every effort 'to induce the villagers to remain, and especially to assist them with loans of corn and animals taking bonds payable next harvest'. However, the villagers refused every offer unless Sherif gave them the assurance that the impending *saliane* would not be demanded. According to Sherif Bey, their resentment was directed exclusively at the government[18] and their desertion was due principally to the coercive actions of the governor, whose repeated extortion 'disgusted' the peasants. The subsequent governor abandoned these policies, negotiated with those who abandoned their lands and persuaded them to return to agriculture.[19]

Such abuses by the local authorities, however, did not distract the Ottoman authorities from overcoming the growing question of the abandoned villages and contemplating a solution to this problem once and for all. Two responses developed by the Tanzimat statesmen were to resettle the once agricultural tribes on at least some of these lands and to fortify these regions and other strategic positions in the desert with soldiers and castles.

Ottoman Settlements and Settlement Projects, 1840–1870

The situation seriously compromised regional security and inflicted severe losses on provincial and imperial treasuries. It was not only a financial problem, but also a political problem that threatened the imperial project of the reinstatement of the Ottoman state in the Syrian and Iraqi provinces, which gained momentum with the Tanzimat process. The deficit of the treasury tended to increase as it proved nearly impossible to effectively tax those groups who abandoned agricultural life and adopted a migrant existence. In order to solve these economic and political problems, the authorities of the various provinces simultaneously developed projects to persuade such societies to adopt a sedentary lifestyle as the tribal willingness was as crucial a precondition as the government's decisiveness for the success of these projects. The easiest to convert was the smaller groups, willing to return to their previous lifestyle, seeking protection against larger groups like the Shammar and Anizah. They were also suitable to be

[18] FO 195/228, Mosul, 18 October 1845.
[19] FO 195/228, Mosul, 24 January 1846.

settled, in contrast to the nomads, as they were 'tribally' organized and usually enthusiastic to ally with the government to protect their lands. Thus, they would create a barrier against the nomads to prevent them from entering the available and potential agricultural areas. Their settlement would also demonstrate to the nomads 'the benefits of civilization' and persuade them to choose settlement.

Aleppo

The Aleppo governorate's initiatives during this period were the most successful as the province contained the largest area of abandoned lands and had a considerable tribal population who were previously engaged in agriculture and thus willing to return to their old lifestyle under government protection. Their manpower was supported by the government's irregular troops to increase their resistance against the Anizah nomads. Besides financial reasons, the repeated government defeats by the Fid'an compelled the Aleppo officials to put settlement activities into practice in order to prevent the nomads' access into the taxable areas. As indicated in Map 2.1, the government undertook to barricade the desert by settling the tribes along its frontiers. In this regard, in 1846, Osman Pasha, the governor of Aleppo, reported that some six Bedouin groups were living on the fertile lands of the Raqqa and Reyhaniye regions settled there with the help of the *kaymakam* of Raqqa and Janufer[?], a member of the Aleppine elite. Some irregular troops were sporadically deployed to protect the newly settled groups from the Anizah attacks. In addition, they were exempted from taxation until they had adapted to their new lifestyle. The governor claimed that he was trying to encourage Anizah groups to change their lifestyle by demonstrating to them the benefits of agriculture through these settlements, an undertaking of *mission civilisatrice*.[20] But the primary concern was to increase tax revenues and provide security against the nomads.

The maintenance of hostilities between the government and the Fid'an through the 1840s and the obvious vulnerable position of the government, detailed in the Chapter 1, encouraged the officials to create more settlements to overcome the 'nomad question'. In 1850, the Bani Said and Rakkash tribes started cultivating land in the Aleppo region in

---

[20] BOA, A.MKT 43/93, Aleppo, 19 Cemaziyelahir 1262 [14 June 1846].

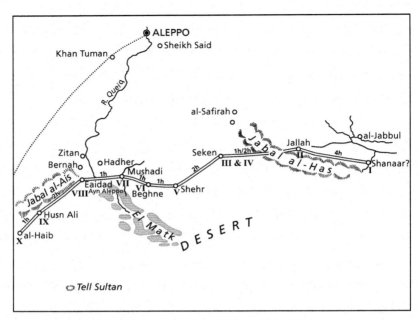

Map 2.1 Map of the settlements around Aleppo by 1852.

appropriate locations and necessary measures were taken to protect
them from Anizah incursions.[21] In addition, Kıbrıslı Mehmed Pasha,
the governor of Aleppo, acquired lands for the Sultan [*çiftlikat-ı
hümayun*] along the provincial frontiers and encouraged tribesmen
and peasants to cultivate these lands.[22] By 1852, thirty different tribes
from the desert had become sedentary and were employed in the abandoned [*harab*] villages of the royal estates to build houses extending
from Geboul by way of old Aleppo to Ma'are, under the authority of
Ferhad Pasha [Baron Stein] and an elite, Rahman Agha, who was
appointed as the administrator of these villages.[23] Some 500 hundred
irregular cavalry and 50 infantry [*asakir-i muvazzafa*] were hired to
protect them.[24] Needless to say that, particularly after the rise of Jed'an
and its alliance with the government, these protection measures helped

21 BOA, BEO.AYN.d. No. 172, 17 Cemaziyelevvel 1267 [20 March 1851], 83.
22 Lewis, *Nomads and Settlers*, 42.
23 BOA, BEO.AYN.d. No. 175, 28 Safer 1269 [11 December 1852], 44; see also:
    FO 195/302, Aleppo, 16 October 1852.
24 BOA, BEO.AYN.d. No. 176, 25 Şevval 1269 [1 August 1853], 32.

the government in its struggle against Dahham of the Fid'an and somewhat strengthened its hand when officials negotiated with the tribal sheikhs although they were far from approaching the power of the nomads.

The process, however, was far from simple and smooth. Some of these tribesmen abandoned their land within three years due to violations by the state officials assigned to facilitate their adaptation to the imperial system. The government of Aleppo initially reported that they had left their land due to overtaxation and the Anizah incursions.[25] When central authorities investigated the issue and inspected the records pertaining to these villages, however, they discovered that their abandonment was a result of Rahman Agha's abuse of authority over the peasants, most likely in collaboration with the Aleppo officials who reported the reason behind the peasants' action as the Anizah incursions: although he had been instructed to do everything possible to assist the newly settled Bedouin and to provide security for the villages, the agha kept much of the harvest for himself and undervalued the income to the government. Furthermore, the Anizah never attacked the villages mentioned, which might suggest a pre-established truce was in force. As a result, the government made further concessions and the governor of Aleppo was ordered to do his utmost to satisfy the villagers.[26] Later documents reveal the success of the central government's intervention; the new peasants were content with their lot, and remained on their land.[27]

The settlement of smaller Bedouin groups around Aleppo continued up until 1860 but so too did the officials' exploitation. In 1856, immediately after the first Ottoman attempt to extend the imperial administration to Deir al-Zor, the Weldah and Ferdun tribes were settled at Deir Hafir in the Zor region through the agency of the *kaymakam* of Urfa and the British consul.[28] The British consul was presumably involved in the process considering that the settlement of the tribes would increase road security which was crucial for the British merchants. A British official, who contributed to settlement negotiations with these communities, visited their district in 1860 and

[25] BOA, A.AMD 64/11, Tezkire, 1271 [1854].
[26] BOA, BEO.AYN.d. No. 177, 29 Zilkade 1270 [23 August 1854], 128; BOA, BEO.AYN.d. No. 178, 1 Rebiulevvel 1271 [22 November 1854], 28–29.
[27] See, for example, FO 195/595, Aleppo, 21 April 1860.
[28] BOA, BEO.AYN.d. No. 180, 4 Muharrem 1273 [4 September 1856], 19.

reported that he 'had found them in a most satisfactory state'. The Ferdun numbered 500 tents[29] and harvested a considerable quantity both of wheat and barley. The government exempted them from taxes during the first two years of cultivation to ensure their commitment to agricultural life. In 1860, before he was appointed as the *mutasarrif* of Deir, Arslan Pasha was involved in the settlement of the Mawali, Hadidi and others in southern Aleppo and this was successful as many of the tribes he dealt with had had prior experience of ploughing.[30] These tribes were also capable of responding to the Anizah attacks when supported sufficiently by the government due to their warlike character.

This policy of settlement, however, was not without its detractors at the local level. The biggest challenge came from Haji Batran, the sheikh of a settled tribe named Hannadi, which had, for many years, been in the pay of the government as irregular troops. Batran recognized that his services would no longer be needed if the tribes were to become peaceful tillers of the soil and take over his position in the region. He contested the new policy by trying to induce Jed'an, the sheikh of the Anizah, to attack and raid the recent settlers, but failed as Jed'an needed to have good relations with the government to have its support against his rival Dahham Haji Batran then went to Aleppo and scared the governor with tales of imminent chaos at the hands of the Bedouins gathering on the outskirts of the city. Duly alarmed, the governor assigned to him supreme control over the tribes and their interests. The Hannadi tribe allowed their horses to graze on the barley of the Weldah, and attacked those who opposed this move. Batran allowed Ahmed Bey of the Mawali Bedouin to move onto the newly cultivated lands, although the tribe was in a state of rebellion and the Hannadi chief had an official order to capture him dead or alive, an interesting case indicating the complexity of the local networks between the officials and tribal leaders. In addition, presumably at the encouragement of Batran, many thousands of tribesmen gathered and overwhelmed the immediate neighbourhood of Deir Hafir. Their flocks, herds and horses grazed unrestricted beside the brook in front of the tent of Muhammad al-Ghanim, sheikh of the Weldah. He was afraid to level

---

[29] A later report figured their population as 8,000 souls: FO 195/902, Aleppo, 2 April 1868.
[30] Lewis, *Nomads and Settlers*, 44–45.

any complaint against the Hannadi, as Haji Batran's position was such that the settlement of these tribes would 'tender his expensive services unnecessary to the government'. The government authorities had to bribe Haji Batran, their indispensable intermediary, not to upset the newly settled tribes.[31]

However, Ismet Pasha's appointment as the governor, his good relations with the Anizah and the completion of the line of small forts in the south-east provided protection.[32] In addition, a later report demonstrates that the Weldah and Ferdun had to pay *khuwwa* to the Bedouin, too, for some time to benefit from their protection against the 'government', that is, Haji Batran.[33] In spite of these difficulties, these tribes progressed considerably in a year: in February 1861, the Ferdun tribe sowed approximately 1,000 bushels of grain, and the Weldah 1,400 bushels. They also built cottages. Additionally, one of the most influential branches of the Anizah, Khaliph al-Kir, of the Rus tribe, joined the Weldah settlement, which, according to the British consul, 'places beyond a doubt the question of the feasibility of inducing the highest class of Bedouins to become cultivators'.[34] Nevertheless, they retained their tents to be able to move short distances in summer in search of pasture for their sheep and cattle, returning in autumn to harvest their crops and remain there for the winter to sow others.[35]

This example demonstrates both the limits of the Ottoman government in the region and the perception of the nomadic potential. The Aleppo government could not prevent its employee from disarraying its project when it was harmful to the latter's interests, which would be impossible for a professional officer. In addition, the Anizah was still perceived by the smaller tribes at that time as a supreme authority that had the potential to replace the empire as their allies and thus had to be satisfied by paying *khuwwa*. Related to that, it indicates the transitivity of the alliances and power relations between the different actors including the government. The government was not a supreme and abstract arbitrator over society: it was an active player in the field using the

---

[31] FO 195/595, Aleppo, 21 April 1860 and the supplement by R. G. Brown in the same file with the date, 12 May 1860.

[32] FO 195/716, Aleppo, 15 September 1862.

[33] FO 195/800, Aleppo, 30 September 1864; see also, BOA, MVL 772/41, 24 Zilhicce 1280 [31 May 1864].

[34] FO 195/675, Aleppo, 4 February 1861.

[35] FO 195/1305, Aleppo, 3 November 1880.

tensions and rivalries between the various local power-holders to put its plans into practice.

It should be finally noted that these settlements were not found by the Anizah groups to be detrimental to their interests.[36] Jed'an's rejection of cooperation with Haji Batran is still worthy of noting although he needed the government's help against Dahham. If these settlements and their consequences had been perceived a vital threat to the nomadic pasture lands, they would resist against the government and against their sheikh by any means as the pasturages were extremely important for them. The settlements in the Aleppo region did not mean the exclusion – or restriction – of the nomads from the pastures there. The newly settled tribes' cooperation with the government and the increase in the number of military fortifications on the desert frontier, however, gradually increased the level of security in the following years as it somewhat reduced the nomads' freedom to raid villages and escape into the desert. Their function vis-à-vis the government was to help the regularization of the nomadic movement rather than their expulsion from the region.

Damascus

Similar projects were being undertaken in other provinces: a settlement plan for the Wuld 'Ali and Ruwalla, the southern Anizah branches, was agreed with the arrival of the head of the army of Arabia, Namık Pasha, in Damascus. The pasha intended to allot Busra in Hawran for the Wuld 'Ali, and Palmyra and that area of the desert to Naif al-Sha'lan, the sheikh of the Ruwalla.[37] The project, however, could not be realized, presumably given the tribes' reluctance to change their lifestyle as well as the lack of a project leader when the pasha was removed from the command of the army.[38] Another important reason was most likely the lack of sufficient financial resources and other infrastructural requirements to accomplish such a large-scale project of settling thousands of the nomads in appropriate regions.

Following the Anizah failure, the Damascene officials tended towards more realistic options and targeted uprooted tribes such as those in Aleppo province. In this regard, in 1848, the tribes who had

---

[36] For details, see Chapter 3.   [37] FO 195/226, Damascus, 16 September 1846.
[38] BOA, İ.MVL 119/2954, 11 Receb 1264 [26 February 1848].

migrated from Hama, Homs, Ma'arre and Husn to Aleppo and Saida ten years earlier returned to their previous homelands at the initiative of the officials specifically appointed for this mission, which demonstrates how the resettlement projects were taken seriously by the government.[39] Three years later, the Muwajibe and Say' tribes, who were forced to leave their lands seeking refuge from the Anizah, settled on the desert frontier in Hama. They offered 800 mares, as tax payment to the provincial treasury, in return for their proper protection against the nomadic exactions, which was by all accounts a handsome addition to the provincial treasury.[40] The latter case proves that the settlement projects were not always one-sided government plans targeted to change the tribes' lifestyle. It demonstrates how the settlers and settled groups were interdependent, contrary to the claims of forceful resettlement put forward by Lewis[41]: the newly settled tribes needed government protection to remain in their lands while the government was obliged to their existence to consolidate its power against the Anizah.

The Ottoman enterprise to transform the substantial area of abandoned territory along Hama's desert frontier into cultivated land[42] continued into the 1860s and new administrative units were established in the frontier regions, such as Ma'arre, to protect the villages against Bedouin attacks.[43] These imperial efforts were not enough, however, to re-cultivate the abandoned lands as the sheer expanse of the agricultural territory was three times larger than when the region was governed by Ibrahim Pasha under Egyptian rule.[44] 'The magnificent plains of Damascus, [which] flourished formerly, had now been abandoned by their inhabitants' following the withdrawal of the Egyptian forces.[45]

It seems that the reason limiting the Ottoman government from undertaking larger settlement projects was the imperial perturbation about the nomadic reaction which would cause chaos in the new settlements and pave the way for the collapse of the projects. As will be explained in the following chapters with reference to specific

[39] BOA, İ.MVL 119/2954, 11 Receb 1264 [26 February 1848].
[40] BOA, BEO.AYN.d. No. 172, 3 Cemaziyelahir 1267 [5 April 1851], 94–95; BOA, BEO.AYN.d. No. 172, 3 Ramazan 1267 [2 July 1851], 131.
[41] Lewis, *Nomads and Settlers*.
[42] BOA, MVL 22/55, 6 Rebiulahir 1264 [12 March 1848].
[43] AMAE, CPC, Turquie, Damascus-7, 18 October 1862.
[44] AMAE, CPC, Turquie, Damascus-7, 18 October 1862.
[45] AMAE, CPC, Turquie, Damascus-7, 21 January 1863.

Figure 2.1 The Munkalli village between the Euphrates and Bilich. İstanbul Üniversitesi Nadir Eserler Kütüphanesi, 90567/0075.

policies, by the late 1860s, the Ottoman policy towards the nomads and other autonomous groups evolved into a new version which further took the nomads into consideration as the Ottoman expansion into the desert and other local, imperial and global reasons necessitated better relations with them. For these reasons, the imperial authorities of Aleppo and Damascus forewent further settlements in the arable lands, that would have restricted pasture lands for the nomads and incited their hostility.

The Jazira Region

The Ottoman approach in the Jazira region was similar. In 1846, Ismail Pasha managed to locate the Jabbur tribe on the western bank of the Tigris, and Abu Salman on the opposite side. The pasha's method to persuade Abu Salman is worthy of mention as it clearly demonstrates the Ottoman technique of creating alliances with the smaller tribes against the larger Anizah and Shammar: some of the Abu Salman horsemen had raided a place called Nimroud and had skirmished with a detachment of the government's irregular troops. Rather than responding with force, Ismail Pasha invited the sheikh to come and meet him. When the sheikh visited the governor, he was kindly treated, given presents and convinced to settle. As both tribal groups were armed and brave people, according to the British consul, this represented 'a valuable fence between the desert and the villages higher up the stream'.[46] They cultivated the land until 1893, when hostility between the two sides and conflicts between the Shammar and Jabbur forced them to retreat to the desert.[47] As will be detailed, they returned to their lands in 1901. Ismail Pasha's successor, Tayyar Pasha, also made significant progress in persuading several of the agricultural Arab tribes to settle in the vicinity of Mosul to create a protective barricade against the Shammar.[48] Similarly, the Shammar sheikh Mani' was settled near Siverek in the Diarbekir region. The sheikh was paid 3,000 piasters and Mustafa Agha, a local elite from Siverek, was tasked with the negotiations, ultimately resulting in the settling of the tribe.[49] As can be inferred from this example, the officials sometimes persuaded the nomads to ally with them against their fellow tribesmen by changing their lifestyle. Intra-tribal disputes presumably enabled the government to establish such alliances.

Another more crucial project of settlement was undertaken in 1864 by Mustafa Pasha, the governor of Kürdistan, to create a 'cordon of settlement',[50] which would contain the agricultural lands against the Shammar by localizing semi-nomadic and mostly Kurdish tribes who had to 'abandon their homelands [*terk-i vatan*] and the settled agricultural lives that they had occupied "since time immemorial"'. As shown in Map 2.2, and similar to the undertaking engaged by Osman Pasha of Aleppo in 1846, they would form a 'line of cordon' [*hatt-ı kordon*] 'a barrier stretching from Mosul in the east to the Khabur River in the west'.[51] The combination of tribal and imperial power would also compel the Shammar to change their lifestyle from nomadism to settlement.

---

[46] FO 195/228, Mosul, 24 January 1846.
[47] BOA, DH.TMIK-M 103/10, 16 Nisan 1317 [29 April 1901].
[48] FO 195/228, Mosul, 10 August 1846.
[49] BOA, A.MKT.UM 177/25, 18 Rebiulahir 1271 [17 November 1854].
[50] I borrow this concept from Samual Dolbee, see: 'The Locust and the Starling', 124.
[51] Ibid., 127.

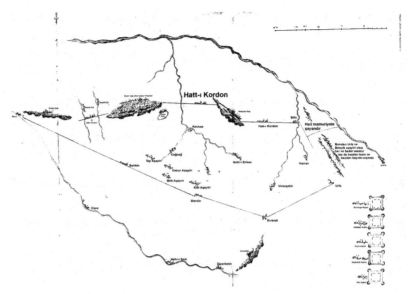

Map 2.2 The Jazira's plan of cordoning by the settlements to ward off the Shammar and Anizah. BOA, İ.MVL 510/23021/3.

One year later, however, the Chechen refugees migrated to the Ottoman Empire from the Balkans and Caucasus and they requested to be settled in the Jazira region in the neighbourhood of Mardin. Although some of them were settled there, they did not engage in agriculture and 'civilize' to a level the government wished. On some occasions, they allied with the Shammar against the Anizah while entering into conflict with them on others. Some of them were not satisfied with the conditions in Mardin and returned to the Caucasus in 1868. Overall, it was a failed Ottoman undertaking to transform the nomad space into 'civilization' and expel the Shammar from the region.[52] To a similar end, the governor of Diarbekir initiated a new project of settlement in Urfa, Siverek, Mardin and Nusaybin and acquired some success in 1869.[53]

Although the new settlements in the desert frontier of the various provinces somewhat consolidated the Ottoman position in the desert frontier, they would not have been intimidating for the nomads unless

[52] Ibid., 124–137.
[53] BOA, İ.DH 600/41825, 14 Agustos 1285 [27 August 1869].

they had been supported by the military presence, on which the following section focuses.

From Offensive Contractors to Defensive Security Providers: The Transformation of the Ottoman Desert Troops, 1840–1870

The maintenance of the new settlements was strictly dependent on their
effective protection against the nomads particularly in the 1840s and
1850s due to the ongoing hostilities and 'state of war' between and
among then and the government. With the augmentation of the new
villages in the desert frontier, the irregular troops' service became increasingly inefficacious due to their uncontrollable character and their back-
door collaborations with the Anizah and Shammar, which undermined
the government settlements and local security system. On the other hand,
as will be detailed below, the primary imperial purpose with their employment was to attack the nomads and defeat them and they were thus not
suitable as 'security providers', which also made their release an imperative. The Ottoman aim of deploying regular troops in the areas where the
nomadic tribes frequented transformed the imperial troops from attacking forces into security providers who protected the new settlements. This
constituted another infrastructural investment for the politics of negotiation that regularized Bedouin migration along the lines of state-tribe
reconciliation from the 1870s rather than as part of a wider imperial
enterprise to push the Bedouin into the desert and to limit their interaction
with the cities which was the aim of officials when hiring irregulars.

The regular troops were rarely engaged in any serious conflict with the
tribes that involved fatalities on either side, but rather performed
a deterrent function against attacks by uncontrollable branches of the
Bedouin on villages and caravans at strategic locations along the desert
frontier, prevented their evasion of government duties and undertook the
return of property stolen by some tribesmen. As will become evident
through this section, the number of new regular troops was by no
means sufficient to maintain total war and to prevent the tribal confederations from entering sedentary areas. Indeed, their number was sufficient
only against a tribal society compromised with a 'social contract', which
would happen following the successful expansion of the Ottoman rule
into the desert territories like southern Syria and Deir al-Zor. The next
section first analyses the irregular forces and their problems for the
imperial government and then examines the regularization process,

which will enable us to understand the military investments in the infrastructure for the reconciliation with the tribes.

The Başıbozuks: *Ottoman Desert Troops and Their Impact on the Tribal Policy*

By 1840, the number of regular troops was by no means adequate to put the Tanzimat reforms into practice, protect the countryside against tribal raids and abolish their domination. According to the British consul in Aleppo, who estimated the number of the Ottoman troops in Syria as 20,000 in 1841, 'at least double the number is requisite merely [for] garrison' in Aleppo.[54] Available documents demonstrate that the regular troops were only deployed in times of crisis when large-scale expeditions were organized[55] and wide-ranging measures were employed against the Bedouin.[56] In addition, the character of the regular troops rendered them ineffectual against the nomads, who could easily flee into the heart of the desert inaccessible to regular troops.[57] Furthermore, although largely failed, the Ottoman policy towards the nomads in the early years of the Tanzimat was to keep them away from the sedentary areas as much as possible and attack them to do this rather than regulating their movement. The regular troops could have defended or protected a certain position but would not have attacked the nomads and pursued them. Given these facts, the Ottoman rulers were repeatedly obliged to hire irregular cavalry and infantry from the semi-settled agricultural tribes and, in some cases, from among the ordinary citizens to boost army numbers and increase its mobility to a level comparable with the tribes.[58] Their commanders were usually a military adventurer 'who offered his services to the government and received in payment a certain sum out of which he

---

[54] FO 195/170, Aleppo, 25 November 1841; for some remarks by the Ottoman authorities regarding the manpower deficit of the army in Syria, see: BOA, İ. MVL 119/2954, Damascus, 11 Receb 1264 [26 February 1848].

[55] See, for example, BOA, İ.DH 149/7754, 11 Cemaziyelahir 1263 [28 May 1847].

[56] See, for example, BOA İ.DH 200/11461, Damascus, 13 Ramazan 1265 [3 August 1849].

[57] See, for example, AMAE, CPC, Turquie, Damascus-2, 23 May 1848; FO 195/170, Aleppo, 2 August 1841.

[58] For an Ottoman report pointing out such problems, see: BOA, MVL 772/41, 24 Zilhicce 1280 [31 May 1864].

then paid to his troops and covered all other expenses'.[59] Employment of irregulars was also financially beneficial to the imperial treasury: as the Bedouin tribes migrated from province to province on a seasonal basis, irregulars could be contracted for a limited period. Another advantage was that they could be recruited quickly if the army urgently needed them for additional manpower in the case of an unexpected Bedouin attack or a quick Ottoman offensive was planned.[60] It is also worth noting that all expenditures relating to the irregular forces were dealt with by provincial treasuries.[61]

The Hannadi tribe, brought from Egypt by Ibrahim Pasha 'as a check upon the different predatory nomadic tribes', was usually recruited in Aleppo against the Anizah and their treatment of the tribesmen also demonstrates the logic of the struggle with the nomads. According to a British report, they would 'without hesitation attack any number of Anazee [sic], and invariably rout them'. Their sheikh was the most fearful figure among the Anizah tribesmen. Their principal aim was not to provide security but to 'attack' and 'rout' the nomads in the case of an Anizah appearance in the districts where they were deployed, which was appropriate to the Ottoman policy of pushing the Anizah and Shammar outside the imperial domains.[62]

The purpose for which they were recruited was suitable to the policies of exclusion adopted in the early Tanzimat years. By 1850, for instance, the irregular cavalry troops [*başıbozuk süvari*] employed against the Anizah Bedouin in the province of Damascus, which provided service along the Aleppo frontier to the southernmost point of Hawran, were to pursue Bedouin groups in the desert, which means that they conducted military campaigns against the nomadic tribes there. They were also to be deployed at strategic positions, supported by four artilleries to prevent Bedouin attacks on the sedentary areas. They would finally patrol the routes where the Bedouin grazed their flocks ready to intervene quickly in the event of a security problem.[63] But they usually acted as if they were in a state of war with the Bedouin;

---

[59] Ma'oz, *Ottoman Reform*, 57.
[60] See, for example, BOA, İ.MVL 167/4938, 16 Safer 1265 [12 January 1849].
[61] See, for example, BOA, MVL 1, 15 Cemaziyelevvel 1269 [24 February 1853], 101.
[62] FO 195/416, Aleppo, 19 July 1857.
[63] BOA, İ.MVL 181/5435, 24 Şevval 1266 [3 September 1850]; BOA, İ.MVL 214/7081, 23 Zilkade 1267 [31 August 1851].

they attacked the Shammar and Anizah groups for booty when they found an opportunity which is difficult to imagine in a regular army providing security service.[64] Such actions were neither prevented nor punished by the Ottoman authorities, as any form of violence was justifiable against the 'savage' nomads. Irregular forces also performed such tasks as the collection of nomadic taxes. But their style of action was convenient to the mentality for which they were employed: as will be detailed in Chapter 6, their frequent method of tax collection was to attack the nomads, capture their flocks and extract them from the amount of taxes they were assigned by the government to pay.[65] This was within the knowledge of the Ottoman authorities.

Both the quality of the irregular troops and the way that they were employed indicate that the principal purpose of their recruitment was to fight with the Shammar and Anizah nomads who came to the vicinity of the towns and cities rather than protecting the countryside, although they were also assumed to protect the newly settled lands colonized by the state analysed in the previous section. Similar to the ways in which they had come and occupied the Arab heartlands of the empire, the nomads would be defeated and sent back to the depth of the desert. As rightly stated by Subhi Pasha, the governor of Damascus, in 1872, who criticized the government's aggressive policy towards the nomads, 'no idea has ever circulated in central government, other than the forcible repression and devastation of the Arabs'.[66] However, towards 1860, the irregular system became almost entirely unserviceable due to the problems caused by these troops. In addition, the augmentation of the new settlements in the countryside made the regularization of the security forces an imperative as their protection now was more important than the operation against the nomads as the imperial policy was progressively inclined to reconcile with the tribal sheikhs.

The Crisis of the Irregular Forces

The troops' irregularity began to seriously impact on regional order, imperial governance and provincial treasuries in the 1860s and became a security issue. The most crucial financial problem was that the

---

[64]   BOA, A.MKT.UM 302/40, 3 Cemaziyelevvel 1274 [20 December 1857].
[65]   BOA, İ.MVL 119/2954, Damascus, 11 Receb 1264 [26 February 1848]; SCR-Urfa 205, 9 Safer 1272 [21 October 1855], 36.
[66]   Quoted in Çetinsaya, *Ottoman Administration of Iraq*, 2.

imperial authorities rarely knew how many soldiers they were employing. Imperial bureaucrats suggest that their number was always much
lower than that declared to officials.[67] The situation was abused by
corrupt officials and other government employees. One such example
occurred when Bican Pasha of Urfa was reported to the Porte for
registering the number of irregular troops as higher than were actually
employed and pocketed some 80,000 piasters, recorded as their
salaries.[68] Around the same time, in cooperation with the administrative council, the governor of Mosul, Mustafa Nuri Pasha, 'nominally
entertained' and paid for 'a large number of irregular soldiers', while
their number was actually low.[69]

Similar conditions prevailed in other provinces where a 'war business' developed. Enabled by the bureaucrats, soldiers and governors,
elites, like Haji Suleiman and Haji Teimur of Diarbekir, who greatly
profited from the irregular troops' business, sometimes encouraged the
Bedouin to commit atrocities, according to the British vice-consul in
Diarbekir, in order to demonstrate the necessity of employing more
irregulars under their command, and 'in the hope of obtaining tickets of
pay for some many more men' who were 'never raised'.[70] In some cases,
they provoked the Bedouin by pitting the settled tribes against them
even though the former conducted themselves with 'great forbearance
and moderation'. Such was the case of Haji Nuh Agha of Diarbekir,
who endeavoured 'to prolong the affair with a view of benefitting
himself as much as possible'.[71] More serious irregulars-related problems were reported by the consul in Damascus:

The Bashi Bozuk [irregular] officer has his partisans amongst the Arab tribes
[nomads], declares war or makes peace with them as he may conceive it to be
more conducive to his own interest or to his personal aggrandizement, and is
only ostensibly subject to the local authority. He seldom has in his employ
more than fifty or sixty per cent of the men whose pay and rations he is
allowed to draw from the government; and in the very rare event of a muster
being called for, he makes up the deficiency with men borrowed or enlisted
for the occasion. Both men and officers universally oppress the villagers

---

[67] BOA, A.MKT.UM 331/49, 23 Rebiulevvel 1275 [1 November 1858].
[68] BOA, A.MKT.MVL 104/83, 18 Cemaziyelevvel 1275 [24 Aralık 1858].
[69] FO 195/676, Baghdad, 13 March 1861.
[70] FO 195/603, Diarbekir, 1 September 1859.
[71] FO 195/676, Diarbekir, 12 June 1861.

without mercy; receiving their pay and rations at headquarters and at the same time obliging the peasantry to feed both them and their horses.[72]

Such problems and the ever-increasing financial burden of the irregulars compelled the Ottoman government to abandon this system and to recruit more regular troops to keep the Bedouin in check. Towards 1860, both the collapse of the system and the successful resistance of the Shammar and Anizah communities against the designs and plots of the empire compelled a fundamental change in the structure of the troops by regularizing them. As the original 'forward policy' choice was foreclosed with the collapse of the irregular system, reconciliation became more reasonable for the imperial authorities to embrace. In this regard, the regularization of the desert army was a remarkable step for the full adoption of the politics of negotiation.

Regularization of the Desert Troops and the Bedouin

As a result, a fundamental transformation took place in the structure of the Ottoman troops employed against the nomads. It also demonstrates the changing imperial mentality regarding the nomadic existence in the imperial lands since this may be interpreted as a major step affirming the Shammar and Anizah as 'natural' and permanent components of the region. But it was necessary for the imperial authorities to minimize the security problems caused by them. The regular troops were extensively deployed as security providers along the desert frontier for a more effective control of the nomads and their migration routes.

The efficient implementation of the regularization policies owed much to the successful recruitment of Ottoman subjects in the 1850s to the imperial army throughout the empire to close its manpower gap. This reduced the imperial dependence on local partners to struggle with the nomads in the 1860s. Unfamiliarity of the regular troops with the region provided another advantage to transform the imperial policy: regularization automatically abolished the possibility of any collaboration between and among the troops, officials and the nomads as they did not have a relationship of interest with any group. Such professionalization of the army was the ideal of the Tanzimat modernizers who imagined the creation of a bureaucratic-professional empire equally

---

[72] FO 195/677, Damascus, 20 August 1861.

efficient in all the imperial domains. But it seems that, during the period between 1840 and 1860, the Ottoman officials also learned their limits about the nomads and used the regular troops purposefully.

Ottoman documents demonstrate that, from the late 1850s onwards, regular troops began to replace irregulars and to be deployed in the villages and along the desert frontier.[73] In spite of problems with the process, many candidates were successfully conscripted into the imperial army across the various regions of Syria and Iraq,[74] and a force of gendarmerie made up of cavalry was established to protect the countryside from the Bedouin incursions.[75] Irregulars were gradually replaced by regulars – or they were drafted into the regular order – in those areas frequented by the Bedouin.[76]

The change in troops employed in the desert was, however, by no means a simple matter. All the agents of governance, who benefited financially and politically from the employment of irregulars and fighting with the nomads, attempted to reverse the regularization of the Ottoman troops. Conflict between 'local' and 'imperial' continued for a while and the decisiveness of the central government ended the resistance of the provincial power magnates including the officials.

The recruitment process of regular troops in Mosul in 1857 highlights the tension generated by the change in structure of Ottoman troops employed in the desert. When Mustafa Pasha was appointed to recruit men to the regular army, the sedentary tribes in government service as irregulars began to attack and plunder the villages together with the Shammar. In addition, they went into various Bedouin encampments and stole their horses so as to create unrest in the province. According to the British vice-consul, they were privately encouraged by Hilmi Pasha, an officer in Mosul, who resisted the orders of the army commander in Baghdad to discharge these corps, retaining them instead. The members of the province's administrative council were staunch allies in the desire to maintain the old system. When Hilmi was dismissed on the grounds of his opposition, he incited his ally tribes to destabilize the region and told those affected by this that, having been

[73] See, for example, SCR-Mardin 244, 2 Muharrem 1278 [10 Temmuz 1861], 17.

[74] See, for example, AMAE, CPC, Turquie, Damascus-8, 15 October 1863.

[75] Colonel Hasan Bey (O'Reilly), for instance, was charged with the creation of the Syrian gendarmerie: AMAE, CPC, Turquie, Damascus-7, 4 January 1863.

[76] See, for example, BOA, A.MKT.MHM 310/95, 3 Rebiulahir 1281 [5 September 1864]; AMAE, CPC, Turquie, Damascus-7, 4 January 1863.

deposed, he no longer wielded any control over his tribes. The consul reported that all sections of society in Mosul believed that he had orchestrated the plundering.[77]

These did not make the Porte retreat from its initial decision and 600 of the irregulars in Mosul were disbanded. Four hundred of the remaining 600 were demobilized two years later, and 200 were retained at the insistence of Mosul's governor.[78] Similarly, the governor of Aleppo reported that elites of the province prevented the discharge of the irregular troops in collaboration with the bureaucrats, and demanded the authorization to expel or dismiss them [*mütehayyızan-ı memleketten mani-i emr-i irade olanların oradan çıkarılması*]. The Porte noted that 'such disorder could have been tackled if the officials acted in unity' and gave full licence to the governor in this matter.[79] The subgovernor of Hawran, Ahmed Pasha al-Yusuf, resigned from his post when he was ordered to disband the irregular cavalries under his command, and instead use the newly created gendarmerie force. The French consul reported that the governor's resignation was due to the loss of a major source of income. He had conscripted fifty irregulars but had received money for 150 horsemen, which constituted a major reason for the dispute between local and imperial in many regions of the empire.[80]

A lack of troops continued to pose a serious problem for some time in areas where the irregular troops had been demobilized. When the regulars assigned to protect the Mosul frontier were transferred to Sulaimania in 1859,[81] the Anizah and Shammar branches attacked twenty-five villages in the province.[82] Similarly, in response to the Bedouin attacks, the governor of Damascus was obliged to instruct the authorities of Homs and Hama to hold them off until he could send troops actually employed in Hawran to help them. The urgency of the situation forced the governor to establish a new corps of irregular cavalry.[83] In places such as Aleppo where 'the nomad question' emerged sporadically, irregulars would occasionally be employed for

---

[77] FO 195/394, Mosul, 13 July 1857.
[78] BOA, BEO.AYN.d. No.181, 6 Cemaziyelahir 1275 [11 January 1859], 37.
[79] BOA, BEO.AYN.d. No.181, 29 Cemaziyelevvel 1275 [4 January 1859], 34.
[80] AMAE, CPC, Turquie, Damascus-7, 4 January 1863.
[81] BOA, İ.DH 451/29874, 23 Muharrem 1276 [23 August 1859].
[82] BOA, İ.MVL 428/18799, 8 Cemaziyelahir 1276 [12 December 1859].
[83] FO 195/677, Damascus, 20 August 1861.

a while in times of emergency.[84] This new method of irregular recruit-ment was comparable to the system used for regular troops as they were 'better paid, constantly mustered and subjected to military discipline'.[85]

A contract signed with Yazıcızade Hasan Agha, assigned to recruit irregulars to protect the villages of Hama against the Anizah, demon-strates the changing character of the irregulars and the Ottoman approach towards the nomads. According to the contract, he was to be responsible to allocate the pastures for the Anizah tribes in the region, to punish disloyal sheikhs, who did not obey the orders of their chiefs through the agency of their sheikhs and to punish the members of the 'loyal' tax-paying Arab and Turcoman tribes who attacked the Anizah and stole their camels, mares and other animals. The contract criticizes these tribes for damaging the peace by provok-ing Bedouin aggression in spite of their loyalty.[86] This contract indi-cates the increasing cooperation between the sheikhs and government forces with regard to the security of the Arab countryside. In addition, it connotes that crimes against the Anizah would be punished which was not referred to previously although the settled tribes occasionally attacked them and stole their animals. It seems that the nomads' status in the imperial perception had been raised from 'savages' to something better. This consequently may be considered evidence for the trans-formation of the imperial policy towards the nomads. It may also prove the nomadic inclination to cooperate as remarks like that would not be included in the text of the contract unless they had not taken place previously.

The regular troops, now constituting the great majority of the imper-ial troops employed in the countryside against the Bedouin, were quite different in nature from the irregulars characterized as they were by their discipline. Their engagement in Bedouin issues required extensive investment in security infrastructure along the desert route. A substantial number of military fortresses and stations were either built or repaired to provide accommodation for these troops and their animals, a major undertaking that had not been attempted on the desert border before 1860. As part of the plan, it was decided to build five

---

[84] See, for example, FO 195/902, Aleppo, 3 December 1867.
[85] FO 195/677, Damascus, 20 August 1861.
[86] BOA, MVL 308/70, 9 Receb 1273 [6 March 1857].

fortresses on Mosul's desert frontier that year.[87] The following year, a decision was made to build two fortresses in Urfa to protect the villages on the desert frontier against the Anizah attacks. The income generated from selling the Bedouin animals seized by government troops was to be invested in the construction and weaponing costs of these fortresses.[88] In 1862, regular troops were deployed to other strategic positions around Urfa.[89] At around the same time, the irregular cavalry was superseded in some areas by a regular force of mounted police.[90] These troops also enjoyed a substantial technological superiority over the Bedouin in terms of weaponry.[91]

In spite of efforts made by some Anizah groups to prevent their construction,[92] a line of small forts covering Aleppo villages to its south east was completed in 1862; and some twenty-eight new villages were created within it, extending greatly the area of highly productive cultivation. As a result of these measures, not 'a single instance of plunder' occurred in the province that year.[93] In the same way, Kethüdazade Mustafa Agha, a local elite and member of the administrative council, and two officers Ömer Bey and Ahmed Effendi were appointed in 1864 by the governorate of Aleppo to determine suitable locations to build military bases on the desert frontier.[94]

The erection of such fortresses and deploying soldiers to the strategic points along the line of Bedouin migration, however, did not result in limiting Bedouin mobility to the desert or preventing their interaction with towns and villages. They were merely security measures to prevent Bedouin attacks on settled areas, regularize their migration routes and protect the newly created villages on deserted land, which amounted to a very small percentage of uncultivated lands suitable for agriculture. The government authorities had to pull out of such projects as they were fiercely opposed by the Bedouin groups. To this end, the Aleppo

[87] BOA, A.MKT.MVL 116/34, 19 Şevval 1276 [10 Mayıs 1860].
[88] BOA, İ.MVL 456/20437, 13 Rebiulevvel 1278 [19 September 1861].
[89] BOA, BEO.AYN.d No. 187, 23 Rebiulahir 1279 [18 October 1862], 5.
[90] FO 195/806, Damascus, 20 November 1866.
[91] For some descriptions, see: Blunt, *Bedouin Tribes* I, 287.
[92] CADN, Serie D, 166PO/D1/57, Aleppo, 1 June 1861; the document is not clear about the reasons behind the Anizah's opposition. It may be either the fear of being 'cordoned' in the desert or the apprehension of losing some pastures occupied by them.
[93] FO 195/716, Aleppo, 15 September 1862.
[94] BOA, MVL 771/9, 26 Şevval 1280 [16 March 1864].

Figure 2.2 An Ottoman military outpost in Dumeir, and a Bedouin on camel in foreground. Gertrude Bell Archives, Newcastle University, P_075.

government proposed a plan to create camel and mule corps to operate against the Bedouin based in the Palmyra and Deir al-Zor regions in 1866. Their aim was to restrict Bedouin access to the towns and villages.[95] The project posed a crucial threat to Bedouin mobility and their interaction with the sedentary areas: the Bedouin, mounted on very fast horses, fled into the desert at the first alarm and the regular cavalry were powerless to follow them there. Although mules were not as speedy as horses, they always overtook them over long distances because they could run much further without resting.[96] Camel corps were also ideal to penetrate into the heart of the desert.

The governor purchased the necessary animals to carry riflemen into the desert which would limit the atrocities carried out by the nomadic Arabs. The Bedouin, however, responded to this measure very aggressively. A thousand Anizah horsemen led by Ibn Murshid, the chief of the Gomussa branch of the great Seb'a tribe, attacked the pastoral tribe of Kayarat at Deir Hafir, an area in the neighbourhood of Aleppo, and carried off 10,000 sheep and 30 mares, killing 7 men, and wounding

[95] AMAE, CPC, Turquie, Damascus-9, 27 May 1867.
[96] AMAE, CPC, Turquie, Aleppo-6, 12 September 1881.

Figure 2.3 An Ottoman fortress at Mudawwarah, 1902. İstanbul Üniversitesi Nadir Eserler Kütüphanesi, 90605/0052.

a dozen more.[97] The following spring, the Fid'an under sheikh Dahham took possession of 5,000 sheep on their way to Damascus, leaving their owners to arrive at Aleppo in protest. The theft could be interpreted as a direct challenge to imperial authority. The British consul states that they only carried out such atrocities once they had 'no longer any hope of being allowed to trade peacefully with Aleppo'.[98] As a result, the plan was abandoned since 'the camel corps would never render services of any value against the nomads'.[99] It appears that the plan was realized in part a few years later through the creation and deployment of the mule corps at Deir al-Zor and at other strategic locations. This was, however, exclusively to increase security on the desert frontier rather than to limit the Bedouin interaction with the cities and their mobility.[100] As will be detailed in the Chapter 3, the Bedouin pasturages had been more or less determined and the empire had officially

---

[97] FO 195/800, Aleppo, 3 December 1867.
[98] FO 195/902, Aleppo, 12 April 1868.   [99] FO 195/902, Aleppo, 23 April 1868.
[100] AMAE, CPC, Turquie, Aleppo-6, 12 September 1881.

recognized the tribal rights to graze their animals by a contract with their sheikhs.

Other measures were also introduced to render the desert and its frontier more secure. The caravans, roads and villages were largely protected by 'a series of small forts and patrols of soldiers',[101] 'all consist[ing] of a square enclosed by a mud wall twelve feet high, and without other opening to the outer world than a single gateway'.[102] By this way, the nomads were surveilled with a technique comparable to Foucault's model of Panopticon. As such, by 1871, a chain of fortresses and military stations were linked by numerous small detachments between Deir al-Zor and Aleppo, and three battalions of mule-riding cavalries were deployed inside the chain. This provided an invaluable advantage to imperial troops as their aim was to protect the neighbour-hood where they were deployed and any attack was generally on the tribes' side. In addition, the improvement in military technology made a significant contribution to the army's success in controlling Bedouin tribes. The effect of the new long-range firearms in the hands of the riflemen was to check the advance of the nomads, and prevent their getting close enough to use their spears on them.[103] As a result of these measures, the desert routes and its frontier became considerably safer: Wilfrid Blunt noted in the early 1870s that the caravan roads were much more secure in comparison with earlier decades.[104] He describes the desert areas 'as safe for travellers as any part of the empire, or of Europe itself'.[105]

After the consolidation of Ottoman rule, security measures were intensified in the regions of southern Syria – today's Jordan – where the new administrative units were established. The main towns were provided security by police [*zabtiye*] and 'guard houses were distrib-uted along strategic villages and intersections for the mule-mounted gendarmes'.[106] The administrative units in the region such as Ma'an, Karak and Ajlun were linked to their surrounding villages with smaller tracks, and police and mounted detachments of gendarmes posted to the strategic points, which remarkably improved state of security along the roads. The roads in the region would later be upgraded for wheeled traffic in the early 1900s.[107] From the 1890s, the Circassian and

[101] Blunt, *Bedouin Tribes* I, 29.   [102] Ibid., 144.
[103] FO 195/976, Aleppo, 17 November 1871.
[104] Blunt, *Bedouin Tribes* I, viii.   [105] Blunt, *Bedouin Tribes* II, 2.
[106] Rogan, *Frontiers*, 67.   [107] Rogan, *Frontiers*, 62.

Figure 2.4 Bedouin sitting in front of an Ottoman fortress at Mudawwarah. İstanbul Üniversitesi Nadir Eserler Kütüphanesi, 90605/0053.

Chechen settlers, many of whom were militarily trained, were employed in the gendarmerie. 'They were to prevent aggressors from entering certain regions, to return stolen property, and to arrest murder suspects. And they were to accompany tax collectors, or indeed collect the taxes themselves from Bedouin and other remote communities.'[108]

The essential function of these troops was to patrol tribal movements and to prevent tribes from attacking the villages and caravans. The increase of the Ottoman military existence in the Arab countryside rarely limited Bedouin mobilization unless they voluntarily requested to be settled. As will be detailed in the following chapters, they maintained their seasonal migrations to their usual pasturages, migrated to the new grazing lands when drought influenced their usual pastures and continued to sell their products and to shop in the town markets. That

[108] Rogan, *Frontiers*, 67.

is why the transformation of the Ottoman desert troops did not create widespread disturbance among the Bedouin tribes.

Conclusion

When the Ottoman state reinstated itself in the 1840s with the Tanzimat reforms, the great majority of the agricultural lands in the Arab provinces had been abandoned due to tribal attacks and heavy *khuwwa* demands by various tribal chiefs. The majority of these lands had been forcefully occupied by the nomads to graze their animals while some others were merely abandoned out of fear of the Anizah and Shammar. The existence of such a great number of abandoned villages both seriously threatened the imperial treasury and constituted a fundamental problem of security in the countryside. As a result, a new undertaking of resettlement was initiated by the imperial authorities which achieved the return of a number of semi-settled tribes to their old lands. Although the imperial aim was initially to restrain the nomads in the desert, the result was further dependence on friendly relations with them as the number of new resettlements was by no means sufficient to wall off the settled areas of the desert where the nomads were supposed to live. But they contributed to the regularization of the nomadic migrations in the following decades as an 'infrastructural investment' given the significant decrease of tribal raids on caravans and settled areas.

Another important investment in the sense of infrastructure complementing the colonization of land was the militarization of the desert frontier by the deployment of regular troops to strategic locations. Chains of military deployments were created along the desert frontier of the Syrian and Iraqi provinces. This was made possible by the transformation of the irregulars who were recruited to be employed against the nomads whose principal trait was to attack the tribes and pursue them in the desert. As outlined in this chapter, however, while the number of regular troops was sufficient to overcome the reconciled tribesmen in the sense of protection of the new settlements and regularization of tribal movement, it was hardly adequate for a complete expulsion of the nomads from the pastures they used in the imperial areas and cutting their communication with the sedentary societies. By these investments, the power balance between the nomads and the empire was ensured, which made the imperial officials more enthusiastic about the expansion of imperial authority into the desert. Chapters 3 and 4 will discuss the Ottoman expansionism that fundamentally transformed Ottoman-nomad relations as it made both parties dependent on each other.

3 Expansion, Reaction and Reconciliation I

Establishment of the Deir al-Zor Mutasarrıfate and Reconciliation with the Fid'an and Deir al-Zor's Shammar

This chapter examines the extension of the Ottoman administration into Deir al-Zor located on the east bank of the Euphrates where the Anizah, Shammar and other tribal groups established strong positions. Towards the late 1860s, the Ottoman officials intensified their efforts to extend the empire's physical presence into the desert regions and more remote rural areas. Besides the Ottoman enthusiasm to expand government control over the remote and inaccessible areas as part of the Tanzimat policies, the Deir al-Zor initiative started and gained momentum by the desire to restrict the Wahhabis in Arabia, the British existence in Egypt and its increasing influence in the Gulf and Iraq, and to minimize the problems caused by Bedouin tribal organizations like the Anizah and Shammar.

This chapter questions how the imperial expansion towards Deir al-Zor transformed the space and society in the region and influenced the Shammar and Anizah tribes and argues that the Ottoman expansion into Deir al-Zor resulted in a partial success in comparison to the preconceived aims due to the tribal resistance, which ultimately compelled the empire to adopt a conciliatory stance, taking tribal concerns and interests into account. To put it another way, the implementation of the imperial expansion into Deir al-Zor diverged from its initial aims and the particular purpose of subjugating the Shammar and Anizah branches had to be significantly revised due to tribal resistance and the change of imperial ideology from 'idealist modernism' to 'pragmatism', which allowed the systematization of the imperial expansionism to fall into place.

In accordance with Tanzimat principles, the primary imperial aim regarding the Bedouin was to restrict the Bedouins' autonomy by

limiting their mobility, imposing taxes on their properties and ultimately colonizing desert territories and thereby forcing the them to
fundamentally change their lifestyle and become settled agricultural
communities. In this way, new human and financial resources would be
generated. However, the expedition and consolidation had to be organized in coordination with, at least, some Bedouin sheiks, who were
treated as partners rather than subjects or citizens of a modernizing
state and who obtained new privileges in the newly occupied territories
such as having the control of new tribal groups or acquiring a superior
position over their tribal rivals. Jed'an's domination over the Fid'an of
Deir al-Zor who rivalled Dahham may exemplify the tribal winners in
the extension of Ottoman rule. With regard to the other tribal advantages, they found new customers for their animals due to the incorporation of the newly expanded regions into the global markets via the
agency of the new merchants settled in the region. They were also
absolved of major responsibilities vis-à-vis the government such as
military service. The concessions given by the tribal groups to the
newly established administration were to pay a moderate amount of
tax and to relinquish their *khuwwa* income. Imperial expansionism
thus signified the beginning of the politics of negotiation based on
reciprocity of concessions.

In light of the Shammar and Anizah examples around Deir al-Zor,
another argument this chapter puts forward is that the imperial expansion did not remarkably change the tribal society of the Shammar and
Anizah as intended by the Tanzimat reformers. The imperial expansion
could neither pacify the tribes by pushing them into the desert nor
dominate them or transform their lifestyle although it was successful
against the other groups detailed below. It also did not convert the
tribesmen into 'ordinary imperial subjects' in the regions where imperial rule expanded; their sheikhs were still the most important authority
for them. The intervention of the imperial authorities into their affairs
was as minimal as it had been in the preceding times and they continued
to visit their old pastures and live within the tribal hierarchy. The
'Tribesmen into Ottomans project' ceased to be realized with respect
to the tribal cases analysed in this book.

Besides the local, tribal and practical reasons, there were imperial
and global reasons for the transformation of Ottoman policy.
Imperially, by the Hamidian era, Tanzimat idealism gave way to
Hamidian pragmatism based on the idea of Pan-Islamism which

stressed the Muslim fraternity and further prioritized the satisfaction of the local, secondary and autonomous groups such as the nomads. The organization of the Kurdish nomadic tribes as the Hamidiye cavalry was a notable example of such policy shift.[1] This evolution of the imperial policy owed much to the changing balance of power in the inter-imperial league: the rise of Germany and the increasing British concerns about India directed the latter to focus on the Persian Gulf and Iraq, and develop relations with the local leaders there. The Russian interests in eastern and southern Anatolia resulted in similar undertakings for Russia. As a result, the Ottoman policymakers felt that they must have better and stronger relations with the local power-holders such as the nomadic sheikhs as they were considered potentially at risk of collaborating with the Great Powers. Thus, the Ottoman government attributed importance to having good relations with the Arab nomads and abstained from policies that would frustrate them.

The key advantage of the Bedouin tribes, which enabled them to counter the imperial expansion and smoothen it was again their ability to destroy the regional order by their coercive tools and to escape into the remote desert regions whenever the Empire attempted to constrain their lifestyle, attacked them, or imposed heavy control on them. The desert, still a vast uncontainable area, allowed the Bedouin considerable freedom from governmental authority even though it was expanding its authority closer. By 1870, although there was a certain control over strategic desert locations such as Hawran, Palmyra and Deir al-Zor, the empire's military and financial situation prevented its rulers from limiting the Shammar and Anizah's mobility in the remote and unreachable desert areas and keeping them away from settled areas, which constituted one major goal of the expansionist policy.

At the Crossroad of the Desert: Deir al-Zor and Its Importance

The Deir al-Zor *mutasarrıfate* was established in a highly strategic position in the desert between Anatolia, Iraq and Syria, at the crossroads of the main caravan routes which connected principal cities such as Aleppo, Baghdad, Basra, Diarbekir, Damascus and Mosul.

---

[1] For a study on this, see: Klein, *The Margins of Empire*.

Its location also linked the northern cities of the region to global markets such as India and Europe via the Persian Gulf.[2] In addition, the location, on fertile land, had agricultural potential situated as it was on the right bank of the Euphrates and irrigated by numerous springs which kept it cool during the heaviest heat of summer and made it attractive for the nomads.[3] Expansionist Ottoman officials believed that the colonization and effective cultivation of the region would immeasurably increase the revenues of the imperial treasury. As stated by an Ottoman official in 1893, if the Bedouin around the city had been settled and the country had been thoroughly cultivated, the region would be as productive as those of the agricultural lands in Egypt.[4]

The town was a local centre of commerce for the Bedouin to buy and sell their goods and their main migration routes, north and south, crisscrossed the surrounding desert. Thus, the imposition of Ottoman authority over Deir would mean considerable control over the tribes in its neighbourhood. The transformation of the Anizah and Shammar tribesmen's nomadic lifestyle constituted the principal target of Ottoman expansionism.[5] On the other hand, it would mean a significant loss for the tribes who enjoyed the pastures in and around the region as well as being deprived of their *khuwwa* revenues. This would force the nomads to adopt a sedentary life which, according to the expansionist Ottoman officials, would ultimately solve the tribal question.[6]

The imperial authorities planned to establish an administrative outpost supported by the military existence as early as the late 1840s. Control of the area was key to Ottoman rule over the Bedouin for several reasons. Firstly, the imperial authorities in Aleppo planned to collect taxes regularly from settled and nomadic communities to meet the needs of the provincial treasury that was severely depleted by the reorganization demanded by the Tanzimat reforms.[7] As the town was

---

[2] For a detailed description of Deir al-Zor's geography, see: Zakariyya, *Rihlatu*, 11–13.

[3] CADN, Serie D, 166PO/D1/54, Aleppo, 1 September 1864.

[4] BOA, DH.MKT 316/40, 13 Ağustos 1309 [26 August 1893].

[5] See, for example, BOA, İ.MVL 167/4938, 2 Ramazan 1265 [24 July 1849].

[6] For such opinions put forward by Ömer Lütfi Pasha, the governor of Baghdad, see: Akyüz, 'Irak ve Hicaz Ordusu', 164–165.

[7] Barout, 'La renaissance', 108; Bostan, 'Zor Sancağı', 214; see, also: FO 195/302, Aleppo, 29 November 1851.

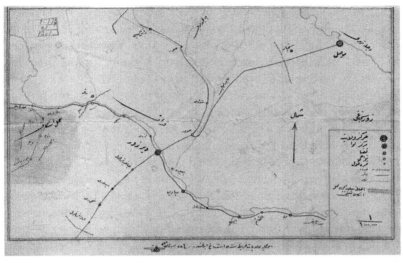

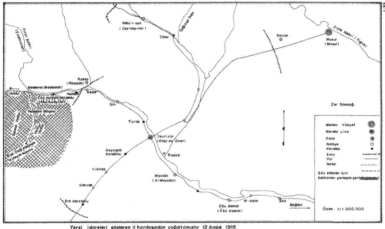

Map 3.1 Road map crosscutting Deir al-Zor. İBB Atatürk Kitaplığı, Vilayet Yolları Haritasıdır, Istanbul: Dahiliye Nezareti Umur-ı Mahalliye Vilayet Müdüriyeti, 1913.

well-known as a market for Bedouin livestock,[8] effective control would facilitate the taxation of tribal animals. Further motivation for the establishment of an administrative outpost in the region was the need

---

[8] For some details on this, see: Blunt, *Bedouin Tribes*, 117.

to secure the routes mentioned earlier, and to open a direct route between Aleppo and Baghdad, which would considerably reduce shipping costs for local and foreign merchants alike. Direct trade between these two cities had almost ceased due to Bedouin attacks after the withdrawal of Ibrahim Pasha's forces from Deir al-Zor in 1840. The Ottoman intention was to create a garrison in the city, fortify it using both regular and irregular soldiers from the neighbouring provinces, and to build military checkpoints along the roads that would force the Bedouin to accede to imperial rule. Once their mobility was limited, they would have to accept the imperial plan to settle them.[9] In addition, the expansion would increase the security of river navigation on the Euphrates that had been subjected to regular attacks by local tribes[10] and would accordingly limit a potential increase in British influence over the Bedouin of the district. The extension of Ottoman rule to Deir al-Zor would also help to undermine Russia's attempt to establish a sphere of influence in the upper Jazira that relied on Kurds, Armenians and Syriacs.[11] Finally, it would prevent the Bedouin from attacking agricultural areas in the wider region. An Ottoman report, prepared by the governor of Damascus and the commander of the army of Arabia, stated that Deir al-Zor's control was critical to sustaining agriculture in Hama, Homs, Aleppo and Ma'arre in Syria and Karbala and Najaf in Iraq, since the Bedouin attacked peasants and agricultural tribes and took refuge across these areas.[12] Another report prepared by the governor of Baghdad demonstrates the existence of many abandoned villages in the east of the Euphrates within the boundaries of Baghdad province due to raids and plunder by the Shammar, which preconditioned the recultivation of these lands to the establishment of a strong government position in Deir al-Zor.[13] Furthermore, proper control over Deir would make the upper and lower Jazira region immune to Bedouin plunder and pave the way for the establishment of many taxable villages in fertile agricultural areas. According to Ottoman officials, the region

[9] BOA, İ.MVL 167/4938, 2 Ramazan 1265 [24 July 1849].
[10] For a description of the security problems on this route that stemmed from the Anizah and Shammar, see: Mehmed Hurşid Paşa, *Seyahatname*, 269–276.
[11] Barout, 'La renaissance', 108.
[12] BOA, İ.MVL 119/2954, 11 Receb 1264 [26 February 1848]; for similar remarks by the French consul in Damascus, see: AMAE, CPC, Turquie, Damascus-2, 2 March 1852.
[13] BOA, İ.DH 401/26573, 1 Şaban 1274 [17 March 1858]; quoted in Akyüz, 'Irak ve Hicaz Ordusu', 165.

was able to support more than 100,000 peasants to cultivate the soil. The plan was to transform the nomads into peasants.[14]

Similar to Midhat Pasha's attempt in Iraq to settle the Shammar, the aims adequately reflect the modernist idealism which believed in the transforming power of the supreme settled civilization and did not calculate the resisting potential of the local population and the Bedouin. In light of the documents on the Deir al-Zor expedition, the government envisaged the target population as if they were ready to embrace Ottoman rule and would not have opposed the imperial expansionism, which would bring civilization to the region. In particular, the Anizah Bedouin were to fight against the Ottoman soldiers and force the Ottoman authorities to fundamentally modify their excessive initial aims. As the French consul observed even in 1864, there was an 'immense distance' between *conception* and *réalisation*.[15]

The First Expansion of the Ottoman Rule over Deir al-Zor

Although 'expansionist' Ottoman local and imperial rulers envisaged a unidirectional process resulting in the subjugation and limitation of the Bedouin, colonization of new agricultural lands and the imposition of the imperial authority over Deir al-Zor, in practice, many revisions had to be made. Many local and imperial officials, the elites of Aleppo and Urfa, who enjoyed close commercial relations with the Bedouin in Deir, expected to benefit greatly from the expansion of imperial authority, and therefore played a very active role in the Ottoman penetration of the region, while others who saw their interests threatened by the expansion strongly opposed it. These competing interests impacted on the pace and implementation of the Ottoman plans. Another more important factor that forced a revision of the initial plans was the need to negotiate with the Bedouin and semi-settled tribal leaders in order to end their opposition, conclude hostilities and secure their compliance with and acceptance of *mutasarrıfate* rule. However, the return to the imperial habit of playing one tribe against the other and fomenting disputes among the various groups brought about chaos in the region which ultimately ended in the failure of the first campaign.

[14] BOA, MVL 772/41, 24 Zilhicce 1280 [31 May 1864].
[15] CADN, Serie D, 166PO/D1/59, Aleppo, 1 September 1864.

It should be noted that it was not the Tanzimat statesmen who first discovered and controlled Deir al-Zor during the Ottoman rule. Following the Ottoman conquest of Arab lands in the early sixteenth century, the imperial authorities constantly endeavoured to pacify the Bedouin of the district by settling the peasants on arable lands. In 1574, Deir al-Zor was a small village ruled by Turkish and Arab tribes who cultivated wheat, barley and cotton, built houses and sold their home-grown produce. More than a century later, in 1696, their way of life remained largely unchanged. Deir was under Bedouin control, who ruled the district on behalf of the sultan.[16] At the close of the seventeenth century, the village was annexed to Diarbekir as part of imperial efforts to increase tax revenues by settling tribes on the wastelands of eastern Anatolia and Bilad al-Sham. This project failed between 1720 and 1725 for several reasons. The Shammar and Anizah migrations from Najd at the end of the eighteenth century and the resultant problems of such a mass relocation rendered the district once again critical to Ottoman regional power.[17] But nothing could be done in the absence of a powerful state. In October 1835, Ibrahim Pasha of Egypt, then ruling Syria, sent a small body of troops to Deir al-Zor and created a garrison there to keep the Bedouin tribes in check and 'the next five years the garrison at Deir and detachments of troops in the fields between it and Aleppo were generally able to do this and to maintain order in the area'.[18] However, when the Pasha's rule in Syria came to an end in 1840, the garrison could not be maintained by Ottoman troops and the governor of Aleppo withdrew the soldiers from Deir within a year. Nevertheless, communication with the Bedouin of the district was maintained and sporadic – and usually unsuccessful – visits were made by the imperial authorities of Aleppo in order to collect taxes and negotiate with the tribal leaders to ensure the security of the roads.[19]

In 1848, Namık and Safveti Pashas, the commander of the army of Arabia and the governor of Damascus were the first to articulate the

[16] Hannoyer, 'Politique des notables', 115–116.
[17] Barout, 'La renaissance', 107. [18] Lewis, *Nomads and Settlers*, 25.
[19] See, for example, AMAE, CPC, Turquie, Aleppo-1, 16 February 1841; some of which were remarkably successful: AMAE, CPC, Turquie, Aleppo-1, 15 March 1842; CADN, Serie D, 166PO/D1/47, Aleppo, 30 April 1842; AMAE, CPC, Turquie, Aleppo-1, 17 April 1842.

necessity of an Ottoman administrative post at Deir al-Zor to keep the Bedouin in check.[20] However, the region was within the boundaries of Aleppo province and the expansion plan could and should have been implemented by the officials there. As such, the Ottoman authorities at Aleppo began preparations to expand imperial rule to Deir al-Zor in 1851,[21] but had to abandon their project in 1852 when all Ottoman troops were mobilized to suppress the Druze revolt.[22]

An expedition for the administrative and military expansion of Deir was organized in 1854 by the Aleppo authorities under the aegis of the Urfan, Şerifbeyzade Yusuf Pasha, appointed as the first *kaymakam* of the region. The pasha was well-regarded in the region given his sustained close commercial relations there, which might serve finding local alliances for the imperial cause and divide regional society. An irregular cavalry of 1,000 men and two artilleries accompanied him, but was too small a force to take on the numbers of Bedouin.[23] Some 5,000–6,000 troops would have been needed to execute these *entreprises importantes*[24] against the major Bedouin groups around Zor, who were subverting the caravan route and attacking villages along the desert frontier in response to the expansion.[25] In addition, a huge amount of money would have been required to establish a sustainable supply chain through the desert.[26] As it was almost impossible for the local governors to mobilize and coordinate the requisite number of soldiers, the authorities tried to gain the support of the major Bedouin groups in the area. At the outset of Yusuf's expedition, the British consul clearly stated that he had 'to control and indeed to conciliate the Anizah tribes bordering the desert frontier, to protect the villages thereto exposed'.[27]

The response of the Bedouin proved that the consul was right and reinforced the necessity of securing their consent to move into the

---

20 BOA, İ.MVL 119/2954, 11 Receb 1264 [26 February 1848].
21 FO 195/302, Aleppo, 8 February 1851.
22 Hannoyer, 'Politique des notables', 122.
23 BOA, MVL 1, 15 Receb 1269 [24 Nisan 1853], 170–171.
24 AMAE, CPC, Turquie, Damascus-2, 2 March 1852.
25 The French consul in Aleppo described the expansion as an 'unpleasant' affair [*désagréable affaire*] that would frustrate the Bedouin and completely destroy the security of the villages and trade roads: CADN, Serie D, 166PO/D1/52, Aleppo, 16 September 1854.
26 AMAE, CPC, Turquie, Damascus-2, 2 March 1852.
27 FO 195/416, Aleppo, 22 July 1854.

desert. When Yusuf Pasha arrived on the outskirts of the desert near Tediff, the Seb'a tribes of the Anizah defeated some of his forces and his chief of the irregular cavalry was severely wounded.[28] Shortly after the defeat, the irregular troops began to desert and many returned to Aleppo.[29] To maintain a permanent and stable imperial presence in the district, the pasha had to initiate another round of negotiations with the principal Anizah sheikhs including Dahham and Jed'an of the Fid'an.[30]

As a result of Yusuf Pasha's efforts, in a matter of months, Jed'an, who had spent the winter in the desert, joined his expedition.[31] Jed'an's plan was to increase his domination over the Anizah groups there and secure their loyalty to him as their sheikhs against his rival Dahham. In addition, as detailed in Chapter 1, he was usually on good terms with the authorities in Aleppo and had been from the very beginning of his emergence as an outstanding Fid'an sheikh. In the following months, the sheikh undertook expeditions against the 'disloyal' Anizah in conjunction with the government.[32] However, Dahham started hostilities against Yusuf Pasha and the governor of Aleppo, and weakened the two men's hold on Deir.[33] By 1856, he finally conceded and consented to the Ottoman existence in Deir al-Zor.[34] The Fid'an's dependence on the sedentary areas presumably forced the sheikh to come to terms. Besides Deir al-Zor, the Fid'an tribes seasonally migrated to the pasturages in other regions of Aleppo province and used the local markets for shopping. Therefore, the tribal leaders had to be careful in their treatment of the government authorities who could prohibit their entrance into these regions. This prevented the tribal leaders, particularly Dahham, from initiating open rebellion against the empire and caused only a limited reaction to the expedition. In addition, Dahham presumably calculated that the expedition would soon fail and the government troops would withdraw from Deir al-Zor.[35]

---

[28] FO 195/416, Aleppo, 4 October 1854.
[29] FO195/416, Aleppo, 13 October 1854.
[30] BOA, BEO. AYN.d. No. 178, 23 Rebiulahir 1271 [22 November 1854], 55.
[31] FO 195/416, Aleppo, 23 November 1854; FO 195/416, Aleppo, 13 December 1854.
[32] FO 195/416, Aleppo, 22 May 1855.
[33] CADN, Serie D, 166PO/D1/53, Aleppo, 3 July 1855.
[34] FO 195/416, Aleppo, 18 April 1856.
[35] For a similar consideration by the tribes of 'Ajlun and Balqa' over the Ottoman expansion towards Transjordan, see: Rogan, *Frontiers*, 180.

Other prominent sheikhs of Deir al-Zor were also 'amicably negoti-ating with the new *kaymakam*'.[36] A considerable number of the small tribes were quickly persuaded by the pasha 'to occupy themselves in agriculture' and they cultivated large tracts of lands, and devoted their time and energy to this.[37] The relative simplicity of reconciling with these tribes might be because they could use the state protection from the Fid'an. They were presumably engaged in agriculture previously and had to abandon their lands due to the heavy *khuwwa* exactions and plunder by rival nomadic groups. Therefore, they seemingly saw the Ottoman expansion as an opportunity to throw off the Fid'an's yoke. Similar examples in other regions, which will be detailed in Chapter 4, make such an analysis possible. Meanwhile, Yusuf Pasha's success in Deir al-Zor saw him promoted to *kaymakam* of Urfa, and his nephew Ali became pasha for Deir.[38]

But the practice of playing off one sheikh against another ruined the initial success and caused the end of the first Ottoman undertaking. Following Ali Pasha, Hasan Bey, from the distinguished Kataragası fam-ily of Aleppo, was appointed desert governor by Ismet Pasha in 1861.[39] According to the French consul, like all the noble families of Aleppo, he had enjoyed a certain patronage over the tribes of Deir. Considering his own interests, the new *kaymakam* supported some of the nomadic tribes and was hostile to some others.[40] After several disputes between the various tribes caused by the act of the *kaymakam*, Fuad Pasha, the governor of Damascus, who was sent to Syria with extraordinary author-ity following the 1860 massacres, abolished the desert governorship.[41]

The Second Expedition: Consolidation of the Imperial Rule and Incorporation of the Bedouin into the Regime at Deir al-Zor

As the very nature of the desert was the major factor in the political unrest, abolishing the desert governorate post could not resolve it.

---

[36] FO 195/416, Aleppo, 23 November 1854; FO 195/416, Aleppo, 13 December 1854.
[37] BOA, BEO.AYN.d. No. 180, 4 Muharrem 1273 [4 September 1856], 19; see also: FO 195/416, Aleppo, 20 January 1855.
[38] FO 195/416, Aleppo, 16 June 1856.
[39] CADN, Serie D, 166PO/D1/57, Aleppo, 21 January 1861.
[40] CADN, Serie D, 166PO/D1/57, Aleppo, 23 June 1861; AMAE, CPC, Turquie, Aleppo-3, 25 June 1861.
[41] FO 195/902, Aleppo, 13 March 1868.

Road security remained an intractable problem. With the imperial authorities unable to open a direct caravan route from Aleppo to Baghdad through the desert,[42] the region still offered the Bedouin a refuge from government control. Thus, proper taxation of the population in the region was still impossible. Consequently, in 1864, Sureyya Pasha, the governor of Aleppo, organized another expedition to Deir al-Zor with authority from the Porte 'to bring the different Bedouin tribes frequenting this district to make their submission to the government, and insure their peaceful conduct in future, and also to force the agricultural tribes located in different parts of the desert to pay their taxes, which many of these tribes had never yet consented to pay'.[43] 'If they [the independent small tribes of Deir al-Zor] decide to abandon the wandering Bedouin lifestyle, important concessions would be made to encourage them and the government will take care of their protection against the desert tribes.'[44] Ömer Pasha, an Ottoman general, was appointed as the commander of the expedition. The idea was also largely supported by the central government and some expansionist elites of Aleppo, who viewed the initiative as a potentially profitable investment.

The Resistance of Aleppo's Notables and Its Elimination

The expansion was, however, strongly resisted by another group of Aleppine elites who enjoyed profitable relationships with the tribal chiefs and thus feared that any governmental penetration into the region might threaten their influence. In addition, there were still others who enjoyed considerable power in the provincial administration and benefited substantially from the recruitment of irregular soldiers to protect villages against the Bedouin. The establishment of proper control over the Bedouin would signify the end to such a profitable business.[45] Consequently they fomented unrest in Aleppo 'to make a diversion in favor of their friends in the desert'

---

[42] FO 195/800, Aleppo, 30 September 1864.   [43] Ibid.
[44] CADN, Serie D, 166PO/D1/54, Aleppo, 1 September 1864.
[45] The governor of Damascus and the commander of the army of Arabia had stated this situation in a joint report on the necessity of the Deir al-Zor expansion: BOA, İ.MVL 119/2954, 11 Receb 1264 [26 February 1848].

and to 'compel Sureyya Pasha to bring back the troops operating in the desert into the city'.[46]

As such, the expansionists' ill-conceived campaign provided a golden opportunity to its opponents: the populations of both city and countryside were harshly requisitioned to meet the operating needs of the army in Deir al-Zor. Low-ranking officers and police forces, assigned to compensate for the demands of the army, abused their positions by seizing more cereals and animals than needed. The French consul estimated that the value of their 'extortions' was some 600,000 piasters, much of which was not spent on expedition forces. In response, the Kurdish, Arab and Turcoman cameleers retreated into the desert and mountains while those who lived in Aleppo or neighbouring villages could not escape the requisitions. Transportation resources were severely impacted in the process, which led to a food crisis in the city in spite of the abundance of the harvest that year. The requisition of the camels and mules also negatively affected the caravan trade, a major factor in the provincial economy.[47]

Taking advantage of this situation, the resisters organized people from the lower classes to attack to houses belonging to the wealthy elites, whom they considered responsible for the situation. According to the French consul, the disorder was deliberately organized by some elites who used the chaos to force the governor into abandoning his decision.[48] Presumably to persuade them to cooperate or to neutralize the resisters a cadastral department was created in Aleppo in 1866, presided over by Raghib Efendi al-Jabiri, a very prominent local elite. It enabled the Aleppine elites to acquire vast tracts of royal lands [*emlak-i hümayun*] in the Euphrates valley. As such, according to Barout, a class of elites emerged in Deir al-Zor, associated with the Ottoman civil and military bureaucracy, who played an essential role in the town's administration and tribal affairs in the years to come.[49] In this way, the resisters were persuaded to abandon their methods and cooperate with the government.

---

[46] CADN, Serie D, 166PO/D1/59, Aleppo, 12 October 1864.
[47] CADN, Serie D, 166PO/D1/59, Aleppo, 29 September 1864.
[48] CADN, Serie D, 166PO/D1/59, Aleppo, 12 October 1864.
[49] Barout, 'La renaissance', 112.

Negotiation, Settlement and Colonization

On this occasion, the imperial authorities were determined to penetrate into Deir al-Zor by dealing with each community individually. The three tribal communities – hunters, semi-settled and nomadic tribes – were targeted to make an impact on each other.[50] Those whose interests could be reconciled with those of the empire were initially approached by the Ottoman authorities to accept imperial rule. The expedition thus first targeted the hunting tribes, *shawayah*, of Deir al-Zor, whose number was estimated at 1,000 tents. They were dependent on the forest around Deir al-Zor and considered easy pickings by the officials. When the troops approached them, they retreated into the desert and sought refuge with the Anizah and Shammar Bedouin. This allowed the expedition troops to progress unhindered towards Deir. After a while, the *shawayah* returned and were dispersed into the forest, where they hunted and could defend themselves. When the troops arrived at the forest, their advance would be obstructed. The government troops made several unsuccessful attacks on the tribal forces, suffering severe losses. Sureyya Pasha responded with a plan to destroy the forest by both burning and cutting down the trees, using 500 peasants recruited from the district of Urfa. But the expense of such labour proved too great. Following considerable losses of men, the pasha entered into negotiation with the *shawayas* and was forced to leave the forest to them in return for a payment of 70,000 piasters as tax.[51]

The second community targeted was the semi-settled tribes, who could be persuaded to turn to agriculture. Similar to the other Ottoman localizations in the Syrian and Iraqi provinces, the resettlement of semi-settled tribes in Deir al-Zor was not merely the result of a one-sided imperial decision to make them settled, increase agricultural production and collect their taxes, though it was a mutually beneficial process. The reasons listed were only those of the empire; while the tribes chose the best option for their interests and cooperated with the empire to protect their positions in the region and to counter their nomadic rivals as they were weak tribes compared to the Anizah an Shammar groups. In addition, since many of them were formerly

---

[50] Bostan, 'Zor Sancağı', 196.
[51] CADN, Serie D, 166PO/D1/59, Aleppo, 12 October 1864.

agricultural tribes, engagement in agriculture was presumably more attractive for them than the nomadic lifestyle.

Shortly after the entrance of the Ottoman troops into Deir al-Zor, Sureyya and Ömer Pashas distributed farmlands on the banks of the Euphrates to the semi-nomadic Arab tribes between 1864 and 1866 in order to encourage the development of agriculture in the district.[52] Similar to the settlement policies implemented in the Aleppo and Damascus provinces previously, the pashas offered to protect these groups from the Anizah's levies in exchange for their paying a smaller amount of taxes to the government. In this way, they changed their loyalty from the nomads to the empire.[53] To protect them against the nomadic attacks, within a matter of months the pashas established a line of military posts manned by regular troops[54] and stationed a battalion of rifles there, while another was sent to seize the ruins of Raqqa, a strategic location that allowed surveillance of the Shammar tribes.[55]

Arslan Pasha, the second *mutasarrıf* of Deir al-Zor, who was described as 'combative yet also constructive',[56] worked energetically and successfully to persuade the semi-nomadic tribes to settle. Part of his policies aimed at 'Ottomanization' of the population in the region which would strengthen their loyalties to the empire. To this end, in the mid-1860s he built the first primary school, a hospital and dozens of villages close to the desert, that were monitored by the soldiers deployed in the military outposts there.[57] These investments were presumably considered to demonstrate to local people the benefits of becoming Ottoman. He also built a series of villages for the Anizah, 'whom he thought he had persuaded or bullied into abandoning their nomadic life and becoming *fellahin* [peasants]'. They, however, never had 'the remotest intention of doing [so], and the huts were never inhabited'.[58]

---

52 Hannoyer, 'Politique des Notables', 123; for details on what they planted and harvested, see, Bostan, 'Zor Sancağı', 196–197.
53 FO 195/800, Aleppo, 3 May 1865.
54 CADN, Serie D, 166PO/D1/60, Aleppo, 1 May 1865.
55 FO 195/800, Aleppo, 30 June 1865.
56 Dolbee, 'The Locust and the Starling', 140.
57 Barout, 'La renaissance', 112; An Ottoman report dated 1870 mentions the agricultural tribes, which also proves that Arslan managed to persuade the semi-settled tribes to engage in agriculture: Bostan, 'Zor Sancağı', 175.
58 Blunt, *Bedouin Tribes*, 84.

Arslan was succeeded by Ömer Şevki Pasha, who persuaded some small Bedouin groups and the Isa tribe, who numbered reportedly more than 2,000 households [hane], around Nusaybin, Ra's al-Ayn, Kawkab and its lower part, and the riverside of Khabur, to cultivate the wetlands and built thirty villages in this district. The pasha also involved some 2,000 households of the Bakkara Bedouin in agriculture around the Euphrates. These were the old inhabitants of Deir al-Zor district who had adopted a nomadic lifestyle and joined the Shammar around twenty years earlier. In addition, the Wahb, Harb and Nu'aym tribes, numbering more than 1,200 households, were settled in the environs of the town. Furthermore, the pasha situated the Tay and Jabbur tribes of Nusaybin, consisting of 1,500–2,000 households, in Busira between the Khabur and Euphrates rivers, procured seeds for them and set about building houses for them.[59]

In spite of such achievements, however, it is difficult to claim that a forward policy towards the nomad's pasture lands could be adopted. Later documents demonstrate that the imperial enterprise could not colonize those lands on which the Bedouin nomads grazed their flocks. They remained the dominant power from the vicinity of the city centre into the depth of the desert.[60] Some lands colonized by the settlement policies were later reoccupied by the nomads. In 1884, for instance, the Sharia court judge wrote that thirty-three villages established some eleven years ago had returned to their old state with the arrival of 5,000 Shammar tents [hane-i seyyare].[61] Similarly, in 1893, the Jabbur, Akidan and Bakkare tribes left their properties at Shirgat and returned to the desert to escape the frequent attacks by the Dulaim and Anizah branches.[62]

Some of these tribes were persuaded several years later by the Deir government to return their lands. In 1901, the *mutasarrıf* of Deir al-Zor negotiated with the sheikhs of Jabbur and Akidan, Musallat and Halef al-Abdullah, respectively, and they made a mutual decision to resettle these communities in the Jazira region, from whence they had fled in

[59]   BOA, ŞD 2213/7, 11 Kanun-ı Sani 1287 [24 January 1872].
[60]   See, for example, BOA, BEO 960/71999, 28 Haziran 1313 [10 July 1897]; BOA, DH.TMIK-M 28/53, 27 Kanun-ı Sani 1313 [9 February 1898]; BOA, DH.ŞFR 248/22, 26 Mayıs 1316 [8 June 1900].
[61]   BOA, Y.EE 11/11, 21 Cemaziyelevvel 1301 [19 March 1884], quoted in: Dolbee, 'The Locust and the Starling', 160.
[62]   BOA, DH.MKT 1942/75, 9 Nisan 1309 [22 April 1893].

1893 due to attacks by the Shammar and Anizah who benefited from the regional chaos and their hostility with Abu Sultan, another settled tribe.[63] The sheikhs were rewarded with a salary of 1,500 piasters as motivation and to facilitate a population census of the tribes. In addition, they agreed to build houses and villages for the tribespeople.[64] The imperial authorities were more cautious this time and deployed camel corps in the region to prevent hostilities between and among the settled tribes and attacks by the desert Bedouin.[65]

Further measures were taken to increase the security level in the region in the 1870s. Several fortresses and military outposts were built and soldiers were deployed in locations near to Bedouin camps and along the strategic stretches of the caravan routes.[66] Ottoman travellers who later described these fortresses and military outposts, commented on the numbers based there which might be demonstrative of the level of reconciliation between the nomadic groups, other tribes and the empire.[67] According to the observations of Fehim Efendi, an Ottoman official in Baghdad, who travelled to the region in 1889 with a caravan to write a travel guide, there were about twenty Bedouin camps around a single military base.[68] This was made possible by the reconciliation with the Bedouin whose majority promised to contribute to – or at least not to oppose – the imperial security lines. The military outposts were established to protect the roads and villages from the small Bedouin groups, who were inclined to raids and plunder.[69]

The investments at Deir al-Zor together with negotiations with the tribal groups there bore fruit in a short time which contributed to the consolidation of the Ottoman position in the region. First, they led to the reopening by 1870 of the direct caravan route between Aleppo and Baghdad that passed through Deir al-Zor, which strengthened Ottoman control in the desert routes against the nomads.[70]

---

[63] BOA, BEO 778/58291, 29 Nisan 1312 [11 May 1896].
[64] BOA, DH.TMIK-M 103/10, 16 Nisan 1317 [29 April 1901].
[65] BOA, DH.TMIK-S 49/4, 1 Haziran 1319 [14 June 1903].
[66] Bostan, 'Zor Sancağı', 164.
[67] For some examples, see: Ali Suad, *Seyahatlerim*, 60; Tozlu, 'İstanbul'a Bir Seyahat', 371.
[68] Tozlu, 'İstanbul'a Bir Seyahat', 371.
[69] For detailed information on this subject, see Chapter 2.
[70] This route was the safest and shortest one in the eighteenth century for the trade caravans which transported goods to Europe and India via Basra. This route allowed the transport of goods within fifteen days at a significant saving

Additionally, 150 houses and 100 shops were built outside the city walls once the authorities had secured a guarantee of immunity from tribal assaults.[71] This would increase the city's influence in the region and enhance urban-desert interaction. In 1871, given its importance to regional governance and economy, Deir al-Zor was annexed to the Sublime Porte as an independent *mutasarrıfate* as Lebanon and Jerusalem were.[72] By 1880, according to the French consul in Aleppo, Deir al-Zor had transformed over some years into a 'productive province' with a capital of 20,000 people.[73] In the mid-1880s, the independent *mutasarrıfate* lost its pivotal role as a centre of colonization and the districts previously annexed to it were partitioned between Diarbekir and Aleppo while the *mutasarrıfate* was transformed into an administrative sub-unit of the Aleppo governorate as it had been to begin with.[74]

The Anizah Revolt

Although the expedition was successful in its subjugation of the numerous semi-settled and hunter tribal groups, reconciliation with the nomadic tribes took more time and was only achieved after a series of conflicts. A year after the second establishment of the *mutasarrıfate*, Dahham of the Fid'an revolted against the Deir al-Zor government. Besides losing ground in Deir al-Zor and devoid of a substantial source of revenue, long-lasting problems between the sheikh and the Aleppo government made a major contribution to the revolt. The rise of Jed'an through the support of the government and Dahham's exclusion from most of the province's territories weakened the latter considerably. The Ottoman campaign gave him a golden opportunity to organize the large Fid'an branches against Jed'an and the empire and reinforce himself as their sheikh defending the tribe against the imperial expansionism that was perceived by many tribesmen to be a serious offense to tribal interests. This might both cause the failure of the expedition and

---

compared with the forty-five days it took via Urfa, Diarbekir and Mosul. But, with the immigration of the Anizah and Shammar from Najd, the road had become insecure from the late eighteenth century. FO 195/800, Aleppo, 3 May 1865.

[71] Bostan, 'Zor Sancağı', 178,   [72] Ibid., 164.
[73] CADC, 4CCC/36, Aleppo, 26 October 1880, quoted in Dolbee, 'The Locust and the Starling', 159.
[74] Dolbee, 'The Locust and the Starling', 160.

pave the way for his reinstatement as the sheikh of the Fid'an by the empire, which he and other sheikhs had achieved several times in the past.

Abd al-Qarim, the sheikh of the Shammar tribesmen in Deir al-Zor, and Jed'an did not ally with Dahham but supported the imperial enterprise. The main reason for the Shammar sheikh was most likely the friendly relations between his fellow tribesmen and the government in the Mosul, Baghdad and Aleppo (Urfa and Mardin) provinces and the creation of a mutual dependence between them and the government. As detailed in Chapter 1, they were also Dahham's enemies as the sheikh had threatened their positions in Urfa, Mardin, Aleppo and Mosul a few years before in search of new pastures for his fellow tribesmen after he was expelled from his pastures in Aleppo by the provincial authorities who allied with Jed'an. As explained before, Jed'an's dependence on the Aleppo government and his ambition to replace Dahham in Deir al-Zor and become the sheikh of the Anizah tribesmen there might have motivated him to support the government. Consequently, the tribal winners of the Ottoman policies in the 1840s and 1850s supported the expedition while the losers opposed it.

Dahham organized a regional revolt throughout the whole province, developed alliances with the Turcoman, Kurdish and Arab tribal sheikhs extending from Ayntab to the frontiers of Damascus province and promoted local resistance in Deir al-Zor which put the Ottoman troops in a very difficult position.[75] The Ottoman officials tried to repress Dahham by brutal force in the beginning which further widened the revolt and caused the pro-Ottoman sheikhs to change side and collaborate with Dahham.[76] However, the imperial plots to divide the tribal front became successful[77] and the rebels were be defeated by the government forces and applied to the officials for pardoning

---

[75] For detailed descriptions of his actions, see: FO 195/800, Aleppo, 31 March 1865; CADN, Serie D, 166PO/D1/60, Aleppo, 1 May 1865; FO 195/800, Aleppo, 3 May 1865; CADN, Serie D, 166PO/D1/60, Aleppo, 22 May 1865; CADN, Serie D, 166PO/D1/60, Aleppo, 12 August 1865.

[76] For instance, in addition to Ahmed Bey of the Mawali, Jed'an and Abd al-Qarim sided with Dahham as a result of the 'thoughtless' imperial policies: CADN, Serie D, 166PO/D1/63, Aleppo, 22 August 1868.

[77] Abd al-Qarim of the Shammar, for instance, changed side and allied with the government troops whose efforts played a major role in the suppression of the revolt. See: BOA, İ.DH 589/41011, 16 Mart 1285 [28 March 1869].

[*aman*]. All of them were forgiven and honoured with medals and robe of honour, which signified a clear victory for the government.[78]

This was however not the end of the game: in 1870, anxious about their privileges in the region due to the continuation of the government operations, the Anizah groups plundered all the villages in Urfa, Mardin and Siverek and 600 villages were abandoned in between Birecik, Mardin and Siverek whose inhabitants took refuge in the Harput region.[79] As a result the governor of Deir was dismissed and succeeded by Arslan Pasha, the first independent governor of Deir al-Zor, in constant conflict with Dahham until he was killed by the Mawali in 1871 in an inter-tribal war which ended the Anizah revolt. Dahham's death signified a structural transformation in the Fid'an leadership from 'fighting' to 'diplomacy'. Jed'an, the more conciliatory and political Anizah sheikh, was invested as the paramount sheikh, and he established relations with the government based on negotiation. Shortly after Dahham's death, Arslan was poisoned by the Bedouin and coercive imperial policies were considerably smoothened. The pasha's death symbolically complemented the process started with Dahham's killing and paved the way for the empire to embrace a negotiating approach.[80]

Reconciliation with the Anizah Branches and Their 'Provincialization' as Partners

The new sheikh was willing to cooperate with the Deir government[81] from the outset of the Zor expansion and recognized its authority in return for a handsome salary and a share of the taxes imposed over the Bedouin. Approaching the Ottoman government also strengthened his position among the Fid'an as the disloyal groups closer to Dahham could be more easily controlled by the new sheikh with the support of the Ottoman troops. His conciliatory attitude was well responded to by the Ottoman government who began to change its modernizing perspective and adopted a negotiating policy towards the autonomous

---

[78] BOA. İ.DH 589/41011, 14 Mart 1285 [28 March 1869].
[79] BOA, İ.DH 41/825, 1286 [1870], quoted in: Öğüt, 'Birecik Sancağı', 134.
[80] FO 195/976, Aleppo, 17 October 1871.
[81] Lewis, *Nomads and Settlers*, 31; Lewis claims that Jed'an was left no alternative but conciliation in order to live around Deir with his tribe. However, Jed'an had been a conciliatory figure long before the start of the expedition.

forces through the empire which gained momentum after
Abdulhamid's sultanate.[82] The increasing rivalry between the
Ottomans and the British in the region and the war with Russia compelled the imperial government to institutionalize good relations with
these autonomous forces as the imperial officials were anxious about
alliances between them and the Great Powers. This consequently
became a new administrative pattern for the empire in its relations
with the autonomous forces while the iron fist of Hamidian authoritar-
ianism was heavily felt in the urban areas. The Fid'an and other Anizah
branches around the province of Aleppo and in Deir al-Zor were
'provincialized' by negotiation as many of their problems were solved
in the province by way of bargain and dialogue. As this method bore
fruit in the solution of the problems between the empire and the
nomads, the tribal leaders more frequently used the imperial mechanisms to solve their problems with each other and with the officials. They
were thus made part of the Ottoman system by way of negotiation.

In this regard, the government and the Fid'an firstly reconciled over
the most important issue for the tribal society: the pastures the tribesmen used. In 1871 the tribe was allocated large tracts of lands between
the Hillah in the south of Baghdad and Deir al-Zor in the west bank of
the Euphrates, which was referred to in many Ottoman reports as
fertile land with a potential for agricultural colonization. The space
allocated to them was situated in an advantageous position which
would allow them to move towards the north in times of drought. It
seems that this compromise reached a certain success. In 1876, for
instance, the troops deployed around the Birecik and Suruç districts
of the Urfa region to prevent the tribal attacks on the villages were
considered to be removed by the Aleppo government on the excuse that
the Anizah had not come to the region for several years. But it should
also be noted that these districts were not vital for the Anizah as they
visited them only during drought years.[83] The tribesmen were required
to pay a tax for the pastures allocated to them, but documents indicate
that they did not do so.[84]

---

[82] Klein, *Margins of the Empire*.
[83] BOA, BEO.AYN.D. No. 867, 1293, 1211 quoted in: Öğüt, 'Birecik Sancağı',
      135.
[84] See, for example, BOA, DH.MKT 467/17, 25 Şubat 1317 [10 March 1902] and
      31 Ağustos 1318 [13 September 1902].

The determination of the Anizah's boundaries made a significant contribution to the decrease of the inter-tribal wars as their migration to the areas occupied by the other nomads was not allowed. Once they crossed their boundaries intending to attack the other tribes grazing their animals in another pasturage, as in 1883 when they moved towards the Shammar territories, the government troops immediately intervened and warned the tribesmen to return to their pastures, a warning which they obeyed.[85] In times of drought, however, it was permitted to search for pastures in other localities as a measure to avoid the death of both 'believers[*ibadullah*] and animals from hunger and thirst',[86] although this increased the possibility of conflict with the other tribes, who were also looking for grazing lands for their animals.[87]

Following the solution of the pasturage problems, the 'provincial-ization' process continued as the tribe was further incorporated into the Ottoman bureaucracy and the sheikhs gradually transformed into partners. In around 1875, together with Suleiman al-Murshid of the Anizah's Seb'a branch, Jed'an negotiated with the Ottoman authorities in Deir al-Zor, consented to make the tribes pay tax and, as a result, was appointed as a major in the Ottoman army. Furthermore, the Anizah received official permission to trade with the towns – not limited to Deir al-Zor – and to use the pastures in the countryside while Jed'an was sent with a mounted battalion of rifles to the Anizah camps to collect the tax from his tribes, albeit unsuccessfully.[88] Reflecting the increase of sheikhly agency in the tribal issues of the empire, Jed'an was described in later Ottoman documents as the *Urban kaymakamı* [the major of the tribes], an official post responsible for the actions of the Fid'an and collabor-ation with the Deir al-Zor officials.

Given the proof provided by the Ottoman documents, he gradually increased his level of cooperation with the Ottoman bureaucracy and contributed to the provincialization of his fellow tribesmen. In 1881, for instance, after a dispute with the *mutasarrıf* when he was mistreated by him, the sheikh went to Aleppo to complain instead of raiding and plundering caravans and settled areas which the Fid'an would have

[85] BOA, Y.A.HUS 175/55, 19 Teşrin-i Sani 1299 [1 December 1883].
[86] Dolbee, 'The Locust and the Starling', 146.
[87] BOA, Y.PRK.ASK 222/57, 22 Eylül 1320 [7 October 1904].
[88] FO 195/1067, Aleppo, 16 August 1875.

done several decades before.[89] It seems that shortly after that the post of *Urban Kaymakamı* was transferred to Aleppo province.[90] The Ottoman documents provide strong evidence that all the Anizah branches around Aleppo were united under the paramount sheikhship of Jed'an at a time around 1880 and were separately salaried to increase their loyalty to the government.[91]

The maintenance of the ban of *khuwwa* and its extension to Deir al-Zor also constituted part of the empire-Anizah compromise. Jed'an had not exacted *khuwwa* on the villages for a long time as a precondition of his agreement with the Aleppo government in 1862 when Aleppo's governor, Ismet Pasha, appointed Jed'an as the sheikh of the Anizah and, in return, they signed a contract assuring his forbearance from demanding *khuwwa* from the province's peasants.[92] The sheikh and his tribe were given certain privileges such as better pastures and handsome salaries. Unlike his predecessors, Ismet Pasha rigorously ensured that the requirements of the contract were fulfilled by the nomads and, if violated, punished the tribesmen.

After Ismet Pasha, Sureyya Pasha successfully managed to sustain his predecessor's policies by partially controlling the nomadic migration routes. He increased the number of salaried sheikhs around Hama and Homs to ensure their cooperation and, in agreement with the Seb'a sheikh Suleiman al-Murshid, deployed a battalion of soldiers in Mashrafa, a village in the desert, to secure the villages from attacks by Bedouin aggrieved by the abolition of *khuwwa*.[93] The Anizah could thus not demand *khuwwa* from the villagers under the authority of Aleppo's governor and Deir al-Zor's *mutasarrıf* until the Russo-Turkish War of 1877–8, when they had 'an opportunity to revert to their old ways, for nearly all the troops were withdrawn'.[94] In 1897, during the Turco-Greek wars, Fahd Bey, the sheikh of the Ibn Haddal branch of the Anizah and the *kaymakam* of Razzazeh, renewed his demands for *khuwwa* from the inhabitants and tribes of Deir al-Zor. In

---

[89] BOA, Y.PRK.ASK 5/77, 8 Kanun-i Sani,1296 [21 January 1881].
[90] BOA, İ.DH 911/72341, 13 Şubat 1299 [26 February 1884].
[91] A document dated 1884 implies that the other Anizah branches had been under the paramount sheikhship of Jed'an for a long time: BOA, İ.DH 911/72341, 13 Şubat 1299 [26 February 1884].
[92] BOA, MVL 762/91, 11 Zilhicce 1278 [10 June 1862].
[93] BOA, MVL 1062/29, 21 Ağustos 1282 [3 September 1866].
[94] Lewis, *Nomads and Settlers*, 32; see, also: AMAE, CPC, Turquie, Aleppo-6, 26 October 1880.

Figure 3.1 The Anizah encampment near the Ga'rah, *wadi* Helqum. Gertrude Bell Archives, Newcastle University, Y_444.

response, Zor's governor made an agreement with him, in the form of a written deed [*sened*] that he would not demand *khuwwa* from the people at Deir.[95] This is a good example of how empire-tribe relations depended on imperial strength. As the nomads did not lose their autonomy and tribal character, they quickly broke the reconciliation and replaced the state as tax collectors when the latter showed signs of weakness.

The Anizah's relations with the government were not sheikh-dependent and did not change following Jed'an's death in 1882. Presumably due to his good service, his son Turki was appointed as the *Urban Kaymakamı* in his place and his authority over the Anizah was widened by the support of the government. He also continued to serve as the paramount sheikh of all the Anizah branches in the province while the Khrissa, Seb'a and other Anizah sheikhs were also appointed lesser positions and salaried by Aleppo province to increase their loyalty to the state.[96] This was a further step in the Anizah's provincialization in Aleppo as the salaries paid by the state somewhat

[95]   BOA, ŞD 2679/40, 16 Ağustos 1313 [29 August 1897].
[96]   BOA, İ.DH 911/72341, 13 Şubat 1299 [26 February 1884].

determined the tribal hierarchy. While the other tribes were previously independent from the Fid'an and their sheikhs were all equals, salarization established a new tribal hierarchy and more or less determined the paramount and lesser sheikhs.

Turki's killing only five years later by the Ruwalla caused the Anizah's division. Following his death, the tribe split into two major groups – the Fid'an Wuld and Fid'an Kharshah. Self-governing, the tribe was divided into several other branches and for the most part integrated into the imperial system.[97] When some branches 'showed irregularity' the responsible sheikh, supported by his fellow tribesmen, commanded the government troops to deal with the problem as Edham Bey, the *kaymakam* of the Anizah in Aleppo, did in 1898.[98] This may be interpreted as a smooth intervention as the involvement of their sheikh would most likely cause less frustration among the tribesmen. In the mid-1900s, all the Anizah branches were again united under the sheikhship of Hajim Bey, whose good service in keeping the Anizah in check was rewarded in 1906 when he was given the title of 'colonel' [*miralay*], most likely the first of its kind for an Anizah sheikh in Aleppo.[99] The vocabulary used to describe the tribes by the government authorities demonstrates the level of the tribal integration and provincialization, as they were referred as tribal subjects [*tebayi'-i aşayir*][100] in place of *aşayir-i ğayr-ı mutia* [disloyal tribes] used previously to depict the state-tribe relations.

The Anizah's provincialization made Aleppo the centre of governance that the tribal sheikhs frequently visited to negotiate tribal issues. By 1906, the Anizah had for a long time employed one of their fellow tribesmen, Ahmed Hafız, as a political and commercial agent in the city to negotiate with the government and mediate between the tribesmen and the officials, while the sheikhs visited him to learn about imperial

---

[97] Lewis, *Nomads and Settlers*, 32; for an Ottoman document praising the loyalty of the Fid'an tribes [Fid'an Asiretleri] see: BOA, Y.MTV 179/142, 20 Haziran 1314 [3 January 1898].

[98] BOA, Y.MTV 179/142, 20 Haziran 1314 [3 January 1898].

[99] BOA, Y.PRK.UM 79/27, 15 Tesrin-i Sani 1322 [28 November 1906]; Davenport notes that all the Anizah branches in northern Syria acknowledged Hajim Bey 'as their highest ruler and on matters of great importance they are bound to obey his orders under their own Sheikh': Davenport, *My Quest*, 239.

[100] BOA, DH.İD 184/22, 3 Haziran 1330 [16 June 1914].

Figure 3.2 Ahmed Hafız, the Anizah's representative in Aleppo, with his Ottoman medal. Davenport, *My Quest*, x.

Figure 3.3 Hajim Bey Ibn Mheid, the Anizah's paramount sheikh, 1906. Davenport, *My Quest*, 150.

developments.[101] The governor of Aleppo told Davenport that 'Haffez [sic] was looked upon as the smartest and shrewdest Bedouin that the Ottoman Empire had ever known'.[102] The appointment and dismissal of the lesser tribal sheikhs also took place in Aleppo as part of the tribe's integration process into the imperial system. In 1906, for instance, Talal bin Farhan, a graduate of the Aşiret Mektebi [the School for Tribes] in Istanbul, replaced the old sheikh in a branch of the Anizah while both were in the city.[103]

As part of the provincialization of the nomads, the tribal sheikhs applied to the provincial authorities for the solution of the disputes among them although this did not mean that they had no impact on the imperial decisions. As the active agents of the government's decision-making process, they both used the imperial mechanisms and benefited from their prestige and authority among the fellow tribesmen to obtain a favourable result. In this regard, in 1907, Sheikh Hajim (not the Hajim Bey of the Fid'an) applied to the Aleppo government complaining that, according to the tribal customs, he should have been appointed sheikh of the Khrissa tribe of the Anizah in place of his late father. But Sheikh Mazwad, another Khrissa chief, had replaced his father and his rights had been usurped. More interestingly, due to his prestige among his tribal fellows Hajim took them to places outside the boundaries of Aleppo where the Milli tribe lived and threatened the provincial authorities that he would not return unless he was granted with sheikhship, indicating the government's dependence on him for acquiring revenues from the tribe. It was a serious problem for the provincial authorities due to the fact that the tax revenues they obtained from the Khrissa amounted to 2,900 liras per year. In the early years of the Tanzimat, the provincial authorities strove hard to expel the tribesmen from the province, the reverse of which now became a concern for them. Hajim was invited with his tribe to the vicinity of the province and he was granted the sheikhship in return for his payment of the yearly tax of his tribe, which indicated his authority among his fellow tribesmen.[104]

[101] Davenport calls Hafız 'the diplomatic ruler of the Anizah' and notes in 1906 that he lived in the city for thirty years. But he did not specify from when he was employed as the tribes' agent in the city: Davenport, *My Quest*, 79.
[102] Ibid., 185.
[103] BOA, DH.TMIK-M 229/58, 2 Eylül 1322 [15 September 1906].
[104] BOA, DH.İD 184/22, 30 Ağustos 1323 [12 August 1907].

Good relations between the Anizah and the Aleppo government continued up to 1914. When the tribe was annexed to the Urfa government at that time, Hajim, the paramount sheikh, opposed the measure and requested to be re-annexed to the Aleppo government, which he presumably achieved.[105] He became a staunch ally of the Ottoman government during the Great War and its aftermath. Hajim's good relations with the Turkish government continued even after the collapse of the Ottoman Empire until he was replaced by the French authorities with Sheikh Muhjim Ibn Mheid.

Faris Pasha and the Provincialization of the Shammar in Deir al-Zor

Another major nomadic group around Deir al-Zor was the Shammar branches frequenting the region and they were also successfully integrated into the Ottoman system. Similar to the Anizah groups of Aleppo and Deir al-Zor, relations between the local officials and the Shammar can be described as provincialization and partnership. As detailed in Chapter 2, in spite of Abd al-Qarim's revolt of 1871 in reaction to Midhat Pasha's project to settle the tribe,[106] the Shammar had also been reconciled by appointing Farhan as their paramount sheikh and his brother Faris as the sub-sheikh of the Zor branches with wide-ranging autonomy in 1875, whose allocated pastures extended from from Deir al-Zor to Mardin. Faris was a crucial sheikh for the Deir al-Zor *mutasarrıfate* and it was almost a must for the Ottomans to win him to establish a sustainable tranquillity in Deir al-Zor.

Faris was thus made an important partner of the Ottoman governance in Deir al-Zor in a few years after the establishment of the imperial control in the region. Shortly after his return from Najd and with increased influence among the Deir Shammar, the sheikh was politely invited by the *mutasarrıf* to come to Deir al-Zor, where he was offered government financing and support 'if he would help the Turkish authorities to keep order in Mesopotamia', which can be interpreted as an open request for partnership. It was agreed that Faris should provide security in the desert, in return for a certain sum of money, to

---

[105] The document is not clear about his application. But given the positive language used, the result most likely favoured the sheikh: BOA, DH.İD 184/22, 3 Haziran 1330 [16 June 1914].

[106] For details, see: Chapter 1.

be paid monthly. The sheikh would also receive the *mutasarrıf*'s support and countenance in his dispute with his tribal enemies – particularly Farhan's sons – that established an alliance between the *mutasarrıfate* and the Shammar.[107] Furthermore, upon the proposal of the governor of Baghdad, he was awarded with a salary and a title of 'Pasha' in 1878 in return for his cooperation.[108] Thereafter, Faris was always ready to help the Zor government to keep the Bedouin in check when the authorities were lacking sufficient troops to protect their town and villages from the Bedouin incursions.[109] An Ottoman report praises the Shammar sheikh's cooperation with the imperial authorities and the 'obedience' of the tribal people.[110]

The relationship was reciprocal and the *mutasarrıfs* defended Faris Pasha against the central government and did their best to prevent Faris from being harmed by the government's activities. During the hostilities between Faris Pasha and Ibrahim Pasha al-Milli, for instance, the *mutasarrıfs* gave exaggerated accounts of attacks by the Milli on the Shammar in a bid to convince central government to punish the Milli.[111] In 1898, Şakir Pasha, who was dispatched to the region to investigate the hostility between the Shammar and Milli tribes, reported that the sub-governor of Zor offered the Shammar protection [*tesahub etmek*].[112] Although the governor of Zor was replaced, they continued to defend their 'tribal allies' and levelled accusations with each renewal of hostilities between the two sheikhs, which could be seen as a sign of institutionalized cooperation between the *mutasarrıfate* and the Shammar.[113]

Abdulhamid's policy of winning the local autonomous forces to secure their loyalty and to prevent their collaboration with the Great Powers paved the way for the institutionalization of the tribes' provincialization. Encouraged by the policies of the central government favouring cooperation with the local autonomies, the provincial

---

[107] Blunt, *Bedouin Tribes*, 323.
[108] BOA, ŞD 2150/32, 10 Ağustos 1294 [23 August 1878]; BOA, DH.MKT 1873/102, 22 Eylül 1307 [7 October 1891].
[109] See, for example, Blunt, *Bedouin Tribes*, 127.
[110] Bostan, 'Zor Sancağı', 199.
[111] For details, see, Ali, 'Le role politique des tribus kurdes', 67–81; see, also: CADN, Serie D, 166PO/D1/87, Aleppo, 27 May 1901.
[112] BOA, DH.TMIK-M 28/53, 3 Mart 1314 [16 March 1898].
[113] For some examples, see: BOA, DH.TMIK-M 102/10, 5 Nisan 1317 [18 April 1901]; BOA, DH.ŞFR 281/65, 19 Mart 1318 [1 April 1902]; BOA, DH.TMIK-M 144/10, 1 Mayıs 1319 [14 May 1903].

officials developed friendly relations with the tribal sheikhs which made them supporters of the provincial administration.

Trade, Urban Dwellers and the Nomads after the *Mutasarrıfate*

The Anizah and Shammar Bedouin sheikhs' willingness to cooperate was strengthened by the development of a commercial axis between Diabekir, Mosul, Aleppo, Deir and Damascus, in which the tribes played a central role and served the increase of 'territorization' between the urban, arable and desert spaces. As such, by 1870, the Deir al-Zor Shammar became the main butter and wool suppliers for Diarbekir, Urfa, Mardin and surrounding areas, and acquired considerable wealth.[114] Flourishing tribal markets had opened with the permission of the government and were known by the tribes' names, thus the Anizah Bazaar [*Bazar al-Anazah*] at Hama.[115] Trade networks established by the Bedouin in city markets noticeably extended their customer base[116]; their animals were purchased by merchants as far away as Ankara in inner Anatolia.[117]

Deir al-Zor's increasing fortune brought about the flow of merchants to the town which enhanced the spatial networks between the town and the neighbouring cities and connected it with the global markets. At the end of 1878, a number of Chaldean Christian and Jewish merchants from Mosul and Aleppo settled in the city for the horse trade. They bought from the Gomussa or Seb'a branches of the Anizah foals of several breeds, and left them with the Deiris or the Anizah to be trained for three years according to Bedouin tradition, and then resold the horses to the merchants of Aleppo. It became the only market for thoroughbreds in Asia. The caravans formed in Deir al-Zor were estimated at 4,500 mules annually, each of which carried between 137 and 170 kg of goods. In addition, as a result of the region's peace and stability, the town became a conduit for flocks of

[114] Bostan, 'Zor Sancağı', 199.
[115] For a reference, see: SCR-Hama 56, Doc. 1479, 1 Zilkade 1277 [11 May 1861]; for another reference to the tribal markets from 1876, see: BOA, İ.ŞD 31/1491, 13 Nisan 1292 [26 April 1876].
[116] Otherwise it was quite difficult to visit them in the desert and find the right animals to purchase. See, for example, Barker, *Syria and Egypt*, 348–351.
[117] See, for example, SCR-Hama 53, Doc. 41, 7 Şaban 1267 [7 June 1851].

sheep from the end of summer, coming principally from the region of Mosul, to be exported to Egypt by the port of Alexandretta, 'red sheep' from Erzurum and 'white sheep' from Mosul were collected in the town to be dispatched to Aleppo, while 'white sheep' from Diarbekir were sent to Istanbul and Egypt.[118] Deir al-Zor also increased its importance as a trading centre for pure-bred Arabian horses[119]; the animals sold there by the Shammar and Anizah were exported far and wide, even to India, which served the 'commodification' of the Bedouin property.[120] The establishment and development of such complicated relations would obviously be difficult in the absence of friendly relations between the nomads and the imperial officials as in the Tanzimat era.

The rise of the sheep and horse trade in domestic and global markets in the following years accelerated the evolution of the Bedouin in the *mutasarrıfate* of Deir al-Zor and its neighbourhood. Some of them chose to change their lifestyle to become agropastoralists. Their basic resource shifted from raiding and booty to a pastoral and agricultural economy in a more stable and secure environment.[121] The great tribal groupings like the Anizah and Shammar maintained the Bedouin lifestyle to respond to the demand by the Ottoman and non-Ottoman traders. However, as a result of their interaction with the sedentary population, they also established more links with the land by bringing in peasants as share-croppers to cultivate the land for them.[122] Thus, although the imperial authorities failed to make the Bedouin relinquish their nomadic lifestyle – or at least not embrace a more settled existence – a new relationship of interdependence was established between the Bedouin and the city-dwellers, which also contributed to the Bedouins' integration into imperial networks.[123] State-tribe conflict was no longer the primary reason for the problems of governance in the district in the following years.[124]

Interaction with the city-dwellers and the imperial authority did not change the sociology of the nomads. The Shammar and Anizah tribes visiting the region protected their pastures in the region, could not be

---

[118] Barout, 'La renaissance', 113 ; Blunt, *Bedouin Tribes*, 117.
[119] See, Chapter 2.   [120] Blunt, *Bedouin Tribes* II, 136.
[121] AMAE, CPC, Turquie, Aleppo-6, 26 October 1880.
[122] Lewis, *Nomads and Settlers*, 31.   [123] Barout, 'La renaissance', 114.
[124] For some examples, see Bostan, 'Zor Sancağı', 216.

forced to change their lifestyle and continued to constitute the great majority of the population in the region. As Blunt's map (Map 0.1) demonstrates, none of the Anizah and Shammar pastures could be colonized by the imperial expansionism. Only some of the sheep pastures presumably used by the settled tribes could be recultivated. It is again clear in the map that none of the Shammar and Anizah branches could be restricted to the districts outside the sedentary areas. Fid'an's (Fedaan) pastures, for instance, were besieged by agricultural tribes such as the Hadidin (Haddadin), Hannadi and Weldi (Weldah). Chapter 2 clarifies that most of these tribes were resettled by the empire after 1840, but there is no reference in the map that these places were formerly used by the Anizah as 'camel pastures'. Many camel pastures presumably allocated to the Anizah or Shammar were located among the agricultural lands.

With reference to the intensity of the nomadic population in the district, an Ottoman report defined the *mutasarrıfate* in 1912 as *urban ve aşayir livası* [sub-governorate of nomads and tribes].[125] Many reports complained about the 'empty lands' and stated the necessity of using them as agricultural lands, which needed to be exploited to increase the productivity of the region and incomes of the imperial treasury.[126] That was mainly due to the adoption of the politics of negotiation which necessitated respecting the tribal interests in return for their submission and loyalty to the empire. Many of the empty lands were indeed tribal pasturages, the colonization of which would have stirred up a great rebellion against the empire and would have made the reassertion of imperial authority very difficult and very costly. For that reason, the nomads remained dominant in the countryside and continued to fight with the rival tribes for the lands they used as pasturage.[127]

---

[125] ŞD 34/30, From the *mutasarrıf* of Zor, 4 Mart 1328 [17 March 1912].

[126] See, for example, BOA, DH.MKT 316/40, 13 Ağustos 1309 [26 August 1893]; BOA, DH.TMIK-M 93/6, 6 Nisan 1316 [19 April 1900]; BOA, DH.TMIK-S 49/4, 1 Haziran 1319 [14 June 1903]; BOA, DH.İD 45/12, From the *mutasarrıf* of Zor, 8 Haziran 1326 [21 June 1910] and 14 Kanun-ı Sani 1327 [27 January 1912].

[127] In this regard, the most notable example was the Shammar-Milli conflict which Faris Pasha fought for years (1895–1908) with Ibrahim Pasha al-Milli to prevent him from expanding to his area of influence at Deir al-Zor. For details, see: Ali, 'Le role politique des tribus kurdes', 67–81.

The initial plans to individualize responsibility to the state had also to be abandoned due to the maintenance of the tribal hierarchy as in the pre-Ottoman times, which means, in the examples of the Anizah and Shammar tribesmen, that the 'tribesmen into Ottomans' project failed to be realized. What the imperial expansion to Deir al-Zor achieved was a sustainable peace between the tribes and government. A durable Ottoman administration at the centre of the desert served the tranquillity in two ways: on the one hand, the reinforcement of the Ottoman existence in Deir al-Zor made the empire more powerful against the tribes as it augmented the imperial military fortifications in the desert. On the other, the expansion increased imperial dependence on the tribes since it was nearly impossible to maintain a governorate in such a place without tribal consent and collaboration. In this way, the interdependence of the parties on each other increased, tribal raids on caravans and villages on the desert frontier almost came to an end from the tribes around Deir al-Zor and the government operation ceased to be a threat to the tribes. The expansion of Ottoman rule made a significant contribution to the systematization of the politics of negotiation which predominated the Ottoman tribal policies from the early 1870s. It must finally be noted that the international calm of these years and the peaceful environment enabled the empire to invest in the desert militarily and to consolidate its rule in the frontier regions. As detailed previously, the periods that the Ottomans fought Russia and Greece, which weakened the imperial presence in the region, were also the times that tribes tried to benefit from the imperial weakness and return to their old habits.

4 | Expansion, Reaction and Reconciliation II

Nomads and the Extension of the Ottoman Administration into the South of Syria

The districts in the south of Damascus – later Syria – province were another region where principal Ottoman administrative units were established to control the nomadic groups of the desert – mostly the Wuld 'Ali and Ruwalla branches of the Anizah – and monitor its frontier in the second half of the nineteenth century. This region was considered crucial by the Ottoman government as they were close to the route of the pilgrim caravan. In addition, it was in the neighbourhood of Hijaz, Najd, the Suez Canal and the Red Sea, all of which were strategic locations for the Ottoman-British rivalry which became an important aspect of inter-imperial global competition particularly after 1870. The region further increased in importance after the British occupation of Egypt in 1882 which made the Ottomans apprehensive about their territories in Syria, Iraq and Hijaz. In addition, Abdulhamid's adoption of pan-Islamism as the empire's official ideology made control of the Arab provinces and Hijaz extremely crucial. The expansion was important in terms of state formation, too, as the reforms necessitated new financial and manpower sources in the form of taxes and soldiers.

As in Deir al-Zor, the major autonomous actors of the region were the nomads and other tribes which made the Ottoman penetration a complicated and long-lasting issue. In the early years of the Tanzimat, the empire's treatment of the Arab nomads was similar that in other regions, but the critical role that the Anizah played in the safety, provisioning and transportation of the pilgrim caravan encouraged a more conciliatory attitude, although it did not mean that nothing changed in the empire-Anizah relations during the early years of the modern Ottoman state formation. They initially adopted a somewhat different approach: As districts like Hawran were crucial

132

for the provisioning of the province and taxation revenues, the Damascene officials intended to separate the 'tribal' and 'agricultural' areas by limiting tribal access into the cultivated lands instead of targeting their migrations to the vicinity of the agricultural areas to pacify them in the desert. As such, they aimed at prohibiting *khuwwa* exactions by the Bedouin groups and thus increasing the tax revenues from the region. As this chapter demonstrates, these purposes were partly fulfilled: the imperial authorities apparently achieved the abolition of *khuwwa* in spite of the resistance of the tribes; but the nomads maintained the ability to graze their animals in the great majority of the newly expanded territories which had great potential to be fertile agricultural regions. They could also enter the town markets to sell their animals and purchase grains. In the process of the consolidation of the Ottoman state in the region which began in the late 1860s, the Anizah tribes continued to be part of the region and became the partners of the empire as in the other regions of the empire. Therefore, the Ottoman penetration into the region may be considered more complicated than being a state-tribe conflict, or an imperial advance against the tribal groups. The Ottoman officials regulated their responsibilities by 'contract' [*sened*] and 'commitment' [*taahhüt*] and had to rely on the tribal declaration, which shows the symbolic aspect of the state-tribe compromise. As rightly stated by Rogan, 'while direct rule was imposed by force, it was maintained by persuasion'.[1] But it should be modified by stating that the tribal means of coercion also benefited during the imposition process of Ottoman rule using local and tribal disputes. Finally, the partnership with the empire assured the Anizah's domination in the regional pasturages and guaranteed its ownership against their rivals such as Ibn Rashid which may be interpreted as another 'mutual dependence' between the empire and the nomads in addition to the pilgrimage business.

For the 'non-nomadic' communities of the region, the aim was obviously to build the mechanisms of the modern state. Inspired by 'European norms of modern statecraft', the imperial project was 'to establish a clear hierarchy of authority and accountability'. In this regard, responsibilities towards the state were to be individualized and tribesmen would be transformed into Ottomans.[2] As Rogan demonstrates, these projects were successfully put into practice roughly

---

[1] Rogan, *Frontiers* 55.   [2] Ibid., 12.

from the late 1860s to early 1890s. Thereby, 'the state entrenched its position in the southern extremities of its Syrian province by infrastructural development and an intensified security presence'.[3]

The region was ethno-culturally different from Deir al-Zor. Besides the Christian and Muslim peasants, which might be considered conducive to the assertion of central authority, the districts in the south of Syria contained the Druze tribes and the settled agricultural Bedouin of Ledjah, all of which had a strong group consciousness and constituted barriers for imperial penetration. They were as difficult as the Anizah groups for the empire to subjugate, which forced many imperial projects to be either delayed or abandoned.

Expansion to Hawran, 1840–1862

Hawran was an extremely crucial region for both the empire and the Anizah tribes as well as the other smaller tribes like the ones settled in Ledjah. It contained fresh pastures for the nomads where the Ruwalla and Wuld 'Ali tribes grazed their animals in spring and summer. The latter enjoyed a dominant position in the region while the former had to consent to the confines of the Hawran's pastures. On the part of the empire, it was a 'grain basket' for the province of Damascus and the agricultural lands there were an important source of taxation. Furthermore, the establishment of a modern army required new recruits and the region's warlike population attracted the imperial authorities to conscript them. As explained previously, the restoration and extension of the Ottoman bureaucracy and army after the Tanzimat edict increased the need for taxes and manpower which necessitated the urgent expansion of imperial rule into fertile and populous areas like Hawran.

The local reaction, however, compelled the officials to change their initial plans. The imperial outposts were restored shortly after the withdrawal of the Egyptian troops in 1840 to secure taxes and cultivation in the region. Although the nomads did not resist the Ottoman attempt to establish state authority in the region, the raids they organized on the villages inhibited the effective taxation of the crops and caused the failure of the first enterprise: in 1845, the *kaymakams*[?] of Hawran, Ajlun and Irbid 'abandoned their posts and ... returned to Damascus in consequence of the emigration of the population', which,

---

[3] Ibid., 18.

as reported by the British consul, was 'brought about by the unreasonable perseverance of the fiscal officers to collect the same amount of
tribute that was levied the preceding year, notwithstanding the late
extensive devastations of the [Anizah] Arabs and the total destruction
of the crops by the locusts'.[4]

The acute need of the provincial treasury for the financial
resources constituted the reason for the excessive taxation, which
paved the way for a second attempt with a moderate policy. A year
after that the provincial officials again reported the necessity of
restoring the *kaymakammate* of Hawran in Al-Ala village two
hours distance from Ajlun for the security and taxation of the agricultural lands of the region.[5] Shortly after that the decision was made
and Hawran *kaymakammate* started to operate.[6] The imperial officials were more cautious this time and made considerable deductions
from the imperial debts due to the Hawranese: as reported by the
kaymakam, only 2,000 purses of the 9,000 purses of the tax arrears
for the years 1841–5 could be partitioned into instalments.[7]
However, the taxes could still not be properly collected in the region
by 1862 due to the practice of *khuwwa* and the solidarity of the
people. As a frequent routine, the peasants harvested the crops and
fled to the tribal regions by detaining the taxation officials in some
way or another, meaning a considerable loss for the provincial
treasury.[8] Similar to Deir al-Zor, a more or less working taxation
mechanism would wait until further expansion of the Ottoman rule
into the region in later periods.

Besides the financial ones, the imperial authority aimed to exploit the
human resources of the region, too, due to the need for troops to
provide security in the Syrian lands explained in Chapter 2, which
resulted in a strong reaction by the local people. In 1849, Hawran
kaymakammate started a population census to recruit the Hawranese
to the Ottoman army, which resulted in a great rebellion in the region
led by the Druze and caused the peasants to escape from their lands into
the Bedouin protection of the impenetrable Ledjah region that then
caused both a cereal crisis for the province and a considerable decrease

---

[4] FO 195/226, Damascus, 23 July 1845.
[5] BOA, A.MKT.MVL 2/48, 5 Şaban 1262 [29 Temmuz 1846].
[6] BOA, A.MKT 45/58, 15 Şevval 1262 [7 October 1846].
[7] BOA, A.MKT 63/5, 3 Safer 1263 [21 January 1847].
[8] BOA, İ.DH 494/33506, 6 Muharrem 1279 [5 July 1862].

in tax revenue.[9] The government ultimately abandoned the population census and the recruitment plan in 1851 and made peace with the Druze leaders.[10] As a result of the government guarantees for the cancellation of the census, the great majority of the peasants returned to their lands and recultivated them.[11] Meanwhile the two consecutive *kaymakams*, Ahmet Efendi and Halil Bey, were replaced due to their inability to deal with the problems.[12]

The result of such stiff resistance was the abandoning of such projects for a long time while maintaining the administrative posts, which produced peace in the region and good relations with the nomads. The Damascus officials made another attempt in Hawran for the census and recruitment in 1862, to which the local people reacted similarly: abandoning their villages and taking refuge in the mountainous districts impenetrable to the government.[13] Understanding the difficulty of persuading – or forcing – the Hawranese to take part in the census and recruitment, the government compromised with them on the payment of an exemption fee [*bedel-i nakdi*].[14]

All in all, the newly created administrative units could not properly function in the region up to 1862. The abolition of *khuwwa* was considered necessary for breaking the alliance of the local groups as it strengthened the peasant-tribe alliance and brought about their mutual action against the government. Before analysing its abolition, the present study will examine the Empire-Anizah relations and its evolution, which will allow us to better understand the reasons behind the Ottoman failure to penetrate into the region in the first two decades of the Tanzimat and the factors that brought the achievements of the subsequent imperial actions.

The Ottoman-Anizah Relations, 1840–1862

A mixture of the needs of the local government and the considerations of the imperial centre determined the imperial policy towards the

[9] BOA, A.MKT.MVL 17/66, 15 Cemaziyelahir 1265 [8 Mayıs 1849].
[10] BOA, A.MKT.MHM 41/32, 18 Safer 1268 [14 December 1851].
[11] BOA, A.MKT.UM 122/78, 9 Rebiulevvel 1269 [22 December 1852].
[12] BOA, A.MKT.UM 7/66, 20 Rebiulevvel 1266 [4 February 1850]; BOA, A. MKT.MVL 36/19, 10 Safer 1267 [16 December 1850].
[13] BOA, A.MKT.UM 562/81, 2 Şevval 1278 [2 Nisan 1862].
[14] BOA, A.MKT.UM 566/56, 20 Zilkade 1278 [20 May 1862].

Anizah groups between 1840 and 1862. The proper fulfilment of the safety of the pilgrims' passage through the Syrian desert towards Hijaz was among the primary concerns of the Ottoman rulers as it was an important source of prestige for the empire. The maintenance of cultivation in the region and regular collection of taxes were essential for the province of Damascus to compensate the expenditures of the growing bureaucracy and army, and for the provisioning of the city. On the part of the nomads, the pilgrim business constituted a significant revenue for the tribal economy through the transportation, provisioning and protection of the pilgrims. These consequently created an interdependence between the two parties, caused them to avoid extreme attitudes and to respect each other's interests in the region.[15]

Another influence on the state-nomad relations in this period was the weakness of the Ottoman authority that prevented the government from playing a decisive role in the tribal and local affairs. Similar to the other Arab provinces, the empire's position was quite vulnerable vis-à-vis the nomads and the latter were usually stronger than the empire, which compelled officials to recognize the tribal prerogatives in the imperial lands. The imperial authority merely approved the tribal conditions which they obtained fighting each other. The Ruwalla-Wuld 'Ali struggle in this case to have a more advantageous position in Hawran and a better share in the pilgrimage business made an impact on the order of things in the district and on empire-tribe relations. Consequently, officials had to collaborate with the winning party and tried to reconcile with them for the smooth conduct of the pilgrim caravan and the safety of the crops of Hawran.

The Wuld 'Ali had been frequenting the region from the early eighteenth century and had fostered 'a working relationship' with the Ottoman authorities in Damascus. 'They were supposed to keep the peace in the area, to provide men and camels to the Hajj caravan and to protect it, for all of which their *shaykhs* [sic] received payment or subvention.'[16] The Ruwalla, who started their regular migrations to the region at the end of the eighteenth century, challenged the Wuld 'Ali and the two tribes competed to be 'favoured' by the Ottoman

---

[15] The Ottoman officials clearly state that these tribes used the imperial dependence on them for the transportation and security of the pilgrims in their dealings with the empire. See, for example: BOA, İ.DH 495/33614, 28 Temmuz 1278 [10 August 1862].

[16] Rogan, *Frontiers*, 55.

Figure 4.1 Armoured Ruwalla horsemen and Sattam al-Sha'lan (in the middle). İstanbul Üniversitesi Nadir Eserler Kütüphanesi, 90567/11.

government during the first half of the nineteenth century. But the prerogative of Hawran's pasturages still belonged to the Wuld 'Ali, whose position would be challenged by the Ruwalla in the late 1850s. As will be detailed, both tribes had already entered into a relationship of interdependence with the Ottoman government by the time the Ottoman expansionist policy gained momentum.

   Due to the imperial dependence on the Anizah for the reasons explained, different from the other provinces in the region, the Damascus government had adopted a conciliatory attitude towards the nomads from its refounding in 1840. Shortly after the restoration of Ottoman rule in Syria, the officials in Damascus opened negotiations with the nomadic tribes of southern Syria following a short period of hostilities that had made the pilgrims' route a risky enterprise.[17] In

[17] AMAE, CPC, Turquie, Damascus-1, 26 September 1843.

1843, an arrangement was concluded between Ali Pasha, the governor, and the Wuld 'Ali, who agreed to be guarantors of the caravan.[18] The cooperation of at least one of the principal Anizah federations was essential for the security of the pilgrims in the absence of effective imperial existence in the south of Syria due to the lack of financial resources to replace their auxiliary services such as providing provisioning to pilgrims.

Besides their services for the pilgrim caravan, another important, and officially recognized, mission the tribes fulfilled in Hawran in collaboration with the government authorities was to keep peace and protect agricultural lands. Since performing this mission carried with it supremacy in the region and obtaining fresh pastures as well as better *khuwwa* incomes, the Anizah groups struggled between each other to 'protect' Hawran's cultivated areas. The nature of their relationship with the empire at that time was one of coercive bargain, by which they 'persuaded' the government to agree to their demands by force directed at both the imperial troops and rival tribes. The empire's inability to forcefully control them compelled the officials to keep the nomads within the imperial system. In this regard, following the restoration of Ottoman rule in Hawran, the safeguarding of the crops was conducted by Muhammad Dukhy, the sheikh of the Wuld 'Ali, who had close contact with the Damascene authorities as the protector of the pilgrim caravan [*Hamledar-ı Hacc-ı Şerif*]. In 1844, however, Naif al-Sha'lan, the sheikh of the Ruwalla, 'usurped the pasture lands' acknowledged for Dukhy, and 'threatened to despoil of its crops to the inevitable injury of the peasantry',[19] due to the 'unusual dryness of the season'.[20] The Wuld 'Ali sheikh applied to the government 'for assistance to expel the intruders which was granted'. The irregular troops and Dukhy were heavily defeated by al-Sha'lan and he conditioned his submission to 'protect the roads and villages in the territory of Kuneitra and Djedur' and be 'allowed to conduct the yearly caravan to Mecca'.[21]

Al-Sha'lan successfully followed a policy of coercive bargain, wasted all the government attempts to subjugate him[22] and subsequently provided between 800 and 1,000 camels for the caravan, an indication that

---

[18] AMAE, CPC, Turquie, Damascus-1, 10 November 1843.
[19] FO 195/226, Damascus, 4 July 1844.
[20] FO 195/226, Damascus, 23 July 1845.
[21] FO 195/226, Damascus, 12 June 1844.
[22] See, for example, FO 195/226, Damascus, 21 August 1844.

he had compelled the provincial authorities to include the Ruwalla in
the imperial system, become a partner of Dukhy and split his profit.[23]
Following that, the provincial authorities planned to allot certain pastures to the sheikhs to prevent their conflict: 'to Muhammad Dukhy and
his tribe Busra or Esky Sham in the Hauran [sic] and to Naif el-Sha'lan,
Palmyra and that part of the desert'.[24] As the later documents demonstrate, although the Wuld 'Ali protected their prerogatives in Hawran,
the Ruwalla continued to migrate to the confines of the country.[25]

Relations between the Anizah groups and the government deteriorated in the following years due to the imperial attempts to reconstruct
the state-tribe relations in which the government would have
a dominant role. A conflict between Mahmud al-Nasr, a prominent
Wuld 'Ali sheikh, and the government troops was considered a suitable
opportunity to break the Wuld 'Ali's power. The sheikh was arrested in
Damascus while he was invited to the city to discuss the pasture
problems despite having been given safe conduct [*aman*] but he later
escaped from prison. In response, the government troops made
a counter raid on the sheikh's encampment to arrest him, captured
some women, and sold them in Hama and Damascus. This was an
obvious violation of the tribal customs and principles of the govern-
ment-Anizah reconciliation and caused the Ruwalla and Wuld 'Ali to
unite against the government and plunder many villages in the desert
frontier of the province from Hama to Hawran. The authorities in
Damascus considered this an opportunity to punish the Anizah groups
and reinforce imperial authority in Hawran by prohibiting their
entrance into the areas of cultivation. But the result was a near-
disaster for the region as the tribes extensively plundered the crops,
Ottoman troops had no success and the government ultimately had to
compromise with the tribes.[26]

[23] FO 195/226, Damascus, 23 July 1845.
[24] FO 195/226, Damascus, 16 September 1846.
[25] See, for example, FO 195/677, Damascus, 12 July 1861.
[26] For details, see: FO 195/320, Damascus, 7 August 1848; FO 195/291,
      Damascus, 23 February 1848; FO 195/291, Damascus, 2 May 1848; BEO.
      AYN.d. No. 171, 22 Şaban 1264 [24 Temmuz 1848], 30–31; FO 195/291,
      Damascus, 21 June 1848; for a petition by the Hawranese complaining about
      the extensive plunder by the Anizah tribesmen, see: BOA, MVL 17/27, 25
      Zilkade 1263 [5 November 1847]; BOA, A.MKT.MHM 16/26, 17 Ramazan
      1265 [7 August 1849].

The tribe-state relations and inter-tribal disputes calmed down for almost a decade after this reconciliation as the Damascene officials learned the limits of imperial strength and the tribes respected each other's rights and privileges. But the year 1858 signified an important turning point in the tribal balance, with the Ruwalla advancing one step further against the Wuld 'Ali and entering into the better pasturages in Hawran, which was a serious threat to the district's peace. In that year, Muhammad Dukhy and Faisal al-Sha'lan, the successor of Naif al-Sha'lan, came to Hawran and its neighbouring districts to graze their animals, which initiated a pasture dispute between the two tribes that lasted for many years. The problem was that the Wuld 'Ali occupied all the uncultivated fresh pastures of Hawran while the Ruwalla had to accept the edges of the country and now struggled with their rival for better pastures.[27] Together with members of the Druze and Muhammad Said Agha, who had been placed in command of a body of irregular cavalry by the governor of Damascus, al-Sha'lan defeated Dukhy and acquired the monopoly of the villages' protection business. Pastures used by Dukhy in Hawran were occupied by al-Sha'lan.[28]

The conflict between these two powerful sheikhs of the Anizah, however, was not promoted by the imperial authorities as it caused the total destruction of regional order, threatening the safe passage of pilgrims from the neighbourhood of Hawran and Muzairib fair as well as the withdrawal of camels provided to the caravan by these sheikhs for transportation of the pilgrims. The government also lacked sufficient coercive means to prevent hostilities among the tribes. The imperial authorities thus – mindful of the need to keep the peace among them – applied the only tool at hand and initiated a meditation process between the conflicting parties. Immediately after the commencement of the hostilities, 'the governor of Damascus and the *mushir* [the commander of the army of Arabia] made all their efforts to put an end to these hostilities'. An envoy consisting of Tahir Pasha, a high-ranking provincial official, and two prominent members of the grand tribunal was sent to the fighting parties to persuade them to cease their hostilities.[29] The

27 FO 195/677, Damascus, 12 July 1861.
28 FO 195/601, Damascus, 3 August 1858 and 19 October 1858.
29 AMAE, CPC, Turquie, Damascus-5, 23 May 1858.

pasha's mission was a great success; both sides entered into negotiation under his auspices,[30] and at the end both sides withdrew to their own pasturages.[31] With the conflict resolved, neither sheikh required his animals for battle and therefore both agreed to supply camels to the caravan.[32] The *Surre Emini* and Tahir Pasha returned to Damascus with about 700–800 camels and 40 horses.[33]

The government's reconciliation of the sides, however, did not solve the problem ultimately as the pastures could not be partitioned among them in a way to which both groups would consent. The Wuld 'Ali and Ruwalla again vied for the pastures of the region in 1861 and several people were killed. But the Ottoman army was sufficiently powerful this time due to the increase in the number of soldiers in the region after the 1860 massacres and the troops encamped between the contending parties.[34] In order to eliminate this contentious situation, Fuad Pasha, the powerful governor of Syria, designated a tract of country in the Hawran and granted each of the two tribes a certain portion of it. However, this arrangement was considered by Dukhy 'as an infringement of his right, and by the representation of the military authorities it was considerably modified'. This time Faisal was exasperated but his requests were not heeded by the authorities. The British consul estimated that al-Sha'lan's alliance with the Druze might mean that Dukhy was 'retained in favor, that in case of its becoming necessary to coerce that people [and] his services may be called into requisition'.[35]

By 1862, however, the attitude of the government changed which again caused the collapse of order in Hawran. Sheikh Faisal al-Sha'lan was presented with a dress of honour by the governor of Damascus, and appointed as the agent responsible for ensuring peace in the neighbourhood of Hawran previously occupied by Dukhy, which meant the occupation of the Wuld 'Ali's pastures by the Ruwalla.[36] He was also assigned to protect the pilgrims' caravans when Dukhy allied with the

30 AMAE, CPC, Turquie, Damascus-5, 7 June 1858.
31 BOA, İ.DH 413/27366, 17 Safer 1275 [27 September 1858]; BOA, A.MKT. MHM 142/67, 5 Rebiulevvel 1275 [14 October 1858].
32 AMAE, CPC, Turquie, Damascus-5, 21 June 1858.
33 AMAE, CPC, Turquie, Damascus-4, 5 July 1858.
34 FO 195/677, Damascus, 10 July 1861.
35 FO 195/677, Damascus, 12 July 1861.
36 FO 195/727, Damascus, 10 July 1862.

Druze against the government, refusing the taxes owing.[37] This provoked hostility between the rival sheikhs, the local tribes and government troops. Although the Ruwalla and the government troops initially
defeated the Wuld 'Ali, the latter ultimately won a decisive victory and
re-established the power balance in the district. Dukhy's victory also
signified a positive change in the government attitude towards him
which had favoured the Ruwalla sheikh.[38] The government was still
far from becoming a determinant power in the tribal issues and leant on
the powerful tribe by giving privileges to it. When the tribes were
almost equally powerful, as in this case, the government's option was
to distribute the privileges among them.

From 1862 onwards, the government consolidated itself in the
region and adopted more decisive policies against the tribes. The abolition of the practice of *khuwwa* was among the first official actions that
established the Ottomans as the only taxation authority and demonstrated the government's power.

The Abolition of *Khuwwa* in Hawran and Consolidation of Ottoman Rule, 1862–1867

Sustenance of the tribal conflicts and the resistance of other regional
communities to the strengthening of imperial authority directed the
Damascene officials to put more radical steps into practice for a more
efficient governance in Hawran. In this regard, the abolition of
khuwwa taxes exacted by the nomads and other tribes represented an
important part of the consolidation of Ottoman rule in the region
which, although they initially resisted it, was be achieved with the
cooperation of the Anizah groups. The consolidated power of the
government and the nomads' dependence on the pilgrimage business
as well as the pastures in Hawran compelled them to obey the government ban on *khuwwa*. As *khuwwa* shares constituted a significant
source of tribal income, the process of its abolition took a long time,
sealed the reinforcement of Ottoman rule in the region and facilitated

---

[37] AMAE, CPC, Turquie, Damascus-7, 10 July 1862; the French consul reported
that Dukhy was dismissed due to his good relations with France.
[38] For details, see: FO 195/727, Damascus, 28 July 1862; AMAE, CPC, Turquie,
Damascus-7, 24 July 1862; AMAE, CPC, Turquie, Damascus-7, 27 July 1862;
FO 195/727, Damascus, 8 August 1862; AMAE, CPC, Turquie, Damascus-7,
11 August 1862.

the Ottoman expansion towards the southern districts such as Balqa', Salt, Karak and Ma'an. However, besides the tribal resistance, the abuses of the local government authorities and their partial actions favouring one tribe against the other contributed to prolonging the process as the Bedouin reacted to the government mishandling by breaking the truce, reasserting *khuwwa* and raiding the villages.

The process that changed the taxation authority in the region started in 1862 when the villages of the district agreed to deliver 32,000 measures [*mesures*] of wheat to the government, which they had previously paid to the Bedouin. In return, the government authorities guaranteed to protect them from Bedouin attacks. This agreement was also endorsed by Faisal al-Sha'lan, the sheikh of the Ruwalla, and by the Druzes at least in appearance.[39] Faisal most likely sided with the government and supported this decision as he tried to consolidate his position in Hawran against Dukhy. Since his pastures in the region were located at the fringes of the region, he presumably did not have substantial *khuwwa* revenues from the villages.

A more radical step was taken the following year with the decision to stop tribes from entering villages to collect *khuwwa*, which the Anizah groups respected. The authorities planned to blockade the passes by building strong garrisons to protect the villages. The sub-governor of Hawran brought together the village chiefs to inform them of the government decision and urged them to be prepared to support the troops in order to successfully rout the Bedouin tribes. Tribal access to the towns and villages for commercial purposes was also proscribed, and markets were established outside the towns. They were told that they could buy their needs from certain villages where presumably the government deployments were strong. In addition, designated pastures were allocated to Bedouin flocks.[40] The reason behind their submissive action was that they were threatened with losing the profitable business of conducting the pilgrimage caravan if they violated the restrictions imposed by the government.[41] By 1863, as a result of the infrastructural investments in the Syrian lands and Hawran, the government's hand became sufficiently powerful to enact such sanctions on the nomads.

[39] AMAE, CPC, Turquie, Damascus-7, 15 June 1862.
[40] AMAE, CPC, Turquie, Damascus-7, 2 February 1863.
[41] See, for example, FO 195/760, Damascus, 17 March 1863.

That was not the end of the story as the reconciliation with the nomads and the abolition of *khuwwa* in Hawran took several years, mainly due to official misconduct and contradictions within the Ottoman government. These new decisions initially met with little resistance from Faisal al-Sha'lan of the Ruwalla and Muhammad Dukhy of the Wuld 'Ali tribes in Hawran. The sheikhs were told by Ahmed Pasha al-Yusuf, the *kaymakam* of the town, to take their flocks to Jarud, far from the sedentary areas. However, this was then changed due to the designs of the pasha. The *kaymakam*, who reportedly received some 100,000 piasters and several pure-bred mares, did not prevent Faisal and other tribes from entering the pastures in Hawran. As a result, Muhammad Dukhy also returned to the pastures in the region he had previously occupied to prevent their permanent occupation. But he was on bad terms with Ahmed Pasha, who was bribed by Dukhy's rival, Faisal. As a result of the pasha's conspiring, the sheikh of Wuld 'Ali, who was given *aman* [surety] and invited to Damascus to accompany the pilgrim caravan, was then arrested there. At the intervention of the French consul, who went in person to the barracks where Dukhy was under arrest, the sheikh was released on condition that he would take his cattle away from Hawran.[42] Some of his men and camels were kept as hostages 'until the due performance of the promise. The service of convoying the Mecca caravan was again confided to Dukhy on condition of his continued good behavior'.[43]

Yet more official intrigue followed in an attempt to use one sheikh against the other and incite intra-tribal hostility, which made finding camels and horses to transport the pilgrims from Muzairib very difficult.[44] In spite of the nomads' conciliatory attitude, the government officials abused the conditions of the former as they were in a difficult position due to the banning of *khuwwa*. The tribes' bribes to convince the authorities to their cause continued to make an impact on the imperial decision which paved the way for the partial actions of the government in favour of one side and led to intra-tribal conflicts. Although guaranteed inversely, the troops plundered many of the

[42] AMAE, CPC, Turquie, Damascus-7, 16 March 1863.
[43] FO 195/760, Damascus, 17 March 1863; the Ottoman reports summarizing these events in Hawran are noticeably censured. Rushdi Pasha claimed that the troops merely punished Dukhy who did not obey the new regulations: BOA, A. MKT.MHM 262/22, 24 Mart 1279 [6 April 1863].
[44] AMAE, CPC, Turquie, Damascus-7, 7 April 1863.

Ruwalla and Wuld 'Ali animals, some of which were restored as a result of the sheikhs' negotiations and veiled threat of rebellion.[45]

The nomads still remained faithful to their promises and did not violate the regional order in spite of these incidents. Before they returned to the desert in the autumn, they requested the governor 'to designate the villages where they could buy their supplies of barley and wheat'. Esjani, Muzairib, Deir Ali and three other villages were indicated to them 'on condition that they would put their tents at a certain distance and they would only buy small fractions'. These conditions were accepted and purchases were made for some weeks at very advantageous prices for the peasants. In spite of their acquiescence to the conditions, the Bedouin were attacked by irregular soldiers and their animals were raided. That was the end of the nomadic patience. In response, an almost impossible alliance was realized among the tribes as they felt their interests vitally threatened by the government action: the Wuld 'Ali and Ruwalla allied with the Bani Sakhr, penetrated into Hawran, defeated the troops and charged *khuwwa* as they had done previously.[46] When Rushdi Pasha, the governor of Damascus, heard the

disastrous defeat, he asked the commander in chief [of the army of Arabia] for another battalion, which the latter refused, basing his refusal on a decree of the military council which states that the Arabs being encamped at the place destined for them by the authority, and no complaints having been made against them, they (the council) cannot advise that an expedition be sent against them.[47]

Upon this, Rushdi Pasha had to go out in person 'to endeavour to pacify the disaffected parties'.[48] The 'intervention of nature' prevented further incursions by the Bedouin: immense rains forced them to retreat to the desert without further attacks on the villages.[49]

The unrest continued the following year with further attacks by the Bedouin tribes on the villages, creating serious problems for the pilgrim business and the caravan's security. The governor of Syria was able to

[45]   FO 195/760, Damascus, 20 June 1863; AMAE, CPC, Turquie, Damascus-8, 6 July 1863.
[46]   FO 195/760, Damascus, 16 September 1863; AMAE, CPC, Turquie, Damascus-8, 5 October 1863; FO 195/760, Damascus, 25 September 1863.
[47]   FO 195/760, Damascus, 16 September 1863.
[48]   FO 195/760, Damascus, 25 September 1863.
[49]   AMAE, CPC, Turquie, Damascus-8, 12 November 1863.

ensure relative peace by compromising with Muhammad Dukhy, who became the most powerful leader of Hawran after the death of Faisal al-Sha'lan, and charged him with providing security to the villages. At the same time, the ban prohibiting the tribal entrance into the sedentary areas was abolished. Dukhy accepted this on condition that the government paid him the price of 100 horsemen, which might be interpreted as part compensation for his *khuwwa* losses.[50] Subsequently, the government agreed with all the other groups, including the minor tribes, to abolish *khuwwa* and, thanks to this compromise, peace was assured.[51] A midway was thus found by allowing the nomads to enter into the sedentary areas in return for the abolition of *khuwwa*.

In the following years, Rushdi Pasha was much preoccupied with the abolition of the practice of *khuwwa* and did not allow anyone – neither government officials nor tribes – to violate the prohibition. By 1865, the Christian and Muslim villagers of Hawran informed the British consul that they had experienced a significant shift from their situation under the pasha's predecessor to their contemporary existence. The Bedouins no longer visited the villages; the villagers were 'saved the enormously expensive involuntary hospitality to which they were formerly subjected'; but the peasants still believed that the nomads might return, and therefore chose to continue to pay *khuwwa* to them, which amounted, in many cases, to more than double what the government demanded.[52] Their fear was justified as the Bedouin, taking advantage of the military weakness of the Damascus government, killed the *mudir* of Muzairib and restarted their collection of *khuwwa* from all the surrounding villages in 1866.[53]

Crucial progress took place in that year towards the proper implementation of the *khuwwa* ban with the support of the nomads. A dispute between Muhammad Said Bey, Hawran's governor and Muhammad Dukhy regarding the distribution of the pasture lands caused the sheikh of Wuld 'Ali to relinquish his protection of the villages and – in the absence of sufficient government troops – the

---

50 AMAE, CPC, Turquie, Damascus-8, 13 May 1864; AMAE, CPC, Turquie, Damascus-8, 31 October 1864.
51 AMAE, CPC, Turquie, Damascus-9, 1 May 1866.
52 FO 195/806, Damascus, 18 March 1865; the French consul reported in 1866 that the Christian villages of Hawran 'enjoyed their crops without being obliged to pay khuwwa': AMAE, CPC, Turquie, Damascus-9, 1 May 1866.
53 AMAE, CPC, Turquie, Damascus-9, 30 June 1866.

smaller tribal groups and sub-units of the larger federations exploited an opportunity to violate the *khuwwa* ban.[54] The issue was settled by the intervention of the governor Raşid Pasha, redistribution of the pasture between Wuld 'Ali, Ruwalla and Bani Sakhr and a new protection agreement made between Bedouin groups and the government.[55] The pasha described the Wuld 'Ali and Ruwalla as 'the greatest of the loyal Bedouin tribes' [*kabail-i urban-ı mutianın en büyükleri olan Ruvale ve Veled-i ali aşiretleri*] and assigned them the responsibility of preventing the smaller tribes of Hawran from imposing *khuwwa* on the villages. According to the pasha, their protection would be influential to end the tribal raids in the region. These tribes also promised to pay the taxes exacted on them regularly, which implies that there was not an established mechanism to collect their taxes. With the support of the Anizah tribes, the governor also finalized the problems between the Druze and the government, obtained strong promises from them regarding the payment of their taxes owing and ensured their loyalty.[56]

The governor and the commander of the troops, Dervish Pasha, paid another visit to Hawran the next year and consolidated the compromise between the tribes, Druzes, others and the government by once again confirming the duties and responsibilities of both sides.[57] In this way, the *khuwwa* question was solved in Hawran, with the support of the Anizah nomads playing a major role. Although the prohibition of *khuwwa* in Hawran was harmful to tribal interests and reduced their incomes, their overall dependence on the local and imperial networks, in which they also took a part, impacted the production of the tribal consent. In addition, disputes between the Anizah groups forced them to maintain good relations to prevent an alliance between their rivals and the government, which would mean their expulsion from Hawran and becoming destitute of major grazing areas and considerable commercial networks.

---

[54] AMAE, CPC, Turquie, Damascus-9, 20 July 1866.

[55] AMAE, CPC, Turquie, Damascus-9, 11 September 1866.

[56] BOA, İ.DH 566/39407, 24 Temmuz 1283 [6 August 1866]; the relations between the Druze and the government deteriorated once again in 1869, and Hiza' al-Sha'lan and Muhammad Dukhy gave full support to the government against the Druze: BOA, İ.DH 1294/201692, 8 Şubat 1284 [21 February 1869].

[57] AMAE, CPC, Turquie, Damascus-9, 28 September 1867; BOA, İ.DH 564/39325, 21 Temmuz 1283 [3 August 1866].

The Ruwalla, Wuld 'Ali and the Ottoman Campaign to 'Ajlun, Balqa' and Salt

The compromise with the Anizah tribes and solution of the taxation problem in Hawran reinforced the Ottoman position in the region and enabled the empire to expand further south, also exploiting the partnership with the Anizah groups. The Ajlun, Balqa' and Salt expedition represents a good example of how the empire benefited from the partnerships made in Hawran while expanding its scope of domination. The nomads also had their reasons to cooperate with the imperial authority: first, it seems that they did not have crucial interests in the region to be expanded; second, imperial expansion towards the south would weaken their rivals such as the Bani Sakhr and would provide a shelter against the Najdi tribes such as the Shammar which began to grow up under Muhammad Ibn Rashid's leadership. Third, they presumably expected new prerogatives from the government in the newly expanded territories in return for their cooperation as it would increase the Ottoman dependence on the nomads.

As a result, in alliance with the Ruwalla and Wuld 'Ali, Mehmed Raşid Pasha organized a military campaign against the tribes of these districts in 1867 to pacify them and establish a permanent Ottoman presence in the region. The pasha put forward two major reasons for the expedition which can be related to the very formation of the Ottoman state in the region: the first was to collect the taxes in the district and the second was to ward off the 'predatory tribes' attacking the villages of Nablus and Ajlun to take shelter in Balqa'.[58] Between May and September 1867, the governor was able to carry out the Ottoman expedition without serious collision and on 4 September 1867, the Ottoman army entered into Balqa'.[59] The sheikh of the 'Adwan tribe, Dhi'ab Humud, who ruled the region until then was defeated after a short battle and fled.[60] In October, the sheikh 'presented himself to the governor in Damascus and was arrested and imprisoned in Nablus'. The Ajlun district was annexed to Hawran *sanjak* while Salt was placed under the newly established Balqa' *mutasarrifate*.[61]

[58] BOA, İ.DH 566/39407, 24 Temmuz 1283 [6 August 1866].
[59] BOA, A.MKT.MHM 390/23, 4 Cemaziyelevvel 1284 [4 September 1867].
[60] BOA, A.MKT.MHM 390/38, 5 Cemaziyelevvel 1284 [5 September 1867].
[61] See, for example, Rogan, *Frontiers*, 48–51; see, also: BOA, A.MKT.MHM 390/38, 5 Cemaziyelevvel 1284 [5 September 1867]; the Ottoman documents show that the *mutasarrifate* was first created and then the expedition was organized:

Figure 4.2 Ramtah in 1900. Gertrude Bell Archives, Newcastle University, A_395.

Prior to the expedition, some infrastructural investments were made in the region to facilitate the expedition; some ruined citadels on the pilgrimage road such as the citadels of Zarqa', Balqa' and Qatran and Hasa were repaired and the sheikhs nearby were given some money as a 'gift'.[62] 'Some other sheikhs and notables' in Hawran were rewarded with medals to secure their loyalty and 'to benefit from their good services' [*hüsn-ü hizmetlerinden istifade olunması mutehakkık olan bazı meşayih ve mu'teberan*].[63] The Wuld 'Ali and Ruwalla supported Mehmed Raşid Pasha's expedition against Ajlun and Balqa', and contributed to the expeditionary force, which facilitated the submission of the townspeople there and in Salt. Partly for the sake of the Anizah's cooperation, no

see, for example, BOA, İ.MVL 584/26261, 31 Kanun-ı Sani 1283 [13 February 1867].

[62] BOA, İ.MVL 534/23951, 13 Mayıs 1281 [26 May 1864].
[63] BOA, İ.DH 565/39347, 12 Temmuz 1283 [25 July 1866].

large-scale fighting took place prior to the establishment of Ottoman control.[64]

The two tribes sided again with the Ottoman troops when Bani Sakhr and Adwan tribes revolted against the empire to reassert their rights to *khuwwa* payments. Muhammad Dukhy of Wuld 'Ali in particular played a major role in the punishment and re-subjugation of the tribes in revolt.[65] Fahd al-Fayiz of the Bani Sakhr and Ali Dhi'ab of the Adwan pillaged Ramtah, a village situated in the plains of Hawran in response to the villagers' refusal to pay *khuwwa*, which that tribe had long demanded. The governor of Damascus was surprised at the actions of the Bani Sakhr, 'who had the privilege of escorting the Pilgrims, never ceased giving trouble to the authorities' indicating how the pilgrimage business created a dependence on the empire. The governor sent a force under the joint command of the *mutasarrıfs* of Balqa' and Hawran, supported by Muhammad Dukhy, sheikh of Wuld 'Ali, with 800 horsemen and Sheikh Ismail al-Atrash with 160 Druze. Thanks to the good relations that the governor had previously established with these Bedouin and the Druze communities, according to the French consul, he did not face any difficulty in securing their support. Another motivating factor for the Anizah tribes was again the pilgrimage: the Bani Sakhr's defeat would mean their exclusion from the pilgrimage business and a considerable increase in the Wuld 'Ali's and Ruwalla's share.

Once the Bani Sakhr were defeated and deprived of the privilege of escorting the pilgrim caravan, Ali Dhi'ab appealed for a pardon, which was granted on condition of payment of 25,000 piasters, 'a sum representing the share allotted to that tribe both of the expenses of the expedition and the value of the property taken at Ramtah'. When Ali Dhi'ab visited the governor of Damascus, he gave, as his justification for the attack on Ramtah, that the news of a war between Turkey and Greece, and of the continued insurrection of Crete necessitating the withdrawal of troops from Syria, led both him and his ally to the belief that this was the most opportune moment to re-establish their authority by levying *khuwwa*.[66] Such reasons demonstrate the relationship

[64] Rogan, *Frontiers*, 51.
[65] FO 195/927, Damascus, 16 July 1869; CADN, Serie D, 166PO/D20/8, Damascus, 4 July 1869 and 18 July 1869.
[66] FO 195/927, Damascus, 16 July 1869; CADN, Serie D, 166PO/D20/8, Damascus, 4 July 1869 and 18 July 1869.

between the strength of the empire and the maintenance of good relations with the tribes. Ali Dhi'ab was later salaried with 1,440 gurush by the Ottoman government to reconcile him and for his loyalty to the state although it was not comparable to the losses incurred with the abolition of *khuwwa*.[67]

Following that, the tribes of the region rarely violated the *khuwwa* ban. Similar to the case at Aleppo, one instance occurred at the outset of the Russo-Turkish War of 1877 when the Syrian garrison was attenuated by the transfer of the troops to the front. Some of the local tribes reasserted their old prerogatives and 'even demanded "arrears" for ten years' from the Ajlun district, where the Ottoman administration in Irbid prevented them from collecting *khuwwa*. But there is no reference to the Anizah groups in this incident and they were presumably not among those demanding *khuwwa*.[68] Similarly, *Lisan al-Hal* newspaper reported in 1886 that the Bani Sakhr tribes demanded *khuwwa* from Ajlun. According to the report, upon the peasants' refusal, they besieged the town and forced the peasants to pay it.[69] A final registered case happened in Hawran in 1893 when the government disagreed with the Druze and conflict with some Bedouin groups increased. Other Bedouin tribes were encouraged to renew their demands for *khuwwa*[70] and threatened an influential Muslim landowner 'with the loss of all his cattle unless their demands are complied with. The sum specified in this case was 20,000 piasters'.[71] It is unclear whether or not they could collect their demands, but such attempts remained exceptional in Hawran and the Bedouin did not revert to former habits due most likely to sustained good relations between the government and the Druze and the major Bedouin groups such as the Ruwalla and Wuld 'Ali.[72]

---

[67] Akarlı, 'Establishment of the Ma'an-Karak *mutasarrıfıyya*', 31; later reports expresses the sheikh's potential to help the government in the extension of Ottoman authority to Ma'an, Karak and Tafila.

[68] Rogan, *Frontiers*, 185.   [69] Saliba, 'Wilayat Suriyya', 206.

[70] AMAE, CPC, Turquie, Damascus-17, 29 November 1893.

[71] FO 195/1839, Damascus, 3 February 1894.

[72] See, for example, AMAE, CPC, Turquie, Damascus-17, 22 November 1895; even during the Great War, the Ottoman army was far below the capacity necessary to force them in a non-negotiated fashion. See, for example: Günay, *Suriye ve Filistin Anıları*, 18.

Cooperation with the Anizah for Further Advancement in the Desert: The Al-Jawf Enterprise and Ma'an-Karak *Mutasarrıfate*

Another attempt to expand Ottoman authority into the northern Najd, Ma'an and Karak took place in the early 1870s with the extensive support of the Ruwalla. The Ottoman expansion into the al-Jawf, part of a larger plan of forward policy into Najd, was the only unsuccessful example in the period discussed here. However, Ma'an and Karak would be incorporated in 1893 into the imperial administrative body. Abdullatif Subhi Pasha, the governor of Syria, was invited into the al-Jawf region in early 1872 by the residents, who wished to be saved from the 'atrocities' of Amir Muhammad ibn Rashid, the newly emerging independent power in the city of Ha'il, who was feared by the

Figure 4.3 A Ruwalla feast organized in honour of Baron v. Oppenheim. İstanbul Üniversitesi Nadir Eserler Kütüphanesi, 90567/13.

Ottoman government to become a second Ibn Saud.[73] The invitation might have been a genuine one when it is taken into account that the al-Jawf was previously controlled by the Anizah groups. The pro-Anizah groups, who were on bad terms with the Shammar, might have tried to provoke the government by proposing cooperation with the officials against Ibn Rashid.

It was also a golden opportunity for the pasha to establish an imperial outpost in Ma'an and al-Jawf to check the tribes migrating seasonally to and from Najd and to initiate preparations for a future expansion into Central Arabia. For this, Subhi prepared a two-stage plan. First, he would establish a *kaymakamate* (*kaza* district) in al-Jawf in northern Najd, which had already been captured by Hiza' ibn Shalaan, chief of the Ruwalla tribe, on behalf of the government and with the encouragement of the governor of Damascus. Another part of the first stage was the expansion of the government authority into Karak and Ma'an, the location of which were closer to the imperially ruled areas. Following this, Ottoman troops would be able to move southeast into central Najd. If Ibn Rashid resisted the establishment of Ottoman control in Jawf, the sheikhs of the Seb'a and Ruwalla of the Anizah, rivals of the Rashidis, would stand ready to assist. These tribal groups would most likely obtain privileges in the newly expanded areas and would become superior to and safe against their tribal rivals. Similar to the Ottoman ambitions in other areas, the reason Subhi wanted to establish administrative districts in Jawf, Ma'an and Karak was to be able to settle, control and benefit the Bedouin tribes there. The other aims were also convenient to the Tanzimat idealism and almost identical with those of Transjordan and Deir al-Zor. He planned to annex the villages of the rich district of Khaybar near Medina to al-Jawf and to post Ibn Sha'lan's brother Sattam there as *kaymakam*, since it was thought that he would act in harmony with the Ottoman administration, perhaps due to his enmity with Ibn Rashid. Similar plans were also made regarding Ma'an and Karak. In this way, the new administrative units would be strengthened both financially and politically. With al-Jawf, Ma'an and Karak thus under control, there would be great economic and political benefits, the pilgrimage route from Syria to Medina would

---

[73]　BOA, ŞD. 2270/19, 23 Eylül 1288 [5 October 1872].

Figure 4.4 Karak in 1913. Gertrude Bell Archives, Newcastle University, A_332.

be secured, Ibn Rashid would be weakened, and the threat posed to Ottoman order in Syria and Iraq by the nomads of the desert would be eliminated.[74] Ultimately, however, the first stage of this plan failed, and at the recommendation of Abdullatif Subhi's successor, Halet Pasha, and the Protector of Medina, Halid Pasha,[75] Ottoman administration over al-Jawf, Ma'an and Karak was abolished in 1873, just one year after its establishment[76] since 'the running costs

---

[74] BOA, İD 2270/9, 12 Mayıs 1288 [25 May 1872]; BOA, ŞD 2270/16, 26 Ağustos 1288 [8 September 1872].

[75] Söylemezoğlu, *Seyahatname*, 78.

[76] Later, Ottoman officials and local elites in the region occasionally advised the central government to reassert its authority in Jawf. But, having learned from Subhi Pasha's experience, the latter refused such suggestions. For some examples, see ŞD 260/43, 27 Ağustos 1291 [9 September 1875]; BOA, Y.PRK. ASK 80/57, 8 Mart 1308 [21 March 1892]; and BEO 78/5797, 17 Rebiulevvel 1310 [9 October 1892]. Reports sent after 1900 highlighted again that the region should be administered by the Ottomans so as not to allow the British to colonize it. DH.İ.UM E-67/11, 17 Nisan 1329 [30 April 1913].

of the new administrative unit far outweighed any revenues'.[77] The region was thus left to Ibn Rashid,[78] with whom an agreement was made stating that an Ottoman officer with eighty soldiers would remain there[79] and an annual tribute of 70,000 piasters would be paid to the treasury of Mecca and Medina. However, these tributes were never paid.[80]

Two crucial challenges, the British occupation of Egypt in 1882 and the rise of Ibn Rashid in Ha'il of Najd, 'provoked a new strategic concern to extend the Ottoman government south ... to protect their Syrian provinces from further British ambitions'[81] and further expansion of the Rashidis into the Ottoman territories.[82] The failure of the first Ottoman campaign and reinforcement of the Rashidis in Najd during the 1880s caused the increase of Ibn Rashid's pressure on the tribes of Ma'an and Karak, whose tribesmen were described as 'harmful people' to the region. In addition, the British activities at Aqaba Bay augmented Ottoman concerns regarding the Ma'an, Karak and Tafila districts, which brought about the expansion of the Ottoman administration into the region. Furthermore, by the early 1890s, the region had become a market for tribes to purchase arms smuggled from Egypt, which, according to Osman Nuri Pasha, the governor of Damascus, necessitated urgent action. In 1892, the pasha paid an inspection visit to the region to 'inquire into the conditions of the local tribes and the adverse activities of Ibn al-Rashid'.[83] The cooperation of the local tribes was considered fundamental for the maintenance of order and security. To that end, Rauf Pasha, Osman's successor, proposed to hire 150 soldiers from the 'appropriately influential Arab sheikhs whose attraction to and favorable disposition towards the government would be useful'.[84]

A good example of how the 'savagery' and 'nomadism' argument was used by the Ottoman authorities to legitimize their positions in the

---

[77] Rogan, *Frontiers*, 52.

[78] BOA, A.MKT.MHM 463/30, 14 Receb 1290 [8 September 1873].

[79] Al-Rasheed, *Politics in an Arabian Oasis*, 205.

[80] Söylemezoğlu, *Seyahatname*, 78.   [81] Rogan, *Frontiers*, 52.

[82] The Ottoman government later compromised with Ibn Rashid and allied with him against the Sa'udis and other tribal leaders in the gulf. But this reconciliation did not contain the imperial tolerance of the Rashidi expansion into southern Syria. For a detailed analysis, see: Çiçek, 'The tribal partners', 105–130.

[83] For some details, see: Akarlı, 'Establishment of the Ma'an-Karak Mutasarrıfiyya', 29.

[84] Akarlı, 'Establishment of the Ma'an-Karak Mutasarrıfiyya', 34.

Figure 4.5 Amman in 1902[?]. İstanbul Üniversitesi Nadir Eserler Kütüphanesi, 90605/96.

intra-governmental debates was displayed during the discussions at the State Council for the establishment of the new *mutasarrıfiya*: the governor of Syria requested some exemptions to the new administrative units to facilitate the incorporation of the people there and higher salaries for the officials to be employed in order to attract qualified bureaucrats into the region. When the members of the council showed unwillingness to accept his requests, the governor played the card that 'Ma'an and Karak are in the middle of an area inhabited by people enmeshed in bedouinism and savagery'. The governor maintained that 'since the administrative organization of this area is conceived as a prelude to the extrication of its people from bedouinism for refinement, recourse to lenient and wise measures, rather than a demonstration of force is requisite for the successful attainment of the desired goal'.[85] Many of the privileges the governor requested were thus given to the new administration.

[85] Akarlı, 'Establishment of the Ma'an-Karak Mutasarrıfiyya', 32.

The process of the establishment had been completed by 1893. Ma'an was first selected as the centre of the new *mutasarrıfıyya* but it was immediately shifted to Karak 'because of the limitations of Ma'an's administrative and geographical relationship with other important locations'. In addition, the willingness of the Majali and Bani Sakhr sheikhs to cooperate with the empire and their influence in Karak made a noteworthy impact on this decision.[86] Salt was also attached to the *mutasarrıfıyya* 'since the tribes of (the *liwa* of) Ma'an seasonally move from Salt to Karak and to Ma'an'. The town was considered by officials to be an indispensable economic and administrative component of Ma'an. The new sub-governorate was thus renamed the *mutasarrıfıyya* of Karak in 1895.[87] Extensive negotiations with the tribes and costly gifts preceded the consolidation of the new administration in order to procure their consent to the Ottoman expansion.[88]

Different from the other imperial expeditions in the region, active Anizah support for the Ma'an-Karak campaign was not reported, presumably due to the fact that there was no major conflict which preceded the establishment of the *mutasarrıfıyya*. But it seems that the creation of the Ottoman administrative units in the region constituted a principal advantage to the Ruwalla and Wuld 'Ali who had long controlled part of these districts.[89] Since the Rashidi expansionism threatened their strongholds in and around the region, they applauded the establishment of the new administrative units as they would create security for the Anizah position in the region against the *amir* of Ha'il. The Rashidis, who monopolized power in the Najd region, threatened the Anizah positions and constituted a primary reason for the maintenance of their partnership with the empire in the region during the 1890s and 1900s.

Ottoman State Formation and the Transformation of the Regional Space

Following the submission of the major tribes and successful expansion of the Ottoman bureaucracy, the whole region of southern Syria experienced an intense state formation and profound social transformation. A year after the military campaign, 300 soldiers were deployed to

---

[86] Rogan, *Frontiers*, 54.
[87] Akarlı, 'Establishment of the Ma'an-Karak Mutasarrıfiyya', 40.
[88] Rogan, *Frontiers*, 55.   [89] See, for example, Ibid., 35.

Figure 4.6 The Circassian gendarme in Southern Syria. İstanbul Üniversitesi Nadir Eserler Kütüphanesi, 90605/97.

Balqa'.[90] Local tribes inclined to cultivate the lands such as Al-Amr, Al-Hirsha, al-Saqta and al-Mazra' were settled within the boundaries of the *sandjak* and 2,035 sheep and goats were collected from them as tax.[91] Circassian refugees were settled in the region and employed as the empire's agents to consolidate its existence.[92] A certain degree of success was achieved in registering the agricultural lands.

In Ajlun, between 1876 and 1879, the registration of the agricultural lands was completed to individualize responsibilities of peasants to the state. But the peasants' fear of being recruited to the army prevented them from registering their lands in their own names, instead they signed away their lands to the urban notables and tribal sheikhs, which somewhat sabotaged the registration process. In Salt, by 1885, the 'land-grant colonies' were carved out and registered to the local tribes. In 1891–2, the title deeds were distributed to the tribesmen cultivating the land in the region. At around the same time, much of

[90] BOA, A.MKT.MHM 401/27, 8 Zilkade 1284 [9 March 1868].
[91] BOA, A.MKT.MHM 415/51, 12 Rebiulahir 1285 [3 August 1868].
[92] For details, see: Rogan, *Frontiers*, chapter 3.

the lands owned by Bani Sakhr were registered in the names of their sheikhs.[93] The Damascus government attempted in 1890, 1892 and 1897 to individualize the lands in Hawran and recruit the Hawranese to the army, but each time the people reacted by abandoning their lands and leaving the province at risk of grain shortage, and compelled the government to retreat.[94] In 1910, although a large-scale military expedition under the command of Sami Pasha al-Faruki gained some success in recruiting people into the army and population census at the cost of some 2,000 Druze killed during the hostilities, it seems that this was a temporary success and the *status quo ante bellum* was restored in a short time and the Druze and the Bedouin of the Ledjah enjoyed larger prerogatives than the earlier ones during the Great War.[95]

As part of the imperial consolidation in the region, merchants from Damascus migrated to the towns, accumulated agricultural lands and became crucial allies of the empire. A growing consumer market emerged while agricultural and tribal production for market expanded. Similar to what happened in Deir al-Zor, the tribes, including the Anizah, became trading partners of the newly emerging merchant class. The newcomers also considerably changed the urban space in the newly established administrative units.[96] The intensity of the agricultural society in the region, the importance of their produce for the provisioning of Damascus, its location vis-à-vis the Hijaz and the perceived threat from the British in Egypt are all possible reasons for further Ottoman investment in the region compared to Deir al-Zor.

There are conflicting theories regarding the state-tribe relations during the Ottoman expansion to the region and its aftermath. Rogan describes the tribes as the obvious losers in the imperial expansion as they 'performed many of the same functions which the state claimed as its prerogative'. The tribal chiefs as the natural leaders of the region before the imperial expansion were deprived of their taxation rights over the peasants as a result of the Ottoman expansion.[97]

In a recent study on Salt, Barakat modifies this approach and argues that, contrary to the presumed animosity of nomadic and settled communities, tribes responded to the new policies after the creation of the modern imperial administrative units, established close relations with

[93] Ibid., 83–88.
[94] Ibid., 184–187, see, also: BOA, İ.HUS 2/21, 5 Temmuz 1308 [18 July 1892].
[95] See, Çiçek, *War and State Formation in Syria*, chapter 6.
[96] See, Rogan, *Frontiers*.   [97] Ibid., 9.

Figure 4.7 The Bani Sakhr camels. İstanbul Üniversitesi Nadir Eserler Kütüphanesi, 90605/22.

the other agents of change, and became the defining factor in the policies' outcome. In her view, 'their participation in implementing these policies shaped the development of modern state institutions in the late nineteenth and early twentieth centuries'.[98] The juxtaposition of the tribes as if they were 'the victims of state-sponsored modernization attempts in the nineteenth century' did not necessarily reflect the 'tribal condition'. With reference to the Sharia court records and through many examples, she convincingly demonstrates that the tribal contribution to the local economy equalled that of the settlers, bureaucrats and merchants. Economic and social data regarding the nomadic communities demonstrate that they played a significant role in the creation of a modern property system in Salt. The court records 'show their key role in creating and maintaining, through their myriad

[98] Barakat, 'An Empty Land?', 9.

property transactions and court cases, a new kind of Ottoman governance in Salt'.[99]

The Provincialization of the Wuld 'Ali and the Ruwalla, and Redefinition of the Empire-Tribe Relations as Partnership 1870–1914

None of the above-mentioned scholars specifically examine the empire's
relations with Ruwalla and Wuld 'Ali nomads during the period when
the state formation process intensified after the 1870s in southern Syria.
Both scholars mainly focus on the Bani Sakhr to understand the development of the state-tribe relations in the region. Studying the Anizah
chieftaincies, however, presents another side of the story which may
reveal a new type of partnership between imperial and local actors, and
uncover a more conciliatory policy of imperial consolidation.

Similar to the endeavours undertaken by Midhat Pasha in Iraq for
the settlement of the Shammar, the successful expansion of Ottoman
rule into southern desert frontiers of the Syria province was followed by
an imperial enterprise of settlement to localize the Anizah groups.
Similar to Midhat Pasha's undertaking and in competition with his
policies in Baghdad, Abdullatif Subhi Pasha tried to colonize the northern and southern pasture plains of the province by settling the Anizah
tribesmen there. This was the first imperial enterprise to incorporate
the nomads into the province. In this regard, the pasha endeavoured to
settle the great Anizah tribes of Ruwalla, Wuld 'Ali, Fid'an and Seb'a.
However, it proved too great a challenge as the Fid'an and Seb'a had
more than 100,000 animals. When they were settled on existing cultivated lands, as the pasha himself observed, the surrounding pastures
would not be sufficient and this would create conflict among them.
Therefore, Subhi adopted a step-by-step approach towards these
immense, mobile populations. He settled 150 households of the Seb'a
around Hama and endeavoured to make a number of tribesmen from
Ruwalla and Wuld 'Ali tillers of the land in the empty fields and the
abandoned villages of the Hawran region. They were to be exempted
from the tithe tax for the first two years of their settlement.[100] It would
appear that Subhi Pasha's project of settling these chieftaincies could

---

[99] Ibid., 25.   [100] BOA, ŞD 253/57, 1 Temmuz 1288 [14 July 1872].

not be followed through when he left Syria since none of the tribes he had tried to settle remained to work on the land.

After this failure, the imperial authorities did not make a second attempt to transform the tribal lifestyle and the relations were based on 'imperial respect' for the tribal lifestyle and 'tribal recognition' of the imperial limits. As in Deir al-Zor, the pastures apparently represented the major issue to be resolved. Keeping their fellow tribesmen within the limits of the grazing lands allotted to them and thus preventing any conflict between the nomads and peasants was the major component of the empire's partnership with the tribal sheikhs. As it was the reason for the tribal migrations to southern Syria, the solution had to be feasible. As already analysed, pasture disputes were the fundamental reason in the 1860s for the hostilities between and among the tribes. It appears that the question of pasturages was resolved as Hawran's pastures were shared between the two powerful sheikhs over the following years. With the reinforcement of imperial authority in the region, their migrations were limited to certain pastures as they were seriously reprimanded by Ottoman authorities when they transgressed these limitations.[101] The sheikhs were made responsible for violation by their fellow tribesmen of the boundaries drawn by the government. Their pastures, however, were located within the boundaries of the province, very close to the sedentary areas which enabled them to sell and purchase their animals in the local markets. An Ottoman document, for instance, refers to the al-Sha'lan's tribe as 'the Ruwalla tribe inside the *sandjak* of Hawran' [*Havran sancağı dahilinde Ruvale aşireti*] as if they were inhabitants of the region.[102] In the estimation of the British vice-consul in Damascus, by 1879, only a fourth of the land in Hawran was settled; 'the rest consisting of vast tracts of fertile, and, in many parts wooded and well watered uplands serving solely as the pasturage grounds during a portion of the year of Bedouin tribes'.[103]

The Anizah Bedouin tended to remain in their allocated pastures and requested the government's permission when they needed additional areas for grazing and watering their animals.[104] This social contract

---

[101] See, for example, MW 5/7, 14 Nisan 1313 [27 April 1897]; 5/8, 18 Haziran 1313 [1 July 1897].
[102] BOA, DH.ŞFR 161/105, 23 Eylül 1309 [6 October 1893].
[103] FO 195/1264, Damascus, 16 August 1879.
[104] See, for example, MW 5/19, 24 Safer 1315 [25 July 1897]; MW 5/12, 23 Safer 1315 [24 July 1897].

with such large groups also facilitated the imperial authorities' job of punishment when one of those groups – or their sub-branches – broke their promise.[105] The Ottoman officers in Amman would write to the sheikh complaining about the disobedient tribesmen and he would stop those loyal to him from violating imperial rules.[106] The Ottoman soldiers were also deployed to strategic locations to prevent the tribal groups from damaging the agricultural products with their animals.[107] Similar to the other regions, some of them were mobile corps [*müfreze-i seyyare*] created to follow the nomads into the depths of the desert.[108]

The British Vice-Consul Jago of Damascus, who journeyed in 1879 to Hawran, reported striking observations regarding the Anizah tribes and their relations with the government, which demonstrates how systematically the relations were regularized and how a partnership was established. In search of forage due most likely to drought, the Ruwalla tribesmen broke from the control of their sheikh and made an irruption into the plain of Ba[l]qa[?]. Their sheikh complained about them to the officials and they were driven back by a few horsemen of the government. But terms were rearranged after the harvest and they were allowed to pasture thousands of camels in the stubble. The owners of the animals carefully guarded the grain floors from possible injury. The vice-consul reported that, although the government troops were withdrawn during the Russo-Turkish war of 1877, 'the prestige of the government was sufficient to prevent serious damage or robbery' by the tribesmen.[109]

Pasturages were not the only component of the empire-Anizah partnership in southern Syria. The decades that followed the 1870s witnessed closer relations between the Anizah branches and the Ottomans in other areas as well. As detailed previously, the increasing influence of Ibn Rashid in the region presumably became an important Anizah concern, motivating them towards further collaboration with the imperial government. On the part of the government, the difficulty of

---

[105] See, for example, AMAE, CPC, Turquie, Damascus-17, 17 March 1894.

[106] For a letter from the commander of Amman to Sattam al-Sha'lan regarding violations by the Ibn Samir branch of the Ruwalla, see: MW 5/23, 21 Zilhicce 1314 [23 May 1897].

[107] See, for example, BOA, Y.PRK.ASK 82/34, 5 Mayıs 1308 [18 May 1892].

[108] BOA, İ.MMS 104/4453, 16 Mart 1305 [29 March 1889]; the document shows that the troops were created long before 1889. But their number had significantly reduced at that time and the central authorities urged the increase of their numbers to 300 souls.

[109] FO 195/1264, Damascus, 16 August 1879.

Figure 4.8 Sattam al-Tayyar, the sheikh of the Wuld 'Ali. İstanbul Üniversitesi Nadir Eserler Kütüphanesi, 90567/12.

maintaining the governance of the newly incorporated territories, the British occupation of Egypt in 1882 and their activities in Aqaba made the partnership with the Anizah desirable and necessitated further investment in their sheikhs. Another risk in this regard was that these tribes might turn to foreign powers such as the British and French, whose influence in the region had visibly increased.

Both sides consequently increased the level of cooperation with the empire, which can be described as partnership and provincialization. Sheikh Sattam al-Sha'lan who ruled the Ruwalla confederation between 1877 and 1901 implemented a strategy which took into account the complicity of Ottoman bureaucracy to increase the level of cooperation with the government. As explained by Lewis, '[h]e tried to maintain good relationships with governors in Damascus and with other officials, bribing the venal ones when he had to, negotiating with

Figure 4.9 Sattam al-Sha'lan, the sheikh of the Ruwalla. İstanbul Üniversitesi Nadir Eserler Kütüphanesi, 90567/14.

them on behalf of the tribespeople and occasionally persuading them to make troops available to help the Rwala [sic] in their conflicts with others'.[110] The Ottoman government was equally willing to keep them at hand and develop policies considering them. In 1892, Sultan Abdulhamid invited the Ruwalla sheikh to Istanbul, gave him a decoration and the title of pasha, which was the confirmation of the empire-Ruwalla partnership at the highest level. He was also requested to 'sedentarize' his fellow tribesmen, which he never attempted to do in the following years.[111]

[110] Lewis, 'Hawran and Palmyrena', 37.   [111] Ibid.

Relations with the Wuld 'Ali were no different. Fearing most likely imperial favour to his rival, Sattam al-Tayyar, one of the most influential Wuld 'Ali sheikhs, requested to visit Istanbul together with the Bani Sakhr sheikh, al-Fayiz, as soon as they learned of the Ruwalla sheikh's invitation, and they were invited to the capital. Osman Nuri Pasha, the governor of Damascus, tried to prevent their visit to Istanbul on the excuse that al-Tayyar was not the paramount sheikh of the Wuld 'Ali, but was a lesser sheikh trying to establish superiority over the Wuld 'Ali sheikhs. However, this intervention was refused by the palace on the grounds that any sheikh who wanted to visit the sultan could not be refused and Istanbul was the best place to solve the problem of sheikhship for Wuld 'Ali. If the paramount sheikh desired to pay a visit to Istanbul, he would also be accepted.[112] This was confirmation of the state's new attitude of collaboration towards the tribes which matured from the early 1870s and Abdulhamid's policy of allying with the autonomous local power-holders to prevent them being influenced by the other great powers and collaborating with them.

Escorting and provisioning the pilgrim caravan continued to be a major area of collaboration and a profitable business for the Ruwalla and Wuld 'Ali tribes. They served as the soldiers of protection [*cerde-i seniyye*] and the conductor of the caravan [*hamledar-ı hacc-ı şerif*], and provided animals for the transportation and provisioning of the pilgrims.[113] Although the construction of the Hijaz railway made the services they rendered to the pilgrims meaningless, they were still employed by the imperial government as the protectors of the telegraph lines and the railroad. They initially cut the telegraph lines to remind the authorities of the vitality of compromising with them.[114]

All the accounts of the Hijaz railroad note a Bedouin resistance around Medina after al-Ula when the railroad approached the region.[115] Yet the realization of this monumental 'trans-imperial'[116] project definitely threatened the basic Bedouin source of income; the protection of the pilgrim caravan and the revenues from its

---

[112] BOA, Y.MTV 56/62, 18 Teşrin-i Sani 1307 [1 December 1891].
[113] See, for example, BOA, Y.MTV 56/62, 18 Teşrin-i Sani 1307 [1 December 1891].
[114] BOA, BEO 1853/138962, 12 Mayıs 1318 [25 May 1902].
[115] See, for example, Gülsoy, *Hicaz Demiryolu*, 120.
[116] I borrow this term from Mostafa Minawi's book, *Ottoman*, 102.

Figure 4.10 Carved stones in the cemetery of the Ruwalla tribes around Sheikh Mubarah (Hawran[?]). Gertrude Bell Archives, Newcastle University, Y_064.

provisioning and so forth, although the territory of the Anizah and Shammar was to the north of the most critical zone of the railway. The weak reaction of these tribes can be attributed to several reasons: first, as detailed above, a high-level integration of the Anizah tribes had been achieved when the project began to be implemented. However, other reasons must be considered as their integration did not abolish their means of resistance. A second reason was the large amount of money, 5,000 piasters, distributed to the tribal sheikhs for their appeasement.[117] In addition, after the completion of the railway, both Wuld 'Ali and Ruwalla protected the lines in return for money until the end of the empire, which partially reimbursed their losses.[118] Third, as reported by the Amir of Mecca and Auler Paşa, the Bedouin could see the opportunities brought by the railway construction as they made a living by selling sheep and camels, and their produce. The Hijaz railway would mean the emergence of new market opportunities for the Bedouin's animals and their produce, which would also be desirable

---

[117] Ibid., 124.
[118] BOA, BEO 4192/314367, 23 Haziran 1329 [6 July 1913]; they attacked the telegraph line when the government did not pay their salaries.

for the Ottoman officials since it would further integrate the nomads into the imperial economy and politics.[119]

As well as these reasons, similar to other Arab cities analysed in this book, the new administrative units in the region and the provincial capital Damascus transformed into centres of tribal governance that the tribes visited to solve their problems and raise their complaints about other tribes or members of the settled communities. The tribal sheikhs played a significant collaborative part in this process and their partnership meaningfully contributed to the 'governmentalization' of the tribal problems. By 1899, a commission had been established in Damascus with the name 'the Commission for the Reconciliation of the Bedouin of Syria and Aleppo [*Suriye ve Haleb Urbanı'nın Te'lif-i Beynleri İçün Mün'akid Komisyon*]' to finalize the tribal disputes. The tribal sheikhs were among the members of the commission as in the example of Sattam al-Sha'lan.[120] The local governments were also transformed into ports of call for their complaints. In 1888, for instance, when the Ubbath tribe of Hawran stole the animals of the Wuld 'Ali, they applied to the government and the animals were returned to their owners by the authorities.[121] Similar to what happened with the Fid'an and Shammar in Deir al-Zor and Aleppo, a provincialization of the Ruwalla and Wuld 'Ali thus took place from the 1870s. This provincialization had a symbiotic relationship with the state-tribe partnership whose agents consisted of sheikhs and officials. The 'governmentalization' of the nomads would not have been possible without the close collaboration of both parties. The same would be the case if the government had not recognized the tribal authority and autonomy.

The hostilities that occasionally broke out between the Ruwalla, the Druze and the Bani Sakhr from the mid-1880s to late 1890s also indicate how the government played a central role in resolving the disputes between and among the Anizah and the other communities. In 1886, when the Druze planned to attack the Ruwalla in alliance with the Bani Sakhr, Sattam al-Sha'lan visited the governor in Damascus and complained about Shibli al-Atrash, the powerful Druze leader, that he incited the Druze and the Bani Sakhr to attack his fellow tribesmen,

[119] BOA, DH.MKT 462/2, 6 Mart 1318 [19 March 1902]; Auler Paşa, *Hicaz Demiryolu*, 14.
[120] BOA, Y.A.HUS 398/7, 24 Haziran 1315 [7 July 1899].
[121] BOA, DH.MKT 1528/47, 23 Temmuz 1304 [5 August 1888].

which would seriously damage the regional security. Security measures were taken by the local government. The hostilities were renewed in 1893 and a conflict took place in Salt where five Ruwalla and twenty to twenty-five Bani Sakhr tribesmen were killed. Two hundred and fifty soldiers were sent to the region to quell the hostilities and because Sattam had not been able to prevent his fellow tribesmen from attacking Christian villages in the region. As Salt was the Bani Sakhr's territory and the Ruwalla were the attacking party, the soldiers were presumably dispatched to protect the peasants and the lands cultivated by the Bani Sakhr tribesmen. The *kaymakam* of Salt was also sent to the region by the *mutasarrıf* of Hawran to reconcile the conflicting parties. Al-Atrash was arrested and questioned in Damascus, and he was compelled to promise that he would no longer incite hostilities. Shortly after that, the problem was completely resolved. When hostilities renewed in 1899, the governor of Damascus went to the tribes in person to conclude the dispute. The governor's intervention firmly finalized the hostilities: he took Sattam with him, visited the Bani Sakhr encampment and reconciled them. The governor also took promises from the sheikhs that both sides would return the plundered animals to their owners.[122] This intense involvement of the government in tribal conflicts is another aspect of the provincialization of the nomads.

Cooperation and partnership made them immune from many responsibilities to the government. Following the consolidation of Ottoman rule in the Hawran, government control over them somewhat increased. As will be detailed in Chapter 6, they paid a moderate *wadi* tax for their animals.[123] Similar to the other Anizah and Shammar branches, the tribal animals were not counted and could be taxed on declaration and none of the Ruwalla and Wuld 'Ali tribesmen could be recruited to the Ottoman army. Like the other nomads, the Ottoman authorities never precisely knew the number of tribesmen and their

---

[122] BOA, DH.ŞFR 161/105, 22 Eylül 1302 [5 October 1886]; BOA, İ.HUS 12/62, 20 Mayıs 1309 [2 June 1893]; BOA, Y.A.HUS 275/85, 24 Mayıs 1309 [6 June 1893]; BOA, Y.A.HUS 275/59, 23 Mayıs 1309 [5 June 1893]; BOA, Y. MTV 78/188, 22 Mayıs 1309 [4 June 1893]; BOA, BEO 213/15910, 22 Mayıs 1309 [4 June 1893]; BOA, BEO 219/16410, 1 Haziran 1309 [14 June 1893]; BOA, 291/21801, 28 Eylül 1309 [11 October 1893]; BOA, BEO 307/22998, 25 Teşrin-i Evvel 1309 [7 November 1893]; BOA, Y.MTV 398/7, 24 Haziran 1315 [7 July 1899]; BOA, Y.MTV 398/71, 13 Temmuz 1315 [25 July 1899].

[123] Lewis, 'Hawran and Palmyrena', 37.

animals until the demise of the empire. That may be interpreted an 'Ottoman concession from its statehood' for the sake of the politics of partnership.

Conclusion for Chapter 3 and Chapter 4

Ottoman expansionism towards the desert and its frontiers intensified at a time when Tanzimat principles were gradually being abandoned – but still influential – in government policies towards the Bedouin. The establishment of the administrative units in the regions where the Anizah and Shammar regularly migrated was an important milestone for the transition to the politics of negotiation although their initiation was the result of the Tanzimat ideals and coercive considerations. During the expeditions and their aftermath some nomadic groups cooperated with the empire while others resisted it and rebelled against the government. As Chapters 3 and 4 demonstrate, for various reasons, many tribesmen took part in the Ottoman expeditions into Deir al-Zor, Transjordan and al-Jawf, and made remarkable contributions to the establishment of a sustainable imperial order in the regions where Ottoman rule was maintained following the expansions. Therefore, the picture is not so clear as to identify the expansion as a state-tribe conflict. The consolidation of imperial rule in the newly expanded areas transformed the collaboration into the provincialization of the nomads and their partnership with the local authorities to maintain the governance of the newly established administrative units and to solve the great majority of the problems that nomads experienced with the settled people and other tribes.

It was not only these local and imperial factors which caused the empire to consolidate its existence in the desert. There were also global reasons which motivated the officials: the increasing British and Russian interests in the Persian Gulf, Iraq and Egypt, and eastern and south-eastern Anatolia. Particularly, inter-imperial competition over the region caused the Ottomans to adopt a more moderate and negotiating approach towards the nomads from the early 1870s as their collaboration and friendly attitude now became more crucial to gain the upper hand in inter-imperial competition over the region. Otherwise, in the Ottoman viewpoint, the nomads might have approached the other great powers who were in search of influence among the various peoples of the Arab lands.

The administrative outposts, however, by no means served the determination of the imperial lands and exclusion of the nomads from these territories. They maintained a considerable domination at certain seasons of the year in the Ottoman territories while sustaining their hegemonic status in the desert territories of Syria and Iraq, which constituted the majority of lands controlled by today's states of Syria, Iraq and Jordan. In the example of the Anizah and Shammar tribes, the social and political structure of the tribal society could not be reshaped by imperial policies such as settlement, although this had been one of the major imperial aims with the expansion of the imperial rule towards the tribal regions. In the same regard, they were immune to obligations imposed on other Ottomans such as military service, which may be interpreted as the results of the state-tribe partnership. The individualization of the duties against the state could also not be realized with regard to the Anizah and Shammar tribesmen. New agents of the empire such as merchants were introduced to the newly dominated regions, but this did not always work to the disadvantage of the Bedouin. The increase in demand for tribal produce contributed to nomadic prosperity. They were also able to have imperial protection in their pastures against their rivals in the same way as the Anizah groups enjoyed in Ma'an against the Rashidis. As for the concessions given by the tribes, they had to pay the price of recognizing Ottoman authority as their legitimate sovereign. They paid the taxes exacted on them more regularly (although these were remarkably moderate compared to the amounts paid by other Ottomans) and had to relinquish the *khuwwa* exactions the tribes imposed on the villages, the most significant 'abnegation' on the part of the nomads. Reconciliation was arrived at as it had been with the Anizah and Shammar tribes in the newly expanded territories.

5 Partnership, Provincialization and Conflict

The Shammar in the Provinces of Mosul, Baghdad and Deir al-Zor, 1870–1914

This chapter analyses the empire-Shammar partnership systematized after the failure of the imperial project to settle the Shammar in the early 1870s, which made it clear to the government that they had to respect the nomadic lifestyle for an effective partnership based on 'mutual concessions'. On the part of the tribes, reconciliation meant proper recognition of the empire as their higher authority and partial fulfilment of the required duties of being an imperial subject. In this regard, they substantially renounced certain tribal habits such as plundering and raiding the sedentary areas. They had to perform their responsibilities towards the government in a more or less organized way: they paid their taxes more regularly, prevented their flocks from damaging crops and relinquished their demands for *khuwwa* from the settled population.

In return, like the other nomadic groups, the Ottoman government had to abandon its aim of making the Shammar tribesmen into 'ordinary Ottomans', such as conscripting the tribesmen to the imperial army, educating them in the imperial schools and settling them on land as the tillers of soil. Bedouin rights in the sedentary areas were recognized: their visits with their flocks to 'the imperially dominated lands' for commerce, shopping and grazing were acknowledged and regularized with the help of the newly recruited regular troops. Their sheikh(s) were employed as the salaried agents of the empire while a quarter share of the taxes collected from their fellow tribesmen was allocated to sheikh. The practical meaning of the appointment of a sheikh by the state was to recognize his privilege of domination over the countryside of an imperial province, the grazing lands where he visited with his fellow tribesmen and hundreds and thousands of animals. Relinquishing these rights meant a considerable loss for the government in terms of human and material resources which were worth trying to retain.

The situation, however, changed after Farhan's death in 1890. The Shammar were divided into three groups, the Deir al-Zor, Baghdad and Mosul branches. While the first two groups were successfully provincialized, mainly due to the designs and plots of the local government, the majority of the Mosuli Shammars conflicted with the state under the leadership of Farhan's oldest son Sheikh 'Asi, who vied for the sheikhship of the Mosul branch. Different from his grandfather, Safuq, he struggled to become a part of the Ottoman desert governance and benefit from its advantages, though he finally achieved this. On the part of the empire, the policies in Mosul province – which increased the tension between the government and the Shammar and provoked intra-tribal hostility – were not approved by central government and the neighbouring governorates such as Baghdad and Deir al-Zor as the intention was to adopt a reconciling approach towards the tribes.

Another challenge for the Shammar-state partnership in Deir al-Zor was to contradict with the outcomes of the Ottoman policies in the Kurdish regions. As a result of employing the Kurdish tribes as the *Hamidiye* light cavalry, the Shammar pastures in the Jazira region were dominated by Ibrahim Pasha, the sheikh of the Kurdish Milli tribe and *Hamidiye* light cavalry brigadier, which ignited a decade-long hostility between the two parties. This challenge noticeably weakened the Deir al-Zor Shammars' position in the Jazira region and caused ongoing hostilities between Faris Pasha and the sheikh of the Milli, in which the latter was usually victorious. However, Faris was not completely abandoned and was always supported by the Deir al-Zor government in his struggle against the Diarbekir party, which contributed to the Shammar's provincialization and his final victory. It should also be noted that the Ottoman central government did not explicitly favour any of the conflicting parties, but adopted a conciliatory stance not to alienate the conflicting sides from the empire. This attitude was convenient to the Hamidian policy of conciliating the local autonomous forces using the Muslim unity principle to prevent them from approaching the Great Powers at a time when Russia and the British were perceived as striving to establish friendship with these tribes against the Ottoman Empire.

The Creation and Consolidation of the State-Tribe Partnership in the Mosul and Baghdad Provinces, 1860–1890

Similar to the previously analysed groups, the regularization of the Ottoman troops, reinforcement of the desert frontier by the new settlements, and abandonment of the Tanzimat policies and settlement plans of the Shammar and the consolidation of the tribal power under Farhan's sheikhship laid the foundations for the empire-Shammar partnership in this era. No intrigue was undertaken by the government authorities against the tribal leadership, while tribal raids on the villages and caravans were considerably reduced as the sheikh did his best to withhold his fellow tribesmen and newly deployed troops actively protected them. All these were part of an imperial policy aimed at maximizing the tribal share in the governance of the desert frontier after the imperial consolidation of power which had been welcomed by tribes already disposed to do so as it would minimize the possibility of state intervention in their territories and would guarantee official protection for the tribal interests both within and without the provincial boundaries.

Figure 5.1 A small caravan travelling in the desert. İstanbul Üniversitesi Nadir Eserler Kütüphanesi, 90605/87.

The Abolition of Khuwwa

Similar to the other cases analysed previously, an important development that paved the way for the state-Shammar compromise was the
abolition of *khuwwa* exactions. The monopoly of taxation was crucial
for the state in terms of both sovereignty and to finance the growing
needs of the army and bureaucracy in Baghdad, Mosul and particularly
in Deir al-Zor. By 1862, the governor of Baghdad 'persuaded' Farhan
to relinquish his collection of *khuwwa*. The growing power of the
Ottomans in the provinces persuaded the sheikh to conciliate with
officials in a bid to protect tribal interests. The sheikh thus prohibited
his fellow tribesmen from imposing *khuwwa* on the villages and merchants in these regions.[1]

This prohibition, however, was not unconditional as Farhan
resumed his extortionist practice on the caravans and the villages if
the government failed to pay his salary, continuing for as long as
needed to force the authorities to make regular payment. It was like
an unemployed weapon in the hands of the tribes which they would put
into service when they wanted the government to be made aware of
their dissatisfaction.[2] When the sheikh's authority weakened in the late
1880s and the tribe dispersed following his death, the Shammar started
again to demand *khuwwa*, especially from peasants cultivating the land
in the Jazira region, proving the cruciality of the compromise for the
maintenance of the Ottoman monopoly of taxation in the tribal
regions.[3] As will be detailed later in this chapter, the collapse of the
order in the region and disputes between the Shammar and the officials

---

[1] BOA, İ.MMS 130/5577, 2 Haziran 1303 [15 June 1887]; the earliest document
    showing that the Shammar demanded *khuwwa* from the peasants and merchants
    goes back to 1862. The British consul reports that Namık Pasha persuaded
    Farhan to abandon this practice that year: FO 195/717, Baghdad, 18 June 1862;
    the absence of any documentation between these dates showing that the
    Shammar demanded *khuwwa* from the peasants proves that this information is
    correct except for the exactions made by Abd al-Qarim during the Shammar
    revolt in 1870.

[2] In 1879, his salary was not paid for fourteen months, which amounted to
    280,000 piasters. In response, he stopped the caravans that brought provisions to
    Baghdad and took the quantity of cereal his tribes needed. To the same end, some
    of his loyals plundered the villages: AMAE, CPC, Turquie, Mosul-2,
    10 March 1879.

[3] BOA, DH.ŞFR 135/104, 28 Nisan 1304 [11 May 1888].

during the 1890s caused the revival of the practice of collecting *khuwwa*.

Urban-Tribal Interactions and Provincialization

The decrease in hostilities also increased the empire-tribe and city-tribe interactions which was an important part of the Shammar's provincialization and an almost infrastructural precondition of the maintenance of the good relations between the 'urban authority' and 'rural autonomy', that is, the state and the tribes. In this regard, commercial relations played a pioneering role in constructing the regional peace which, along with the other factors, played a framing part in the empire-Shammar compromise from which both sides would benefit. Even in 1863, shortly after the restoration of peace between the Shammar and the government of Baghdad, Farhan was visited by the French consul in Baghdad to negotiate the potential export of the wool produced by the Shammar to France, this would mean a significant income for the tribe and a valuable tax revenue for the empire.[4] Similarly, companies were established by the city-dwellers to engage in animal trade with the Shammar.[5] The increasing dependence on cities also resulted in the decrease of the Shammar's mobility beginning from the 1860s. The tribes associated with Abd al-Qarim moved between Mosul and Urfa while those who accepted Farhan's authority migrated between Baghdad and Mosul. A recent study identifies this transformation as 'provincializing the Shammar' with reference to the tribesmen's increasing interaction with the Ottoman provinces and integration into their political and commercial life, and more or less limitation of their movement within the provincial boundaries without any coercion on the part of the government.[6]

The relationship of the Shammar with the cities increasingly flourished and diversified in the early 1870s, mainly stemming from the state-tribe compromise that cemented the sustenance of the partnership. For Mosul, for instance, 'a continuing and regular interaction existed between nomadic animal herders and settled urban and

---

[4] Dolbee, 'The Locust and Starling', 107.
[5] See, for example, SCR-Urfa 214, Doc. 84/169, 10 Cemaziyelevvel 1287 [8 Ağustos 1870] quoted in Kahraman, '214 Numaralı Urfa Şer'iyye Sicili', 210–212.
[6] Dolbee, 'The Locust and the Starling', 108.

agricultural communities'. The nomads were important '*because they were nomads* at a time when animal products were the most important exports, and intensive animal husbandry did not provide a viable alternative to pastoral production'.[7] Although from a later date, an Ottoman report clarifies how the settled and nomadic societies were integrated with each other as a result of the construction of a sustainable peace. In a Shammar encampment in the neighbourhood of Mardin, there was 'a considerable contingent of Armenian Catholic and Assyrian Christians from Mardin' who visited the tribe 'to sell dry goods and work as blacksmiths in the moving camp of the Shammar'. Eighty to eighty-five men from Mardin, both Christians and Muslims, were in the camp for trade. Many of them devoted a considerable amount of time to the nomads, one or two months for some of them. A camel trader from Hama accompanied the Shammar for twenty-five days while a Mosuli merchant was with the tribe for one and a half months; a blacksmith from Mayadin lived in the encampment for four months.[8] Together with other outputs of the present study, this encampment can be interpreted as a panoramic picture falsifying the desert-town contrast which is still a dominant theory in discussion of city-desert interactions.

The Shammar's Protection of the Desert Frontier and Caravan and River Routes

As detailed in the previous chapters, the protection of the provincial countryside had to be assigned to the Anizah and Shammar sheikhs to prevent them from plundering and in order to establish friendly relations with them. From the mid-1860s onward for the Shammar, they performed this mission without violating the state-tribe agreement except for a Shammar revolt in 1870 in reaction to Midhat Pasha's plan of settling them. In a letter by Abd al-Qarim, the Shammar sheikh, addressed to Mustafa Pasha, the governor of Kürdistan, he presented himself and his colleagues as follows: 'we are the sheikhs of the Jazira [sic] from Aleppo to Baghdad and it is our duty to protect the peasants [*reaya*] and the people [*ahali*]'.[9] This was not only lip service given the

---

[7] Shields, *Mosul before Iraq*, 181.
[8] BOA, Y. PRK UM 54/8, 26 Nisan 1317 [9 May 1901]; quoted in Dolbee, 'The Locust and the Starling', 181.
[9] Dolbee, 'The Locust and the Starling', 124.

significant decrease in the tribal attacks against the villages. As noted previously, they protected the agricultural lands against both their fellow tribesmen and the members of the rival tribes which constituted a crucial part of the empire-Shammar partnership in the Jazira region and elsewhere.

In addition, the Shammar sheikhs performed well in their protection of the main caravan routes from attacks by their own fellow tribesmen and other tribes. They became the major partners of empire to make the desert and rivers safe zones although it took some time and government investments in the desert frontier to establish a sustainable peace along the routes that connected the main cities. The Baghdad-Damascus caravan road had often remained closed up until 1870 due to the security problems in the desert and the caravans had to divert goods through Aleppo rather than using the shorter route via Damascus.[10] Following the consolidation of Ottoman rule in Deir al-Zor, fortification of the desert frontier and establishment of the sustainable good relations with the Shammar and Anizah tribes that led to a truce with the tribes on the route, it was reopened to the caravan traffic. Several chiefs of the Shammar received annual salaries from the government to ensure the safety of the caravan roads between Diarbekir, Aleppo, Mosul and Baghdad. In some locations, an escort of combined Anizah and Shammar protected the caravans in return for the payment of a toll.[11] An arrangement, informally recognized by the authorities, had established the rules of peace in the early 1860s between the powerful Shammar sheikhs and Uqayl tribe, who provided security and transportation between the provinces, in return for immunity from attack for Uqayl caravans as they passed through their respective district.[12]

The Bedouin tribes, who previously constituted a major security problem for the river routes,[13] also protected the rafts sailing on the Euphrates and Tigris from attacks by their own tribesmen and others. A member of the Shammar accompanied the rafts sailing from Mosul to Baghdad, under whose 'potent guardianship' the boats were to 'be secured from the attacks of any of his powerful and plundering tribe'.

---

[10] FO 195,927, Damascus, 3 April 1869.   [11] Blunt, *Bedouin Tribes*, 292.
[12] FO 195/676, Baghdad, 18 December 1861.
[13] Hurşid Paşa, who remained in the region and wrote a detailed account on the tribes between 1848–1852, describes the routes from Baghdad northward as unsecure: Mehmed Hurşid Paşa, *Seyahatname*, 269.

The raft that Ussher travelled on from Mosul to Baghdad in the early 1860s came across a plundering faction of the Bedouin. The Bedouin did not attack them, however, although they heard that the passengers 'were a party going down with money to pay the troops at Baghdad a year's pay', which they had on board in cash, together with some very valuable gifts from the sultan to the pasha.[14] Such a service was not provided by the nomads for free. It was in return for the imperial recognition and guaranteeing of the Shammar's rights on certain grazing lands: the pastures on the right bank of the Euphrates around Shirgat were allocated to the Shammar, who, in return, provided security for the river navigation and prevented the neighbouring minor tribes from attacking the boats.[15]

Farhan Pasha played a revolutionary role in the evolution of relations towards compromise by adopting a negotiating and conciliatory stance towards the government and bargaining with the officials about the prerogatives of his fellow tribesmen that permanently transformed and institutionalized the empire-Shammar relationship. As stated by the British consul in Baghdad, Sheikh Farhan 'represented the changing' and 'was diplomatic, occasionally visited Baghdad; and when a raid was committed by his kindred, always had a letter ready ascribing it to his unruly sons' which prevented a conflict between the imperial troops and the tribesmen. As part of his partnership with the Ottoman government, the pasha also did his best to restore the plundered property to its owners, including to foreigners, when the Shammar occasionally organized raids against villages, flocks and caravans. He negotiated with government authorities and accepted an Ottoman title (Pasha) and a stipend from the state that demonstrated his respect for (and loyalty to) the imperial authority.[16]

The new situation of partnership was described by the French consul in Baghdad as 'some sort of dependence' of the Ottomans 'on these tribes'.[17] However, this analysis reflects only one part of the dependence. The partnership was also the result of the vulnerability of the tribal position in the imperial lands to the imperial expansionism which required a peaceful co-existence with the settled communities. The security measures and military fortifications detailed in Chapter 2

---

[14] Ussher, *A Journey*, 421, 432.   [15] Ibid., 421, 432.
[16] FO 195/1682, Baghdad, 26 June 1890.
[17] Dolbee, 'The Locust and the Starling', 116.

strengthened the imperial position and increased the tribal dependence on the imperial decision makers although the officials were still not able to limit the nomads' actions by coercive means and needed negotiations with their sheikhs. If the dependence had only been one-sided, the maintenance of the reciprocal relations explained in this section would not be possible.

Besides Farhan's agency, the transformation of the imperial policies towards the tribes and other autonomous forces played a part in the state-tribe conciliation. The increasing influence of the British in the Iraqi territories made the Sultan anxious about the loyalties of the Shammar sheikhs and directed him to satisfy them. To counter the British within and outside the imperial territories and to develop a new imperial vision, Abdulhamid appealed to the ideal of Muslim unity around the authority of the caliph, gave new prerogatives such as the title of Pasha to the sheikhs and recognized the existing ones, which equally determined the realization of the state-Shammar partnership.[18]

One Step Forward: Disintegration and Consolidation of Provincialization

Farhan Pasha's death greatly increased the state-tribe partnership as each province appointed its own sheikh. The Shammar was divided into three branches in Mosul, Baghdad and Deir al-Zor as a result of the combination of the tribal dynamics and the policies of the Mosuli officials who conflicted with the Baghdad authorities over the Shammar's unity. The Baghdad government defended its view that the Shammar could be better controlled if the Ottoman government recognized a paramount sheikh for all the branches dispersed in Urfa, Aleppo, Mosul, Deir al-Zor and Baghdad. The Mosul government, however, opposed this claiming that the geography the Shammar frequented made such a practice impossible. As the powerful tribal leaders such as Faris Pasha and 'Asi favoured the latter and the Ottoman government did not want to antagonize them as part of the Hamidian policies of sustaining good relations with the nomads, the Shammar had to be recognized as three separate tribes shortly after Farhan's death.

[18] See, for example, Çetinsaya, *Ottoman Administration of Iraq*.

Initially, tradition was observed and, as Farhan's eldest and most charismatic son, 'Asi was considered as the paramount sheikh in place of his late father. However, he refused to appear before the governor of Baghdad as a result of the intrigues of the Mosuli authorities who defended the Shammar's division into three; this can be interpreted as the beginning of the division. Instead, given his close relations with the Mosul authorities, the sheikh chose to go to Mosul to be 'crowned' there.[19] 'Asi enjoyed good relations with the Mosuli authorities at that time and was presumably used by them in their plans to divide the Shammar. In response, the insulted governor of Baghdad appointed one of Farhan's other sons, Mujwal, as the paramount sheikh. He was unsuccessful in ruling the large number of tribesmen and that compelled the imperial authorities to divide the Shammar.[20]

It is difficult to interpret 'Asi's attitude towards the governor of Baghdad. If he was opposed to recognizing the authority of the government, he would not have accepted an appointment by the government of Mosul to a lesser position. The most reasonable explanation is that he was misdirected by the Mosuli local notables and officials who wanted the division of the Shammar and annexation of a branch of it to the province in expectation of increasing the revenues of the provincial treasury by having a share from the Shammar taxes. Annexation would also increase the influence of the Mosul government among the Shammar tribesmen. 'Asi was a powerful sheikh and thus it was quite convenient to use this for a division plan. But later, 'Asi would dispute with the Mosuli authorities, too, since they replaced him with his brother, most likely because of his independent character which made him inadequately 'useful'.

To give more details about the process of division, following the disturbances among the Shammar branches in Mosul under 'Asi's leadership, the province demanded that the Mosuli Shammar appoint 'Asi as their sheikh and pay him accordingly. In a bid to minimize the central officials' and Baghdad authorities' reactions, the governor highlighted the widespread support for 'Asi's appointment in Mosul noting that the administrative consul, elites and Mosuli merchants all supported 'Asi's appointment as they felt he would provide security to the

[19] BOA, DH.ŞFR 145/85, 5 Eylül 1306 [18 September 1890].
[20] BOA, DH.MKT 1782/49, 5 Teşrin-i Sani 1306 [17 November 1890].

city from the Shammar attacks.[21] As a result and given his influence among the Shammar branches around Mosul, his appointment was confirmed as the sub-sheikh of the Mosul branch.[22] Subsequently, Faris Pasha, the brother of Farhan, was reconfirmed as the sub-sheikh for the Zor Shammar, a position he had held since 1878. But in practice, the paramount sheikh Mujwal did not have any authority in Mosul and Deir and the Shammar was divided as per the requests of Farhan's sons, with the support of the Mosul government.

The disintegration process gained momentum in the following years and was officially accepted by the imperial government who adopted a policy of minimizing dissatisfaction of local leaders to win their hearts. In 1891, Faris Pasha sent a telegraph to the minister of the interior requesting the division of the tribe into two parts. According to his proposal, the Deir al-Zor branch would be totally independent of the others and Faris Pasha would be responsible for their actions. He issued a veiled threat to the central government, warning that he would not be responsible for the incursions of the Zor Shammar if his proposal were refused.[23] This letter presumably played an important part in central government's disintegration decision. Encouraged by Faris Pasha's success, by 1893, the Mosul government had recognized its own sheikhs as the sheikhs of the Shammar in the province.[24] Since the potential candidates demanded the division of the tribe and because to achieve that regularly generated unrest, there was, indeed, no other option for the government but to accede to them, especially given the absence of a strong leader like Farhan. Thus, the Shammar were eventually divided into three independent official sheikships, annexed to Baghdad, Mosul and Zor where they were provincialized, but protected their autonomy under the leadership of their sheikhs.

The maintenance of the politics of negotiation was relatively straightforward for the Deir al-Zor and Baghdad Shammar. As detailed in Chapter 4, Faris Pasha (d. 1904) and his son Hamidi ruled the Deir Shammar until the end of the Ottoman rule in harmony with the imperial officials in Deir al-Zor and helped the local authorities both protecting the tribal interests and abiding to the

---

[21] BOA, DH.ŞFR 145/85, 5 Eylül 1306 [18 September 1890].
[22] BOA, DH.MKT 1784/69, 13 Teşrin-i Sani 1306 [23 November 1890].
[23] BOA, HR.TO 395/84, 22 Nisan 1307 [5 April 1891].
[24] BOA, BEO 306/22879, 14 Teşrin-i Evvel 1309 [27 October 1893].

imperial limits.[25] Similarly, Mujwal remained as the recognized
sheikh of the Baghdad Shammar and worked with the provincial
authorities to synchronize the tribal and imperial interests until
1910 when he was replaced by Humaidi at the proposal of Nazım
Pasha, the powerful governor of Baghdad, who was sent there to
resolve the tribal unrest caused by 'Asi of the Mosul Shammar.
Humaidi was a graduate of the tribal school [*Aşiret Mektebi*] in
Istanbul,[26] established to educate the sons of the tribal leaders[27]
and as Farhan had done, he lived in Istanbul for a long period,
spoke Turkish and was well acquainted with Ottoman bureaucracy.
He thus cooperated effectively with the imperial authorities to keep
the Baghdad Shammar in line with Ottoman rule.[28] Presumably, as
a result of his good service, and in similar circumstances to Farhan,
Humaidi was appointed as the paramount sheikh for all the
Shammar around 1912.[29] However, this was not sufficient to
become a successful sheikh: Humaidi could not rule the tribe effi-
ciently as he presumably could not keep the balance between the
tribal interests and the imperial policies and acted like an Ottoman
official. By 1914, 'Asi consequently undermined Humaidi's authority
by gaining the majority support of the Shammar and retreating into
the remote areas of the desert.[30] As a result, the imperial project of
uniting the Shammar under the authority of a paramount sheikh
failed due to the tribal resistance.

The Shammar's disintegration, however, increased each group's
integration into the provincial administrations. Shortly after the

[25] For a very positive report by the governor of Zor on the services performed by
Faris for the Shammar's peacefulness in Deir Zor when he died, see: BOA,
DH.ŞFR 325/100, 30 Mayıs 1320 [12 June 1904].

[26] Humaidi's assignment was proposed in 1907, by the governor of Baghdad:
BOA, DH.TMIK-M 242/36, 12 Teşrin-i Sani 1323 [25 November 1907]; but the
assignment was confirmed in 1910: BOA, MV 139/15, 28 Mart 1326
[10 April 1910]; there is no information in the Ottoman documents regarding
the reasons for this delay, although 'Asi's opposition might be one reason for it.

[27] For a detailed examination of this school, see: Rogan, 'Aşiret Mektebi', 83–107;
Akpınar, *Aşiret Mektebi*.

[28] See, for example, FO 195/2415, Summary of events in Turkish Iraq for the
month of February 1912; FO 195/2368, Summary of events in Turkish Iraq
during the months of February and March 1911.

[29] BOA, ŞD 34/30, 14 Haziran 1328 [27 June 1912] and the document dated 19
Haziran 1328 [2 July 1912].

[30] Günday, *İki Devir Bir İnsan*, 199.

disintegration of the Shammar, the provinces limited their responsibility with the tribes annexed to them and inclined to protect them against the intervention of the other provinces which may demonstrate an improved level of provincialization and mutualization of interests. The tribes observed government concerns, while the officials knew what would cause tribal disturbances and would deteriorate the state-tribe relations.

An Ottoman undertaking of 1892 to subjugate the Shammar exemplifies how the relations between the Shammar and the provincial governments became sophisticated and intermingled following the disintegration. Reform troops [*kuvve-i ıslahiye*][31] under Ömer Vehbi Pasha's command were established to carry out tribal reforms including retrospective taxation, settlement and conscription, and conducting a population census in the Iraqi provinces of Mosul, Baghdad and Basra. However, the pasha's mission failed largely due to the resistance of the local officials. He reported that some members of the Shammar were protected by Baghdad province and complained about the lack of support for his mission from the surrounding provinces and *mutasarrıfates* like Aleppo, Deir al-Zor and Mosul in spite of his broad mandate.[32] Conversely, local administrators complained of the difficulty of cooperating with him since the pasha viewed the local rulers as his subordinates, and wanted to use disproportionate force against the nomads implying that the pasha did not know the sensitive balance between the tribes and the state and the limits at which the officials had to stop. Many complaints were levelled against him by local people, elites and officials alike. Ultimately, the Porte had to abandon their aims in order to avoid further dissent.[33]

It seems that the local officials were quite aware of the limits to involvement of the state in the tribal affairs and thus prevented the pasha and central government from making fatal mistakes which would destroy all the infrastructure of the state-tribe reconciliation at the provincial level. A serious attempt to realize the pasha's project would most likely cause a large-scale tribal uprising and would destroy the foundations of the empire-tribe conciliation which provincialized the Shammar in Mosul, Baghdad and Deir al-Zor as separate groups.

[31] For details, see: Hut, 'Musul Vilayeti', 121–131.
[32] BOA, BEO 79/5924, 27 Eylül 1308 [10 October 1892].
[33] Hut, 'Musul Vilayeti', 123.

They were also suspicious about the decisiveness of the Ottoman government. This 'reform attempt' could only have remained as an initiative which deteriorated the state-tribe relations in the region as the central authorities might have abandoned it in future. Such attempts are also important to indicate that there were still official factions within the Ottoman government defending the adoption of a more radical stance against the nomads in order to benefit from their human and material sources in a more effective way by transforming them into more controllable societies.

Contrary to common belief, the provincialization also provided benefit to the Shammar and increased the tribal radius of action as it made synchronization of the government forces more difficult. When, in 1894, the governor of Mosul planned an expedition to punish certain branches of the Shammar presumably loyal to Sheikh 'Asi who had plundered flocks in Zimar, a region in Mosul belonging to the royal estates, he petitioned central government to engage neighbouring provinces in military support of his expedition. Without this, the governor alleged, the enterprise was bound to fail as it had on numerous previous occasions.[34] As a result, provincial synchronization could be achieved and the governor quickly recovered the stolen property from the Shammar.[35] However, Shammar incursions in Zimar did not cease due to the problems stemming from the dismissal of 'Asi, which caused branches of the Shammar to frequently break the peace and attack the villages and caravans. In this case, the provincialization of the tribes increased their capability to counter as they were able to escape to places like Deir al-Zor where they had a good relationship with the officials.[36] Given the disturbances in Mosul detailed in the next section, maintenance of good relations with the tribes and respecting their limits was almost the only option for the authorities of Mosul, Deir al-Zor and Baghdad to maintain peace in the regions the Shammar frequented and dominated, a sizable percentage of the lands available in these provinces' countryside.

Disputes between the neighbouring provinces regarding the tribes further clarifies the level of provincialization and how the provincial authorities adopted the tribes annexed to their administration. Even

---

[34] BOA, BEO 382/28630, 31 Mart 1310 [13 April 1894].
[35] BOA, BEO 395/29619, 16 Nisan1310 [20 April 1894].
[36] The sub-governor of Zor, however, denied all the allegations: BOA, BEO 474/ 35539, 10 Eylül 1310 [23 September 1894].

the administration of provincial capitals like Baghdad preferred favouritism when their tribes were in conflict with people from other regions. In 1902, for instance, a number of tribesmen from the al-Silka Bedouin of the Baghdad Shammar plundered a great number of animals belonging to the Tiyane village of Deir al-Zor and escaped beyond the Baghdad frontier. During the skirmish, according to the report by the sub-governor of Zor, the villagers also captured the relatively small number of nineteen camels and three guns from the al-Silka.[37] When the Deir al-Zor authorities appealed to the governor of Baghdad to restore their plundered property, the latter made his assistance conditional on the villagers' return of their attackers' animals which was an obvious action to favour their 'fellow tribesmen'.[38]

Although, at first glance, the competition of the provinces for 'their tribal comrades' harmed the bureaucratic harmony and consistency of the state, and caused 'official partisanships', it unintentionally served the imperial purpose of consolidating relations with the nomads as in the example of the Shammar-Milli conflict. The state-tribe consolidation at the provincial level manifested itself in competing partnerships during the hostilities between the Zor Shammar and Milli tribe that lasted from the mid-1890s to 1908. The Shammar maintained the struggle with the support of the Deir al-Zor government and elites, and finally won with the discontinuation of support to the Milli by the Diarbekir province with the 1908 Revolution in spite of the former's loss of ground in the early 1900s.

The Shammar-Milli Conflict for the Domination in the Jazira and Consolidation of the Empire-Tribe Partnership in Deir al-Zor

The Deir Shammar's supremacy in the Jazira region was seriously challenged in the mid-1890s by the Kurdish Milli tribe of Viransehir annexed to the Diarbekir governorate. Ibrahim Pasha, the sheikh of the tribe, was generously supported by the Diarbekir authorities and his tribe was appointed as a *Hamidiye* brigade, part of whose mission was designated by the Diarbekir officials to be the protection of the desert frontier against the Shammar and Anizah. By 1897, the Milli tribesmen

---

[37] BOA, DH.TMIK-M 110/23, 2 Kanun-ı Sani 1317 [15 January 1902].
[38] BOA, DH.TMIK-M 110/23, 13 Nisan 1318 [26 April 1902].

occupied the neighbourhood of the Khabur River used as pasturage by the Shammar, which ignited a long-lasting hostility between the Shammar and the Milli, patronized by the *mutasarrıf* of Deir al-Zor and the governor of Diarbekir, respectively. Although Diarbekir's support for the Milli has been much highlighted in the available scholarship, the Shammar's cooperation with the Zor authorities has not yet been analysed. The Shammar-Milli conflict has accordingly been interpreted as the Ottomans' proxy war against the former in alliance with Ibrahim Pasha. However, the different factions of the Ottoman government at the local level supported the different parties: the Deir government sided with the Shammar while the Diarbekir province made a common cause with the Milli, which makes the colour of the imperial favour blurred.

The conflict between the two parties stemmed from their attempts to control the major regional caravan routes at a time when Ibrahim Pasha emerged as a regional power broker around Urfa, generously supported by Abdulhamid II, seizing control of the commercial networks established along the Diarbekir, Aleppo and Damascus axis as well as those routes between Zor, Mosul, Diarbekir and Aleppo that benefited from and were principally controlled and 'protected' by the Shammar. As the rise of Ibrahim Pasha also meant the commercial and political rise of Diarbekir against Deir al-Zor as a regional hub, the officials and local mercantile elites of the province backed the pasha while the power-holders in Deir joined with the Shammar for similar reasons.[39]

In a short time, the tribal conflicts transformed into a tribal-based rivalry between the governorate of Diarbekir, and *mutasarrıfate* of the Deir al-Zor and Shammar's provincialization constituted a major mainstay in this struggle. Both the relationship between Ibrahim Pasha, sheikh of the Milli tribe, a man who had a Kurdish origin but much respected by several Arab Bedouin tribes, and the governors of Diarbekir, and that of the government of Zor with Faris Pasha of the Shammar offer strong examples of 'official partisanships'. They formed such 'strong alliances' that the governors appeared to be their advocates before the central government to set it in motion against the other side. The governor of Diarbekir gave exaggerated accounts of attacks

---

[39] For details, see, Ali, 'Le role politique des tribus kurdes', 67–81; see, also: CADN, Serie D, 166PO/D1/87, Aleppo, 27 May 1901.

Figure 5.2 Ibrahim Pasha, the sheikh of the Milli tribe, in his *Hamidiye* brigadier uniform. İstanbul Üniversitesi Nadir Eserler Kütüphanesi, 90506/87.

by the Shammar on the Milli in a bid to convince the central government to punish the Shammar and instruct other provinces to help Diarbekir in its struggle against them. In return, Ibrahim Pasha paid a significant proportion of the *bakhshish* to the governor and other provincial bureaucrats which can be interpreted as the 'official share' in

Ibrahim Pasha's financial benefits from his regional expansion since he controlled widespread commercial networks extending from Diarbekir and Aleppo to Baghdad. The relationship between the *mutasarrıf* of Deir al-Zor and Faris Pasha of the Shammar was along similar lines.[40]

The two tribal leaders clashed over more than one decade, from the mid-1890s to 1908, with a parallel dispute running alongside between their sponsors, the governor and the *mutasarrıf*. In 1895, the *serasker* reported to the Grand Vizier regarding the Shammar-Milli conflict that the governor of Diarbekir exaggerated the extent of Shammar sheikh Faris Pasha's attacks on the Milli to exact punishment on the sheikh, thereby rendering Ibrahim stronger than his enemy.[41] The *serasker* was correct in his assessment; after minimal negotiation, Faris Pasha soon withdrew his tribe from Diarbekir's frontier without any further incident.[42] Similarly, in 1898, Şakir Pasha, who was dispatched to the region to investigate the hostility between the Shammar and Milli tribes, reported that the sub-governor of Zor offered the Shammar protection [*tesahub etmek*] just as the governor of Diarbekir defended the Milli.[43] Although the governors of Zor and Diarbekir were replaced and their successors were cautioned on numerous occasions by the central government to cooperate on tribal matters and made their efforts to reconcile the conflicting parties, they continued to defend their 'tribal allies' and levelled accusations at one another with each renewal of hostilities between the two sheikhs.[44] The institutionalization of the tribes' provincialization and their partnership with the local authorities constituted a major reason for the sustenance of official support to the tribes at the local level independent from the officials that followed each other.

Ottoman documents include an abundant number proving the devoted 'partisanship' of the imperial officials for their tribal comrades in both localities, which made it difficult for central government to determine the truth. When the Milli's pasture land around Urfa and Mardin was burned in 1895, the Diarbekir government accused Faris

---

[40] For details, see, Ali, 'Le role politique des tribus kurdes', 67–81; see, also: CADN, Serie D, 166PO/D1/87, Aleppo, 27 May 1901.
[41] BOA, BEO 632/47341, 12 Mayıs 1311 [25 May 1895].
[42] BOA, BEO 638/47792, 24 Mayıs 1311 [6 June 1895].
[43] BOA, DH.TMIK-M 28/53, 3 Mart 1314 [16 March 1898].
[44] For some examples, see: BOA, DH.TMIK-M 102/10, 5 Nisan 1317 [18 April 1901]; BOA, DH.ŞFR 281/65, 19 Mart 1318 [1 April 1902]; BOA, DH.TMIK-M 144/10, 1 Mayıs 1319 [14 May 1903].

Pasha.[45] The *mutasarrıf*, however, responded that Diarbekir officials had burned the land and organized the villagers to complain about the Shammar.[46] According to the accounts of the Diarbekir governors,[47] the Shammar were entirely responsible for the failure of regional security and the wilful blindness of the Zor government towards their atrocities, while the *mutasarrıf* repeatedly accused the Milli tribe and bemoaned the unconditional support of the Diarbekir authorities for Ibrahim Pasha.[48] The governor and *mutasarrıf* so exaggerated to defend the 'righteous' position of their allies that at one point in 1898, in order to conclude the endless disputes between the different governors, central government was forced to adopt the following attitude: 'After that we will pay no attention to further discussion. Since it is vitally important to conclude this issue, you are expected to communicate in good faith with one other or exchange officials for the resolution [of the hostilities] ... the telegraphs should not be occupied by this issue, as they are intended for the urgent [business] of the state.'[49]

The dispute only came to an end in 1908 when Ibrahim Pasha's power was curtailed by a broad alliance of his rivals spanning Aleppo, Zor and Diarbekir when the sultanic support to him evaporated with the 1908 Revolution.[50] The conflict represents a significant example of mutual dependence between local governments and the Shammar, who created a united front against the Milli attacks. Although the Milli was obviously favoured by Diarbekir province – and to some extent by the sultan – the Shammar's close relations with the Deir government and its provincialization there prevented the tribesmen from rebelling against the empire. In response, the Ottoman government did not identify the Shammar as enemy or rebels although the Milli was officially recognized as the *Hamidiye* forces, the troops of the empire. The Shammar front, however, could only gain the upper hand when the Milli 'de-provincialized' in Diarbekir province with the 1908 Revolution. In this way, Ibrahim Pasha was declared

[45] BOA, DH.MKT 408/61, 22 Ağustos 1311 [4 September 1895].
[46] BOA, DH.MKT 408/61, 15 Eylül 1311 [28 September 1895].
[47] See, for example, BOA, DH.ŞFR 208/128, 30 Nisan 1313 [13 May 1897]; BOA, DH.MKT 2220/13, 26 Haziran 1315 [9 July 1899].
[48] See, for example, BOA, DH.TMIK-M 38/39, 27 Ağustos 1313 [9 September 1897].
[49] BOA, DH.TMIK-M 50/44, 11 Mart 1314 [24 March 1898].
[50] For details, see: Barout, 'La renaissance', 114–115.

a rebel, delegitimized and taken out of the imperial system while the Shammar again returned to its dominant position in the Jazira region.

Turmoil in Mosul: Sheikh 'Asi and His Struggle to Become a Partner

The story in Mosul was somewhat different from the others as the tribal division did not resolve the rivalry between the various candidates for the sheikhship and partnership between the local government and the tribal sheikh could not be established. The appetite for conflict of Farhan's descendants – 'Asi, Abd al-Aziz, Jarullah and Shellal – led to sustained hostilities and paved the way for the total eradication of security and an unsettled state of affairs in the province. The corruption of provincial rulers and elites who decided the Shammar leadership according to their own interests significantly exacerbated the tribal chaos. It occasionally became a crisis of governance, influencing the relations between the Mosul governorate, the neighbouring governments and the central administration as the discontented Shammar groups caused disorder throughout the region.

From the very beginning of the Shammar's official disintegration in 1893, local notables frequently changed the recognized sheikh with various excuses, many of which did not reflect the authentic reason. An attempt in 1899 to appoint Shellal as the sheikh of the Mosul Shammar in place of 'Asi is illuminating in helping to understand the provincial administration's role in the ongoing disputes. The British consular agent in Mosul reported that the governor received 200 liras from Shellal to support his appointment although 'Asi was more popular in the tribal society – but most likely had a clash of interests with the governor and the provincial elites. Ziya Pasha, the head commissioner of the crown lands [*emlak-ı hümayun*] and 'Asi's protector, opposed the appointment of Shellal and sent several telegrams to the minister of the sultan's private treasury, providing reasons to invalidate his candidacy for sheikh.[51]

Once this initiative failed, the provincial authorities and notables made another attempt, and they achieved 'Asi's replacement with another son of Farhan Pasha. In 1901, the provincial administration replaced 'Asi with his brother Jarullah, who had closer relations with

---

[51] FO 195/2055, Mosul, 16 February 1899.

the provincial authorities and merchants.[52] According to the governor of Baghdad, Jarullah was the leader of a small branch, but the livestock of the Mosul elites were under Jarullah's protection and he had thus long been championed by the Mosul administration.[53] As 'Asi's sponsor, Ziya Pasha opposed Jarullah's appointment and produced an account book that detailed the latter's plundering.[54] Aware of the pasha's influence over central government and his ability to depose Shellal in the past, the governor reminded the minister of the interior that it fell within the jurisdiction of the governor and the administrative council to appoint the sheikh.[55] Most likely due to the resistance of the central government to Jarullah's replacement with 'Asi, who was the strongest among others, shortly afterwards, the governor of Mosul explicitly stated that central government had no authority to overrule the appointment of a sheikh decided at the provincial level.[56]

The incidents that followed 'Asi's removal demonstrate how the designs of provincial bureaucrats and elites provoked the internecine war between the various branches of the Mosuli Shammar and deteriorated state-tribe relations in the region. Inevitably, the replacement of the sheikh gave rise to internecine hostilities and, during the fighting, 'Asi's son was killed by Jarullah's. Subsequently, according to the governor of Baghdad, rather than mediating between the two sheikhs, the provincial gendarmerie accompanied Jarullah to punish 'Asi and seize his livestock.[57] Fighting between rival groups prompted peasants around Sinjar to leave their lands and seek refuge in Mosul.[58] Due to the chaos that stemmed from the tribal hostilities, two governors of Mosul – Mustafa Nazım and Ahmed Rashid – were dismissed between 1901 and 1902.[59] As is obvious in the Ottoman documents, neither

[52] BOA, DH.TMIK-M 102/45, 29 Mart 1317 [10 April 1901]; Ebubekir Hazim Bey, the governor of Mosul at that time, claims in his memoirs that he dismissed 'Asi just because the sheikh wanted to be involved in the hostilities between the Shammar and Milli. But the contemporaneous documents make no reference to such a reason. See, Tepeyran, *Hatıralar*, 459–464.

[53] BOA, DH.TMIK-M 150/12, 12 Ağustos 1319 [25 August 1903]; the British consul also describes Jarullah as the leader of a small branch of the Shammar: FO 195/2137, Aleppo, 24 February 1903.

[54] BOA, DH.ŞFR 279/12, 20 Şubat 1317 [5 March 1902].

[55] BOA, BEO 1648/123578, 7 Nisan 1317 [20 April 1901].

[56] BOA, DH.ŞFR 260/69, 15 Mayıs 1317 [28 May 1901].

[57] BOA, DH.ŞFR 318/17, 11 Teşrin-i Sani 1319 [24 November 1903].

[58] BOA, DH.TMIK-M 156/11, 19 Teşrin-i Evvel 1319 [2 November 1903].

[59] Hut, 'Musul Vilayeti', 149–153.

central government nor Baghdad province approved the activities of the Mosul governorate whose relations with the nomads were quite different than those in other localities and did not conform to the general imperial policy of establishing good relations with the local autonomous forces by respecting the grazing and that belonging to others within the provincial territories.

Such dissatisfactions, however, did not change the order of the things in Mosul as the inter-tribal conflicts contributed to by the provincial policies transformed into a regional crisis threatening the security situation from Urfa and Aleppo to Baghdad. The hostility between the two chiefs escalated quickly, causing the closure of the caravan route between Aleppo and Mosul via Deir al-Zor as the sides created new alliances with other sheikhs of the Shammar and the Anizah.[60] 'Asi positioned himself around Mosul with 10,000 mounted forces, joined forces with the Shammar and Anizah from Baghdad, Aleppo and Zor, and they heavily defeated Jarullah's supporters.[61] The latter appealed to the powerful Kurdish tribal leader Ibrahim Pasha, the sheikh of the Milli tribe, for support. A long-time enemy of the Zor branch of the Shammar, Ibrahim agreed to help that would also allow him to extend his influence over the Mosul province.[62] At around the same time, the Baghdad Shammar were attacked by Jarullah since they allied with 'Asi and this extended the area of conflict.[63] In response, Mujwal, the sheikh of the Baghdad Shammar, made an attack on Jarullah's followers and then retreated to his zone of security, that is, the boundaries of Baghdad province.[64] In fear of a harsh reaction by the Ottoman central government, the Mosul authorities accused the governor of Baghdad of supporting 'Asi and undermining provincial order. Any attempt to mediate met with little success due to both party's insistence on their positions – for the province of Mosul, not to reappoint Asi, for the sheikh, being reappointed to the sheikhship.[65] The spatial scope of the disorder demonstrates the intertwined character of the relations

---

[60] CADN, Serie D, 166PO/D54/10, Damascus, 28 February 1905; BOA, DH. TMIK-M 156/11, 1 Teşrin-i Sani 1319 [14 November 1903].

[61] BOA, DH.TMIK-M 156/11, 5 Teşrin-i Sani 1319 [19 November 1903] and 15 Teşrin-i Sani 1319 [28 November 1903].

[62] BOA, DH.ŞFR 293/67, 13 Eylül 1318 [26 September 1902].

[63] BOA, DH.TMIK-M 156/11, 23 Teşrin-i Sani 1319 [6 December 1903].

[64] BOA, BEO 2026/151918, 9 Mart 1319 [22 March 1903]; BOA, BEO 2038/152832, 22 Mart 1319 [4 April 1903].

[65] BOA, DH.ŞFR 324/67, 10 Mayıs 1320 [23 May 1904].

between the tribes. The large-scale provincialization of the Shammar and collaborative partnerships between the local governments and the tribal leaders did not weaken the tribal potential as a regional actor playing a determining role in regional affairs.

In early 1904, most likely as a result of the pressures by the Ottoman central government, 'Asi was called to Mosul to negotiate, but in response to – or more probably under the colour of – the complaints of proprietors of the plundered caravans and decimated herds, and the authorities in Mosul imprisoned him in spite of guarantees of immunity offered by the governor. In response to further disorder by 'Asi's supporters objecting to his arrest and in a bid to curb the local authority's designs, an imperial decree was issued in early 1905, forgiving 'Asi for his past crimes and appointing him as sheikh in place of Jarullah. He left the city centre after being presented by the governor and the members of the Administrative Council with his supporters. He, in turn, promised to reimburse the property plundered by his supporters. Knowing about the informal 'rules' of the state-tribe relations at provincial level, the sheikh did not neglect to satisfy the governor, presumably so as not to be caught up in intrigue once again. According to the French consul, 'Asi had bribed the governor Nuri Pasha for his appointment and even the sum, the consul claims, that changed hands was known.[66]

A report detailing the incidents sent by the minister of the interior to the Grand Vizier identified another key reason for the incidents. The minister defined this as the appointment of 'Jarullah as the sheikh by the governorate [of Mosul] without taking the consent of the Shammar tribes into consideration', which highlights an important aspect of the politics of negotiation. According to the minister of the interior, the actions and attacks of the Jarullah family paved the way for the spread of the tribal disorder.[67] These were most probably government-supported punitive expeditions to eradicate 'Asi's influence among the Shammar and consolidate Jarullah's authority over who mutualized whose interests with the officials and elites in Mosul.

Although hostilities between the rival groups and raids on villages occasionally took place, the Mosul Shammar were mostly peaceful until 1912 when the Baghdad and Mosul Shammar were united

---

[66] CADN, Serie D, 166PO/D54/10, Damascus, 28 February 1905.
[67] BOA, DH.TMIK-M 181/7, 27 Ağustos 1320 [9 September 1904].

under the authority of Humaidi Bey. This calm confirms both analyses: the plots of the provincial authorities to design the Shammar sheikh-ship according to their interests played a considerable part in the tribal disturbances around Mosul. Equally important was to ensure the tribal consent, its negligence made the control of such a 'liquid' society impossible and paved the way for a reign of chaos and disorder.

The turmoil in Mosul following the death of Farhan Pasha demon-strates that reconciliation between the state authorities and tribal leaders remained a precondition for the maintenance of state-tribe relations until the later periods of the empire. The alternative was chaos, conflict and disorder. Therefore, and in light of the Ottoman documents referred to earlier, it was not a deliberate imperial policy but a local action caused by the complex relations and disputes between the local authorities, notables and rival sheikhs brought about by the 'misinterpretation' of the new imperial policy with regard to nomads. In addition, it clarifies that the Shammar did not lose their coercive means and fighting capability during Farhan's sheikhship and stayed peaceful for the sake of reconciliation. They were as powerful as in the Tanzimat period vis-à-vis the empire. Furthermore, it indicates that the tribal sheikhs who were supported by the majority of their tribe were still among the most influential actors of the region and could ruin the regional order in spite of the considerable government investment in regional security in the sense of recruiting new soldiers and establishing new villages. Finally, 'Asi's opposition and frustration stemmed from his exclusion from the system by the local elites and state authorities. Different from his grandfather Safuq, he struggled to become a partner of the empire rather than resisting imperial designs and attacks to expel the Shammar from the imperial lands.

The Reinstatement of *Khuwwa* in the Shammar Territories

An important outcome of the Shammar-Milli conflict and disputes in the Mosul province was the restoration of the practice of *khuwwa* in the region. As the abolition of *khuwwa* constituted an important precondition of the state-tribe compromise, dispute and hostility nat-urally resulted from its restoration. The reinstatement of *khuwwa* may also be considered a tribal weapon to force the state into partnership as with the Mosuli Shammar. As the Shammar's pastures were located in the same place, neighbouring the agricultural lands, it was difficult for the imperial authorities to dissuade them from imposing *khuwwa* on the peasants and settled tribes cultivating the district without the cooperation of the Shammar sheikhs.[68] The help of the pro-government sheikhs like Shellal[69] and the deployment of troops in some districts that the nomads used for pasture to protect peasants[70] were ineffective as the major Shammar branches broke the truce. This caused a regional disorder which gave an opportunity to the lesser sheikhs to obtain maximum profit from the situation by reimposing *khuwwa*.[71]

By 1900, the resurrection of *khuwwa* brought about serious eco-nomic consequences harmful to the Ottoman treasury. The nomads' plunder and double taxation forced some agricultural tribes and peas-ants to emigrate to Iran depriving the Ottomans from their tax revenues.[72] The following year, as a result of some Shammar groups' plunder of the harvest and *khuwwa* exactions, other peasants, having lost all their crops, considered leaving their lands in the Jazira.[73] The potential loss of such fertile lands compelled the Ottoman central and local authorities to take fundamental steps to release the peasants and agricultural tribes from the burden of double taxation. To achieve this, they started to build two military outposts, one in Zimar and another in the village of Abu Wahya on the desert frontier.[74]

All coercive measures applied by the imperial authorities were, how-ever, hopeless as the nomads maintained regionwide plunder in the form of *khuwwa*: the *mutasarrıf* of Urfa reported in 1907 that some 250,000 camels and 10,000 sheep owned by peasants and settled tribes in the region were forcibly taken over a number of years and around 100 members of the plundered settled tribes and peasants were killed

[68] BOA, DH.MKT 1961/108, 2 Haziran 1308 [15 June 1892]; BOA, DH.MKT 1945/30, 19 Nisan 1308 [2 May 1892].
[69] BOA, BEO 338/25348, 25 Kanun-ı Evvel 1309 [7 January 1894]; later documents demonstrate that 200 camel corps were conscripted for Shirgat and Zimar and the construction of military barracks was planned: BOA, BEO 345/ 25862, 9 Şubat 1309 [22 February 1894].
[70] BOA, BEO 254/19037, 29 Temmuz 1309 [10 August 1893]; BOA, BEO 306/ 22916, 24 Eylül 1309 [7 October 1893].
[71] BOA, BEO 329/24639, 6 Kanun-ı Evvel 1309 [19 December 1893].
[72] BOA, BEO 1443/108210, 6 Şubat 1315 [19 February 1900].
[73] BOA, DH.TMIK-M 114/60, 17 Teşrin-i Evvel 1317 [30 October 1901].
[74] BOA, BEO 2027/152012, 10 Mart 1319 [23 March 1903].

by the Bedouin nomads during hostilities. The Bedouin were so out of control that they even took animals from the outskirts of Urfa, a major area of the Shammar-Milli conflict. Consequently, annual imperial tax revenues from their animals and agricultural products dropped considerably.[75] By 1908, the extortion of *khuwwa* was so widespread around Mosul that even the villages in the immediate vicinity of the city centre were taxed by the Bedouin groups: they demanded 5 gurush for every sheep and goat and 20 gurush per camel.[76]

Another reason for the increase in demands for *khuwwa* was the significant drop in numbers of the mobile corps during the decade-long hostilities between the Shammar and Milli tribes up to 1908, and the mobilization of these troops to suppress the Milli uprising of the same year.[77] In the absence of a powerful reconciled sheikh to keep the Shammar in check and effective security measures to complement it as well as fewer, if any, camel and mule corps, the Bedouin were able to resume their demands for *khuwwa*.[78] In early 1910, in cooperation with the Dulaim tribe, they were able to plunder 7,000 sheep belonging to the Abu Hamid tribe on the outskirts of the devastated city of al-Hadra. Shortly afterwards, similar raids were made on other tribes.[79] An unsuccessful expedition was organized to return stolen animals,[80] as only a very small number of the animals plundered by the Dulaim were restored to their owners.[81]

The hostilities and regional chaos also resulted in the renewal of the tribal exactions on the caravans.[82] In 1910, for instance, the French vice-consul in Mosul, reported that 'none of the cameleers or herdsmen could cross the desert without paying these nomads [the Shammar] a fixed fee per head of cattle, or some of the levies they transported'. They prevented a flock of sheep going from Mosul to Syria through the

---

[75] BOA, DH.TMIK-M 238/21, 2 Mart 1323 [15 March 1907].
[76] BOA, DH.SYS 26/2-1, 8 Eylül 1324 [21 September 1908].
[77] BOA, DH.MKT 2676/88, 19 Teşrin-i Sani 1324 [2 December 1908].
[78] BOA, DH.MKT 2861/30, 16 Mayıs 1325 [29 May 1909].
[79] CADN, Serie A, 18PO/47, Aleppo (Transmitting the vice-consul at Mosul), 15 February 1910.
[80] CADN, Serie A, 18PO/47, Aleppo (Transmitting the vice-consul at Mosul), 21 April 1910.
[81] CADN, Serie D, 166PO/D54/10, Mosul, 21 April 1910.
[82] See, for example, FO 195/2095, 'General Report upon the Vilayet of Aleppo', 13 May 1901.

Jazira desert and forced its owner to pay *khuwwa* which was higher than in previous years, and, according to the merchants' claims, amounted to 1,000 Ltq for 200,000 sheep. It was significantly more than the amount demanded by the government. The merchants of Mosul applied to Nazım Pasha, the governor of Baghad, and sent telegrams to their deputies in the Ottoman parliament to put pressure on local government to force them to act against the Bedouin. Local newspapers criticized the governor's inability to prevent such demands.[83] As a consequence of their lobbying activities in Baghdad and Istanbul, Nazım Pasha mobilized a force of 1,500 horsemen against the Shammar from Baghdad, and a number of other troops from Mosul, Deir al-Zor and Mardin also took part although there is no report regarding its achievements or failure.[84]

The collapse of regional order also caused the friendly sheikhs to return to the practice of *khuwwa*. The description by Gertrude L. Bell of the Tikrit-Mosul road is interesting in terms of disclosing the exactions by the sheikh of the Baghdadi Shammar, Mujwal Bey on the caravans:

The road from Tekrit to Mosul is in Shammar territory, so far as it can be said to be in the territory of any one. Not a caravan passes up and down but it pays tribute to Mejwal [Mujwal] ibn Farhan [sic], a beshlik (three piasters) on every mule, and half a beshlik for a donkey, unless the travelers happen to be escorted by a zaptieh as I was. Muleteers cannot afford zaptiehs, and when they see two spearmen of the tribe upon the road, they pay and lodge no complaint in deaf ears. Sheikh Mejwal, who is the strongest of Farhan's fourteen sons, levies a tax from all the Jebbur [Jabbur], the tribe that camps along the river, and I was told that whereas the Jebbur had once been breeders of horses, now they breed none, finding it an unprofitable labour with the Shammar sheikhs alert to seize every likely mare.[85]

The difference for a reconciled tribe was that when there was a Zabtiye [Ottoman police] accompanying the caravan then the tribesmen did not demand exactions, demonstrating their recognition of government authority.

<hr>

[83] CADN, Serie A, 18PO/47, Aleppo (Transmitting the vice-consul at Mosul), 4 November 1910; CADN, 18PO/47, Aleppo (Transmitting the vice-consul at Mosul), 29 December 1910.

[84] CADN, Serie D, 166PO/D54/10, Mosul, 20 January 1911.

[85] Bell, *Amurath to Amurath*, 125.

Conclusion

When Ottoman rule was reinstated with the Tanzimat reforms from
the early 1840s, the existence of nomadic groups like the Shammar and
Anizah was perceived by the imperial authorities as a threat to the
consolidation of state authority. As this chapter demonstrates, by
1870, in the case of the Shammar tribes, due to the tribal resistance
and the transformation of the imperial ideology to 'pragmatism' stemming from the obvious failure of attempts to subjugate the nomads as
well as the transformation of the imperial and global circumstances,
rivalry replaced affirmation, containment and collaboration, and the
sheikhs became the partners of empire. A similar transformation took
place in the position of the tribes; Farhan Pasha, who already understood that he had to give some concessions to the government to put an
end to antagonism with the empire, dominated the Shammar
tribesmen.

The unity of the Shammar under the authority of one paramount
sheikh constituted an important component of the politics of negotiation which prevented further imperial intervention into the tribal
affairs and transformed the tribal confederations into a single political
unit. By the 1890s, the death of Farhan who had successfully controlled
his fellow tribesmen increased the tribal dependence on the provinces
and this may be described as the 'provincialization' of the nomads. On
the other hand, the Shammar-Milli conflict and disputes between
Sheikh 'Asi and the Mosul government demonstrate the level of the
empire-nomads partnership: the Deir al-Zor government acted before
the central government as if they were the advocates of Faris Pasha and
wholeheartedly defended the tribal interests. As for the incidents in
Mosul, Sheikh 'Asi fought for the favour of the empire which was
almost a precondition for full control of the tribe as they were incorporated into the imperial system.

The result of the conflict with the Mosuli Shammar was the restoration of collection of *khuwwa* in the region, which can be seen as an
example of the limits of the compromise: as in the case of Sheikh 'Asi,
when the sheikhs were not reconciled as partners by the state, they
chose to reinstate the old system to force the state into partnership. Due
to the difficulty of determining their responsibilities, even the reconciled groups resumed the collection of *khuwwa*, which was detrimental
for the imperial system of taxation.

6 | Taxation

The Collection of the Shammar and Anizah Duties

If the sole objective of the government was to collect a certain amount of revenue for the imperial treasury, this might easily have been accomplished by imposing a duty on wool, butter and lambs brought for sale to the towns on the outskirts of the desert, and the burden of tax would equally have fallen on the nomadic tribes through an equivalent reduction of the price of their produce. But the collection of taxes from the Bedouins seems to have been contemplated as a means of bringing them into subjection, which end would not be attained by that simple mode of levying them. Still, it was not by sending troops to fire upon them if they refused to pay that such a purpose could be realized, and this attempt, like the previous experiment, only had the effect of driving the tribes to an inaccessible distance.[1]

Taxes are assessed on account of the *sheikh* . . . the assessed taxes are again collected by the sheikh.[2]

To support the cost of their occupation, the British, like the Turks, taxed the local tribes, using the sheikhs to collect the money and giving them a percentage as a reward. Like all his colleagues, [Captain] Dickson [the British Revenue officer at Suq al Shuyukh] was challenged continually by the cleverness of the local Arabs . . . Since there were no records of how much money their predecessors, the Turks, had received, Dickson asked the first sheikh he encountered how many date palm trees he had been taxed on by the Ottoman administration. 'By God, O Dickson, I know not,' the sheikh answered. 'Rot,' Dickson said, 'of course you know quite well. Now how many trees did you pay on in 1914?' 'By your head, mine eyes, I know not,' the sheikh responded. 'Write fifteen hundred!' he commanded. Dickson jotted down that number in his book and collected from the man the

---

[1] FO 195/1067, Aleppo, 16 August 1875.   [2] Günday, *İki Devir Bir İnsan*, 202.

appropriate tax. Several days later an informer showed Dickson an old Turkish tax receipt stating that the sheikh owned 5,000 trees. Dickson ordered the sheikh to appear at his office and asked him to explain. 'Five thousand, sayest thou, my dear?' asked the sheikh. 'By God, it is very strange!' Then, with a generous sweep of his hand, he ordered Dickson, 'Y'Allah! Write down six thousand, my friend. Let us not quarrel.' It was only several months later, however, after the sheikh had become a friend, that Dickson asked him how many date trees he really owned. 'God alone knoweth,' the sheikh replied, 'but there cannot be less than ninety thousand.'[3]

The Question of the Nomad Taxes: An Overview

The British consul's report very well describes the Tanzimat practice of tax collection by the irregular troops. However, he dismisses that the Ottoman authorities had abandoned such practices at the time when this report was sent and adopted the method he advised for the taxation of tribal produce. The proposed method was also ineffectual for the tribal animals which constituted an important amount of the tribal duties due to the mobility of the nomads and insufficient means of coercion available to the government.[4] The remarks of Ahmet Faik Bey, who worked in the various districts of Iraq including the tribal areas as the *mutasarrıf*, and the story conveyed by Gertrude L. Bell after the British occupation of Iraq demonstrate the transformation of the Ottoman tax collection practices after the establishment of the state-tribe partnership which was merely a return to the centuries-old practice of tax-farming based on a bargain between sheikh and the officials.

The increase of the sheikhly role in the process did not transform collecting the Bedouin taxes into an easy job as it constituted a fundamental problem up to the late 1880s until the creation of the mobile corps who increased the government authority in the tribal society and consolidated the sheikh's position against his fellow tribesmen when they refused paying the allocated amount. Supporting the sheikhs with troops not only increased the imperial revenues, but also made their authority in the tribal society stronger and enhanced their

---

[3] Wallach, *The Desert Queen*, 293.
[4] A document dated 1876 for instance informs that the Anizah taxes could not be collected in the market established at Hama due to the fact that they did not come there that year: BOA, İ.ŞD 31/1491, 13 Nisan 1292 [26 April 1876].

loyalty to the Ottoman Empire, which was a major goal of the Hamidian policies adopted towards the local autonomous forces.

It is worth mentioning here that the tribal taxes were not only an instrument to establish a hierarchical relationship between the empire and the nomads, and provide the tribal recognition of the imperial authority. The taxes economic value was also the target of the imperial officials. Although the taxes exacted on them did not aggregate a sizable amount, their addition to the Ottoman treasury was still important as it seriously lacked revenues in an age of reforms. As explained in a recent study,[5] different from the European industrial powers, the Ottoman economy remained largely agricultural until the very end of the empire and did not produce a generous industrial output, which compelled the government to take each taxable piece into consideration, including the duties of the nomads, to be able to survive against the European empires. This acute need for new tax resources multiplied after the loss of the Balkan territories after the Ottoman-Russian War of 1877–1878 which necessitated the government to organize mobile corps to pursue the nomads in the desert for the effective collection of their taxes.

The government officials thus made an effort to tax tribal produce and property. However, it was the tribal animals that were difficult for the officials to tax, not the produce that the British consul mentioned: mobility of the tribes enabled them through a series of manoeuvres to evade the *wadi*, a special and profitable tax imposed by the government on the nomads' animals.[6] The proposed measures had, indeed, already been carried out by certain Ottoman authorities long before the cited dispatch to the Foreign Office, and Bedouin access to sedentary areas had been contingent on their regular tax payments.[7] These measures also remained ineffective as a major problem regarding the taxation of Bedouin property was catching and counting their animals and calculating the precise contribution to the imperial treasury, which, as

---

[5] Özbek, *İmparatorluğun Bedeli*.

[6] The *wadi* was usually collected as camel, horse, sheep and goat. Camels were not preferred by the government as it is difficult to sell it in the market. Sheep were the ideal was as they were easy to sell and could be used to feed the soldiers: MW 1/14, 8 Teşrin-i Evvel 1310 [21 October 1894].

[7] See, for example, BOA, İ.DH 213/12410, 7 Cemaziyelevvel 1266 [21 April 1850]; in some years they did not come to the regions they regularly visited and their taxes could not be collected. For an example from Hama, see: BOA, İ.ŞD 31/1491, 13 Nisan 1292 [26 April 1876].

indicated in the conversation between Dickson and the sheikh, could never be appropriately achieved until the end of the Ottoman era. As such, the government took several ineffectual steps: in 1867, for instance, the Ottoman government tried to count the animals of the Bedouin by issuing them ownership documents, thus officially registering them. Animals without documentation would automatically be considered stolen property. However, implementation of this measure was no simple matter as, in many locations, the Ottoman authorities could only register the animals of agricultural nomads. In 1872, the State Council issued a proclamation requiring animals to be sold in designated town markets in a bid to limit tax evasion by the Bedouin and livestock merchants. Due to the practical challenges of this initiative, however, it was declared optional in 1897. Similar unsuccessful attempts were made in 1910 and 1913 to count the Bedouin's livestock animals to calculate appropriate taxation.[8]

Given such complications, the taxes of the Bedouin were largely collected on the basis of estimation. Although the tax collection was known as animal counting [*ta'dad-ı ağnam*] in the desert, as is also clear in Dickson's story, the imperial authorities never knew precisely how many animals – or trees – the Bedouin had, and throughout the imperial period they were forced to rely on the numbers that the tribesmen volunteered although they bargained over the declared amount as the British revenue officer did. Even given such a concession, imperial authorities faced obstacles in collecting the Bedouin duties which necessitated extensive effort. During the Tanzimat period, in the absence of a sufficient number of Ottoman fortifications on the desert frontier and the lack of sufficient troops to visit the nomads' camps peacefully to exact their duties, coercive measures were put into practice using irregular troops. But such methods increased the number of tribal attacks on the villages where the nomads frequented to compensate the taxed property. Consequently, even after the consolidation of the Ottoman position in the desert frontier and completion of the expansionist expeditions in Deir al-Zor and southern Syria, they had to be treated with great sensitivity [*hüsn-i muamele*] and persuaded to pay their duties largely by the agency of their sheikhs.

As exemplified in the conversation between the sheikh and Dickson, after the adoption of the politics of negotiation based on reconciliation

---

[8] Barakat, 'Marginal Actors?'.

with the tribes, taxes imposed on the Bedouin became a matter of negotiation and were often collected by means of a negotiated compromise with Bedouin communities and the cooperation of their sheikhs although the sum did never reach an amount the imperial authorities desired as the sheikhs had also to observe the conditions and interests of their fellow tribesmen. Compromises were hard-won in such a delicate matter and the imperial authorities had to make considerable concessions including dropping their intention to count Bedouin animals, handsomely remunerating their sheikhs and giving 1/4 share of the *wadi* to sheikhs. Consequently, the desert remained an impenetrable area for imperial authorities, which inevitably established the Bedouin realm as a locus of tax evasion for urban livestock traders, as late as the early 1890s. However, the co-optation of the sheikhs to imperial tax collection by paying them made a significant impact on the abolition of *khuwwa*, a deconstructive tribal activity in the Arab countryside for the Ottoman taxation. In addition, the *wadi*'s efficiency and regularity increased with the establishment of the mobile camel and mule corps which enabled the imperial army to penetrate into the depth of the desert to collect the taxes under the guidance of the sheikh who also profited from tax collection. The amount was still moderate and not heavy for the tribal groups, but, as mentioned previously, important for the Ottoman treasury. In addition, the appearance of the imperial troops near the tribal encampments made the state more visible, which contributed to the improvement of the security situation in the desert frontier and persuaded the nomads to reconcile with the officials. Furthermore, the *wadi*'s regular collection automatically augmented the provincial revenues that made the nomadic taxes an issue of competition between the neighbouring provinces who contested to win central government's favour by increasing the revenues of the provincial treasury. The Bedouin nomads exploited the rivalry, and thereby won extra concessions from the authorities while maintaining the payment of their duties.

Although studies of the modernization of the Ottoman state and its changing taxation practices in the modern era have increased in number in recent years,[9] there remains virtually no research into the Ottoman experience of taxation of the Bedouin. Addressing the issues mentioned above, this chapter represents the first serious examination

---

[9] For a recent study, see: Özbek, *İmparatorluğun Bedeli*.

of how the Bedouin paid their duties and those techniques employed by the imperial authorities to achieve effective taxation as well as its impact on the transformation of the empire-tribe relations in the modern era.

Early Tax Collection Practices and Challenges

Collection of the Shammar and Anizah taxes had been problematic for some time prior to the Tanzimat reforms and their establishment of an Ottoman bureaucracy. This was in large part due to the lack of a 'social contract' between them and the Ottoman government as the nomads in practice denied the empire as their superior authority. This was accompanied by regional chaos that resulted from their mass migrations along with their hundreds and thousands of animals from Najd at the close of the eighteenth century. Their dispersal across the Syrian, Anatolian and Iraqi provinces had greatly impaired the Ottoman taxation system in the desert and rural countryside. In addition, the minimization of the Ottoman state in the Arab provinces due to conflicts between central government and the ruling elites of the provinces – the likes of the Jalilis, Azms and Mamluks – and wars with Mehmed Ali of Egypt had almost totally destroyed the Ottoman authority and system of taxation which granted almost total freedom from government pressure to the nomadic groups in the regions to which they had recently migrated. These communities thus vigorously opposed any modernization of the state apparatus and attempts to regularize their payments.

Irregular Troops, Coercive Policies and the Bedouin Taxes

As a result of the 'government-free conditions' of the first decades of the nineteenth century, the Ottoman officials of the 1840s were faced with great difficulties in getting the nomadic groups' consent to pay their taxes. The ambiguous form of relationship between the state and the nomads, and both sides' ignorance about the other caused frequent hostilities and created contradictory and arbitrary taxation practices. From the outset, the Bedouin groups refused to recognize the Ottoman bureaucrats as the superior authority of taxation, with associated rights to impose taxes on them, and thus withheld payment. Great difficulties arose when Ottoman tax collectors paid an initial visit to the Bedouin groups and informed them of imperial orders requiring payment of their duties, *wadi*: in many places, the tribesmen humiliated the tax collectors by expelling them from their tribal districts.

The Ottoman struggle was twofold in almost all the tribal districts: enforcing the nomads to pay taxes to the imperial authority and collection of the taxes from the lesser tribes associated with the Anizah and Shammar nomads. The lesser tribes initially refused payment as they already had the nomads as their taxation authority in the form of *khuwwa*. In 1841, for instance, tribes around Deir al-Zor refused the pasha of Aleppo's tax demand and rebelled against him since they had just signed a treaty with the Anizah, accepting their protection in return for the regular payment of a certain sum of *khuwwa*.[10] Thus, the Ottomans had to both prevent the practice of *khuwwa* and collect the duties from the nomads – and their associates – in order to become the taxation authority.

The acute need of the provincial – and imperial – treasury for revenues to reinstate the government and expand it, however, directed the officials to use every means to collect the tribal taxes. The Aleppo government organized a military expedition to the region the next year under the command of the *Mutesellim* [deputy governor] and the taxes were collected without opposition from all Arab tribes even those who were less willing to pay.[11] The expedition was most likely prior to the Anizah's arrival in the region and thus the *Mutesellim* could take two-thirds of the revenues demanded of the Bedouin in the Deir al-Zor region without much resistance. They also promised to pay 100,000 piasters, the remaining amount that was required from them.[12] Later reports, however, reveal the difficulty of regular collection of tribal taxes in the district presumably due to the continuation of the structural problems which stemmed from the double taxation.[13] The absence of a physical Ottoman presence in the region which would protect the lesser tribes against the nomads and break the alliance between them most likely constituted the prime reason preventing the regular collection of taxes.

---

[10] CADN, Serie D, 166PO/D1/47, Aleppo, 15 March 1842.
[11] CADN, Serie D, 166PO/D1/47, Aleppo, 31 March 1842.
[12] CADN, Serie D, 166PO/D1/47, Aleppo, 30 April 1842.
[13] CADN, Serie D, 166PO/D1/49, Aleppo, 1 January 1846; AMAE, CPC, Turquie, Aleppo-1, 29 January 1846.

The great amount demanded by the officials due to the needs of the treasury, the lack of protection against the nomads and the uncompromising imperial attitude to exacting taxes also caused reaction from the smaller tribes who would normally be less resistant to changing their taxation authority. The authorities *ex parte* decided on a certain amount and instructed the tribe to pay it without providing a protective shelter against the nomads who also maintained to request their share, that is, *khuwwa*. When a sheikh was unable to pay the duty imposed on him, he, or some of his relatives, were seized and imprisoned by troops, and the tribe was compelled to pay the fixed amount. Following the liberation of the sheikh, members of the tribe would lie in wait and plunder the first caravan passing through their region, or attacked a village that paid its taxes regularly, which could 'yield them three times the amount'.[14] Thus, the regular collection of the duties of the smaller tribes would not be possible until the abolition of *khuwwa*, the recognition of the Ottoman government as the sole authority of taxation and the adoption of a more flexible policy of taxation by imperial officials.

The methods employed against the nomadic groups were not essentially different. As detailed previously, in cooperation with local elites and employing mainly irregular troops, the government authorities initially introduced coercive measures, organized military expeditions and captured their animals to subjugate the nomads and 'collect' the official revenues.[15] An important reason for using these methods was the 'state of war' between the nomads and the Ottoman state at that time. Another related cause was the lack of infrastructural tools like the fortifications in the desert frontier and the mobile corps to collect the tribal duties peacefully.

The Aleppo and Damascus governments followed these practices against those nomadic groups who were reluctant to pay their duties. Their animals were seized in a number of places and sold in return for long-standing 'tax arrears'.[16] As rightly noted by the British

[14] Wellsted, *Travels*, 167–168.
[15] For the Shawaye in the Aleppo region, see: FO 195/170, Aleppo, 30 December 1841; for the Jabbur tribe in the Mosul region: FO 195/228, Mosul, 29 November 1844; for the Anizah at Deir al-Zor, see: FO 195/207, Aleppo, 27 September 1845; for the Wuld 'Ali tribe of the Hawran, see: FO 195/196, Damascus, 10 May 1842.
[16] See, for example, BOA, İ.DH 231/13860, 3 Cemaziyelevvel 1267 [7 March 1851].

consul in Aleppo, these campaigns established a pattern of 'acts of oppression and injustice' carried out by local authorities.[17] In a similar vein, the tax-paying peasants were forbidden to sell grain to the nomads to force the latter to pay their camel, horse and sheep taxes. In response, the nomads fell upon the government revenue sources plundering the tax-paying tribes and peasants, and emigrated to the boundaries of another province to escape taxation – at least temporarily – and 'to get their grain at more moderate rates'.[18] What the Ottoman troops collected as tax at that time in cooperation with the provincial power magnates was indeed the booty that was captured by the irregulars from the nomads as a result of their punitive expeditions explained in Chapter 1. They were legitimized as 'tax' to add them to the provincial treasuries.

These hostilities were however never resolved to the government's advantage and never solved the financial deficiencies of the provincial administrations due to their weakness vis-à-vis the nomads. As detailed previously, government troops were defeated on a number of occasions by the Anizah and Shammar, and a great number of casualties were inflicted on both sides between 1841 and 1846. As there was no restriction and rule detaining the sides, 'state of war' – or 'state of nature' in the Hobbesian sense – is the best descriptive phrase explaining the relations between the nomads and the government during this era during which they fought for the maximization of their booty. The government's irregulars targeted the nomads' flocks while the latter captured the products and animals of the settled tribes and the peasants on the desert frontier, an important source of tax revenue for the government.

Imperial rulers soon appreciated the inefficacy of coercion in dealing with the nomads, which resulted in significant losses for both the provincial and imperial economy, and instead invited them to the negotiation table, concluding ultimately in an agreed settlement that generated certain revenues. This half-hearted agreement in 1846 with the Anizah of Damascus and Aleppo, addressed both sides' obligations, with the state benefiting rather more. Ottoman documents imply that other Bedouin groups had similar experiences. These arrangements appear to echo the proposal made by the British consul in the

---

[17] FO 195/207, Aleppo, 14 June 1845 and 9 August 1845.
[18] FO 195/228, Mosul, 6 September 1845.

correspondence quoted at the start of this chapter, although its implementation varied significantly from one year to the next.

The government initially proposed the following conditions to the
Anizah: the Bedouin were required to 'promise that they would not
plunder the provinces in Arabistan [Syria and Iraq] and the Urfa
province'; doing so would be considered a 'violation of the promise
[*muğayir-i taahhüt*]' and they would be forced to compensate for all
damages. In addition, the government would take 20 gurush tax from
each camel sold in the city and they would be compelled to provide
1,000 camels to the Ottoman army. To avert the violation of the
contract, four principal tribesmen would be held hostage in Aleppo
and Damascus. In return for adhering to the contract, the tribesmen
would be allowed to sell their products and buy what they required in
Aleppo as their trade with the peasants was proposed to be conditioned
to the official permit. Predictably, the Anizah rejected the proposed
contract as they derived no benefit from it and as it merely confirmed as
'privilege' what they were already enjoying. The government
responded by arresting 117 Anizah, who were on the city outskirts to
trade, thereby forcing the sheikhs to accept the government offer.[19]

The Anizah tribe was coerced by the army to fulfil some of its
'promises' the following season. They delivered 782 camels to the
provincial treasury and considerable taxes were raised from the sale
of their camels in Aleppo. A sign of their discontent at the imposed
contract came immediately after the tribesmen's departure from the
city when they plundered 250 camels of a Hamidi village to compensate
their 'losses'.[20] The following year, collection of Bedouin taxes and
ensuring tribal peace was only achieved with the mobilization of
a substantial number of troops and recruitment of many irregulars.
This incurred more expenses for the local treasury than was generated
by the tax income from the Bedouin. The great tribal confederations of
Hawran like the Ruwalla, Seb'a and Wuld 'Ali paid the *wadi* 'reconciled' a year earlier with the 'assistance' of these troops. Bedouin
incursions around Hawran, Hama and Homs were prevented by
deploying numbers of troops in various positions. However, in spite
of this military intervention, it proved impossible to compel the

---

[19] BOA, İ.MVL 81/1597, 21 Receb 1262 [16 July 1846]; see also, BOA, A.MKT
      50/45, 28 Ramazan 1262 [19 September 1846].
[20] BOA, A.MKT 56/34, 1 Zilhicce 1262 [20 November 1846].

Bedouin to act against their will. Many tribes united against the government around Hama and Homs, refusing to pay the heavy taxes imposed on them. Hostilities ensued between government troops and the Bedouin around Ma'arre, Tel Sultan, Hazira and Abd al-Jabbar fought with 6,000 troops. The Bedouin also attacked tribes like the Hadidin, described by the Ottoman officials as 'the loyal tribes' [*aşayir-i mutia*] who paid their taxes to the government regularly. The government failed to retaliate effectively as the Bedouin simply vanished into the desert when pursued by Ottoman soldiers, and the troops became tired quickly in the extreme heat.[21]

The method was similar in other provinces: in Aleppo, the Anizah were forced to accept a figure of 750 camels in taxes by the government officials in response to their offer of 600. In return, the Arabs were allowed back into the towns.[22] The Anizah sheikhs reconciled with the *mutesellim* receiving the camels agreed in a treaty with the Anizah sheikh Dahham, whom the government had to recognize as their sheikh.[23] However, the *mutesellim* was only able to take 200 camels as the nomads were to have free trade with Aleppo and so they paid the usual due of 3 gazis per head on all sales.[24]

Everlasting conflict was not sustainable for the tribes either, and reconciliation was beneficial for them, given their dependence on sedentary areas for trade and shopping, and thus both sides eventually engaged in negotiations. The Bedouin sheikhs objected to the overtaxation and argued that their fellow tribesmen would rebel against them if they were forced to pay such amounts in a single instalment. Some local elites stood as guarantor for the Bedouin and, as a result, an agreement was reached by breaking down the *wadi* demanded of the Bedouin into several instalments.[25] This was a strategic request for the nomads as the revenue collection was not an easy task for the government. Applying the same measures such as the mobilization of the troops several times in a year would definitely make already weak government mechanisms tired and reduce the efficiency of revenue

---

[21] BOA, İ.DH 149/7754, 11 Cemaziyelahir 1263 [28 May 1847] and 14 Cemaziyelahir 1263 [31 May 1847].
[22] FO 195/302, Aleppo, 29 May 1847.   [23] FO 195/302, Aleppo, 19 June 1847.
[24] FO 195/302, Aleppo, 24 June 1847.
[25] BOA, İ.DH 149/7754, 11 Cemaziyelahir 1263 [28 May 1847] and 14 Cemaziyelahir 1263 [31 May 1847].

exaction. This would give an opportunity to the nomads to evade at least some of the instalments.

The agreement could not be sustained too long for reasons that stemmed from both sides. As explained in Chapter 2, the lack of sufficient regular troops to put the state-tribe agreement into practice and the 'state of war' between the Fid'an and the government analysed in Chapter 1 constituted the primary reasons for its failure. Although they initiated a process of reconciliation, neither side renounced their old habits entirely as the hostilities carried on. Reciprocal raids continued even in times of peace. The difficulty for the officials to prohibit the irregular tribal troops in the government service from organizing 'punitive expeditions' against the nomads and for the sheikhs to detain sub-branches from attacking the villages made the sustenance of a compromise almost impossible unless the sides maintained good relations. In 1849, for instance, a group of government troops attacked several Anizah branches from the south and north and forcibly extracted their tax payments.[26] In response, branches of the Anizah launched an assault on the Karakechili tribe of Diarbekir and stole a considerable number of animals and goods from their villages.[27]

The difficulty in collecting the Anizah taxes mainly stemmed from the Fid'an-state conflict during the 1840s which ruined the rural order and made the collection of the tribal taxes impossible due to the fact that they usually revolted against the Ottoman authority. The rise of Jed'an in the early 1850s, however, somewhat facilitated tax collection as the sheikh was more reconcilable. As detailed in Chapter 2, he also enjoyed good relations with the commanders of the irregular troops such as Hajı Batran which smoothed the state-Fid'an relationship and made consensual tax collection among the nomads possible although not to a desired level. To that end, the governor of Aleppo, Muhammad Pasha, visited the Anizah sheikh Jed'an several years later near Deir al-Zor, secured his loyalty by agreeing the amount of tax to be paid to the imperial treasury and presented him with a robe of honour.[28] This represented a major step for the imperial government which demonstrated at that time that the it implicitly accepted the sheikh's authority, but this, too, met with little success.

---

[26]   BOA, İ.DH 200/11461, Damascus, 13 Ramazan 1265 [3 August 1849].
[27]   BOA, İ.MVL 145/4072, 16 Şaban 1265 [8 July 1849].
[28]   FO 195/302, Aleppo, 5 April 1851.

The diplomacy between the government and the Anizah over the following years led to more acceptable agreements for the nomads and further concessions were made, in particular reducing the amount or value of the property to be paid to the treasury. Equally, a more flexible approach was adopted: in 1851, for example, as a requirement of the contract [*mukavele*], the Anizah paid 800 sheep and 10 camels, which was much less when compared to the previous years and there is no record of any plundering that year by members of their branches.[29] In later years, the officials had to accept the postponement of tax payments to the following year, inevitably meaning some debts were never paid.[30] The lack of sufficient number of troops was the primary reason for the government to accept such compromise, which was obviously to the detriment of the imperial treasury.

If the governors wanted Bedouin groups to pay their taxes in full, they had to spend a great deal of money and mobilize substantial numbers of soldiers. Sustaining such a state of emergency soon became unworkable. When the commander of the Ottoman army in Iraq demanded 2,000 camels, 100 horses and 6,000 sheep from the Anizah, presumably as the amount of the taxes in arrears, he had to mobilize 1,200 soldiers just to secure the roads around Baghdad to prevent the tribes from escaping. In addition, further troops and batteries were deployed at intervals along the road from Deir al-Zor to Muntafiq to limit the tribes' movement. Clearly, the Ottoman government – or any government at that time – could not afford financially and militarily to repeat such measures every year.[31] Moreover, even the Ottomans' taking of influential Bedouin hostages failed to achieve its ends of forcing tribes to pay their taxes as tribesmen united and rejected Ottoman demands.

Although we do not have much evidence about the taxation of the Shammar it is not difficult to estimate the situation. The Baghdad government presumably could not exact any taxes from the Shammar during the hostilities with Safuq and taxation became possible when there was peace with Farhan. But, as explained in the previous chapters, the tribal sheikhs continued to exact *khuwwa* till 1862 from the caravans and villages and a salary was paid to them for the protection

---

[29] This time the term contract [*mukavele*] substituted the word promise [*taahhüt*], which indicates that a written proof was taken from the Bedouin: BOA, İ.DH. 236/14227, 4 Şaban 1267 [5 June 1851].

[30] For some examples, see: BOA, MVL 2, 9 Ramazan 1269 [16 Haziran 1853], 41.

[31] BOA, İ.DH 399/26448, 17 Receb 1274 [4 March 1858].

of the countryside. Consequently, it might be difficult to claim an efficient taxation for the Shammar, too.

The Employment of Contractors

By the 1860s, in accordance with the changing government policy from conflict to compromise, local authorities were cooperating closely with the local elites and sheikhs by subcontracting the *wadi* collection to them in many districts while supporting them with regular or irregular troops. It was merely a return to the pre-modern tax farming practices which delegated tax collection to the local power magnates by selling this right to them or giving them a share from the total amount. Some of the contractors were themselves sheikhs, but this system created problems among the Bedouin as particularly the non-sheikh tax contractors [*Mukataaci*], in partial cooperation with officials, attempted to maximize their profits by overtaxing the tribal groups. In 1861, for instance, a branch of the al-Izza'a (Shammar[?]) tribe of Baghdad refused to pay the contractor any more than they owed. Suleiman Bey, *kaymakam* of Khurasan, sent a detachment of regular cavalry and irregular horsemen to coerce them, which led to hostilities in which nine Bedouin were killed, several more wounded and numerous properties were raided. When the incident looked like becoming a security crisis, the governor of Baghdad intervened, dismissed the *kaymakam*, had him put on trial and returned some of the property seized by the tribes.[32] In such instances, the tax-collectors' ambitions to maximize their profit frequently conflicted with the nomads' legitimate reaction to over-taxation which intercepted the creation of a working revenue-raising system.

Other testimonies support this argument and reveal additional problems of this system such as sharing of the tax revenues between the collectors and officials instead of adding them to the imperial treasury by understating the collected amount. The British consul in Damascus considered the officials, rather than the Bedouin, guilty of such disturbances: they were 'often organized by officers in command of troops in outlying districts'. The officials retained 'the best part of the booty for themselves', sending only a small portion back to headquarters. It was 'unreasonable' to expect the nomads not to respond in kind, 'whilst

[32] FO 195/676, Baghdad, 17 July 1861.

such a system [was] allowed by the civil and military authorities'.[33] Not only did these practices incite tribal revenge, but they were rarely profitable as the Bedouin learned of the intended expeditions against them, decamped and drove their flocks before them into the desert where the contracted collectors, together with the troops assisting them, were unable to pursue them. Consequently, they often had to demand a reduced amount from the Bedouin.[34]

The mobility of the nomads posed another obstacle for the regular collection of their taxes via contractors. As they remained at the imperial pastures for a certain period of the year under the tents, the Bedouin's migration to the same region the next year was not guaranteed. The yearly condition of the pastures they frequented most likely determined the nomadic routes and this constituted a major problem for the tax farmers who bought the nomads taxes in advance agreed with officials for a certain amount. Thus, they frequently requested correction in the previously agreed amount. The *mültezim* of Homs who bought the Anizah taxes requested in 1877 that his debts to the treasury belonging to the year 1872 be written off as the nomads did not migrate to the region and his request was fulfilled.[35] A similar incident happened in Hama two years later as the nomads did not visit the Anizah Bazaar that year where, as proposed by Aleppo's British Consul in the introductory quotation, their taxes were collected.[36] It was reported in 1881 from Mosul that the taxes imposed on the Shammar camels were almost completely collected,[37] while the duties of the tribe could not be collected in 1887.[38] Such problems continued until the early 1890s when the local tax collectors were deactivated with the creation of the camel and mule corps and their effective use in the collection of the tribal taxes.

Another issue of this era that stemmed from the lack of state control over the nomads' tax collection process was the tax evasion by the animal traders who entrusted their flocks to the Bedouin for grazing. Due to imperial inability and tribal refusal to count the Bedouins'

---

[33] FO 195/806, Damascus, 30 August 1866.
[34] For an example, see: BOA, ŞD 2878/7, 29 Kanun-ı Sani 1289 [11 February 1874].
[35] BOA, İ.DH 735/60253, 2 Haziran 1293 [15 June 1877].
[36] BOA, İ.ŞD 31/1491, 13 Nisan 1292 [26 April 1876].
[37] BOA, Y.PRK.ASK 10/23, 8 Kanun-ı Evvel 1297 [21 Aralık 1881].
[38] BOA, MV 21/3, 8 Haziran 1303 [21 June 1887].

livestock, the animal traders could easily move their animals to tribal regions to avoid them being taxed. Their deception was only revealed if their animals were captured by another tribe and liberated by imperial authorities.[39] The Ottoman government had issued some redundant regulations to punish tax evaders with double taxation when they were caught by the imperial authorities.[40] The documents do not specify when this method of evasion began although they imply that it continued for an extended period, and that the bureaucrats were aware of the situation. It is evident, however, that the evasion was checked immediately after Ismail Hakkı Pasha's reforms of the 'mobilization' of the desert corps, which will be detailed in the next section. Interestingly, such incidents did not take place following these reforms despite the ongoing tribal protection of traders' animals.[41] It is thus plausible that the influence of local elites over tax collection enabled these traders to keep their animals from being taxed, which prevented effective taxation and decreased the state revenues.

Compromise, Regularization and Co-optation of the Sheikhs

It appears that in the Arab provinces the contracting process was not the only method, and in some places tax collection was directly handled by the state beginning in 1860, through till the late 1880s. The establishment of the state-tribe compromise brought about the sheikhly support of the officials in their effort to collect the tribal taxes. Similar to the tax-contractors, the sheikhs became the collaborators in return for a share from the collected amount, which can be interpreted as a new version of tax-farming. The number of regular cavalries was increased, officers or *mutasarrıfs* were appointed to command them, the elites and sheikhs were co-opted into this arrangement and the use of irregular troops was stopped, thereby reducing the abuses by

[39] BOA, DH.MKT 1638/51, 3 Temmuz 1305 [16 July 1889].
[40] BOA, DH.MKT 1638/2, 1 Temmuz 1305 [14 July 1889].
[41] In 1892, a certain Lieutenant Esad Bey recovered Karmozade Yahya's animals which were grazed by the Rashidi branch of the Tay tribes and plundered by the Shammar. Instead of returning them to their owners, he counted them as government animals and took them with him. When Yahya applied to the court to retrieve his animals, the court recognized his demand and decided that all the animals should have been returned to him unconditionally. There is no reference to taxes in this case: SCR-Mardin, No. 179, Document 1, (Hüccet) 27 Cemaziyelâhir 1309 (28 Ocak 1892).

the various players in the process. These changes, for instance, allowed Ismet Pasha of Aleppo to successfully collect nomads' taxes in his province regularly for some time in the early 1860s. Wealthy individuals with significant public debt who bought the Bedouin taxes were made to pay off longstanding arrears.[42] Likewise, the Bedouin tribes like the Ruwalla and Wuld 'Ali in southern Syria finally accepted an agreed sum owing and were thus integrated into the imperial system of taxation. Midhat Pasha reported in 1879 when he governed the province of Syria that the value of the *wadi* collected from the Syrian Bedouin amounted to 40,000 purses, which could be considered relatively satisfactory compared with 53,000 purses generated by the *ashar*.[43] A document from 1903 details the local elites' and sheikhs' contribution to the *wadi* collection: Fahd al-Sha'lan, the sheikh of Ruwalla, and Ribatzade Hisham Efendi were rewarded for the contribution their tax collection made to the imperial treasury.[44] As it did elsewhere, the presence of the mule corps [*estersüvar*] in the early 1890s ensured more effective government control over the Bedouin in this region and reduced sheikhs' excuses for exempting their subjects from paying tax.[45]

In addition, the consolidation of Ottoman rule in southern Syria and the profitable business of escorting the pilgrimage caravan contributed significantly to the Ruwalla and Wuld 'Ali tribes' co-optation, and enabled the Syrian authorities to exercise more effective control over the nomads, facilitating regular tax collections in the district. As a result, these Bedouin groups tended to adhere to the truce with government authorities and would be punished by government troops if a branch violated the contract.[46] The amount owed was agreed in consultation with the sheikhs who visited cities in order to resolve this, and they signed and sealed a written document [*sened*] to that effect.[47] But tribes around the northern and central provinces of Baghdad, Mosul, Aleppo and Diarbekir could not be controlled by the Ottomans and required further action. The Shammar-Milli conflict

---

[42] FO 195/716, British Consulate Aleppo, 30 June 1862.

[43] Gedikli, 'Suriye Layihası', 186.

[44] BOA, DH.MKT 720/7, 25 Mayıs 1319 [7 June 1903].

[45] For a reference to the employment of the camel corps in the province of Syria, see: Söylemezoğlu, *Seyahatname*, 47.

[46] For an example, which belongs to 1867, see: BOA, A.MKT.MHM 391/21, 13 Cemaziyelevvel 1284 [12 September 1867].

[47] See, for example, MW 1/9, 1 Haziran 1313 [14 June 1897].

and hostilities among the various Shammar groups around Mosul for the sheikhship reduced the sheikhly authority and gave a considerable freedom to the small branches to escape from taxation, which constituted a major reason for the incorporation of the mobile corps into the tax collection activity. The Ottoman troops in the desert thus adapted their methods to the mobile character of the Bedouin, and co-opted their sheikhs into the process.

Tax Collection, the Mobile Corps and the Co-optation of the Sheikhs

The early 1880s were the formative years for the Hamidian regime that ruled the empire for about thirty years. After its consolidation, the new regime sought new revenue sources to increase the state income which had reduced considerably after the loss of the Balkan provinces in the Russian-Ottoman War of 1877–1878. It would also make the imperial economy more self-sufficient and would enable the government to undertake new infrastructural projects such as the extension of railroad and telegraph lines into the remote corners of the empire. It was mandatory for the Hamidian officials to find funding before they undertook any investment which necessitated expenditure from the treasury.

On the part of the tribe, like many communities, taxation was never a voluntary action and always required sheikhly guidance and military support. The large number of shares allocated to the sheikhs in the tax-farming system persuaded them to cooperate and the mobile corps and other infrastructural investments convinced the ordinary nomads not to resist the government demands, which did not amount to an unbearable sum. It is also worth noting that this system became practicable once the state had sufficient means of discouraging alternatives, such as prolonged continuation of collection of *khuwwa*, and just as importantly, providing credible force to support the authority of the co-opted sheikhs within their tribes.

As a result, the imperial authorities fundamentally changed the structure of the troops employed in tax collection in these provinces and co-opted the tribal sheikhs into the process in order to establish a more effective tax collection system in northern and central Syrian and Iraqi provinces as well as to increase security in the countryside. To this end, they created the mobile mule corps [*estersüvar*] and camel corps [*hecinsüvar*], and used them to raise revenue from the nomads, increase the imperial army's mobility in the desert and facilitate the sheikhs' control of his subjects' mobility.[48] As indicated in the previous chapters, from the 1860s, Ottoman officials included sheikhs to some extent in the process of governance. They paid the sheikhs handsome salaries in return for preventing their subjects from attacking the cities, villages, roads and rivers as well as protecting their own territory, thereby contributing to regional security. Negotiations with and payments to the sheikhs ensured a degree of government authority over the Bedouin and kept them in check. The sheikhs also helped officials in the collection of taxes which somewhat satisfied the government although the amount collected did not reach a level desired by the imperial authorities.[49] However, the death or weakening of the powerful sheikhs like Farhan and Jed'an, the division of the tribes into smaller branches and ongoing hostilities among the tribal groups worsened the situation further and made the collection of their taxes difficult. The introduction of the regular camel corps[50] and their incorporation into the tax collection system remarkably increased effective taxation, as they followed the tribes into the desert under the guidance of sheikhs and secured the regular collection of the Bedouin duties.[51] There were exceptions: in a few locations the old system of selling the collection of

[48] It should be noted that the mule corps were also available in southern Syria in 1880s. But they were not effectively used in collecting the Bedouin taxes, instead they accompanied the pilgrim caravans and protected the villages at the desert frontier, which indirectly facilitated the tax collection. An Ottoman report dated 1889 states that many of their animals perished and they were ineffective as their number reduced: BOA, Y.MTV 38/99, 15 Nisan 1305 [28 April 1889]. They would be reinstated around 1914: Günay, *Suriye ve Filistin Anıları*, 13.

[49] For a report expressing that the Bedouin sheikhs around Aleppo were salaried to gain their cooperation, see: BOA, MVL 1062/29, 21 Ağustos 1282 [3 September 1866]. But the author of the report warned that the number of the mobile regular troops must have been increased to be able to benefit from the employment of the sheikhs effectively; for another report by the Governor of Baghdad, Abdurrahman Nureddin Pasha, dated 1880 highlighting the need for the mobile corps, see: Ebubekir Ceylan, 'Abdurrahman Nureddin Paşa', 93.

[50] It seems that the Ottoman army tried to create irregular Dromedary corps [*hecinsüvar*] in 1867 and organize regular camel corps in 1868 to be employed against the Bedouin. FO 195/800, Aleppo, 3 December 1867; FO 195/902, Aleppo, 12 April 1868. However, the minister of War, Namık Pasha, vetoed the project due to the tribal opposition and their employment was abandoned: FO 195/902, Aleppo, 23 April 1868.

[51] For a document exemplifying the sheikh's guidance, see: BOA, ŞD 2178/13, 16 Kanun-ı Sani 1314 [29 January 1899].

tax to local elites persisted most likely due to the low amount of the taxes to be collected that made any infrastructural investment meaningless.[52]

In late 1886, an imperial initiative was launched under the aegis of Ismail Hakkı Pasha, commander of the reform troops [*Kuvve-i Islahiye Kumandanı*], the aim of which was to regulate Arab and Kurdish tribal affairs in the provinces of northern and central Syria and Iraq, and to increase the imperial revenues collected from the tribes. As stated above, the purpose was to find new revenue sources for the Hamidian regime that aimed at establishing a self-sufficient economy. To this end, the pasha advocated the establishment of the mule corps in Deir al-Zor, Aleppo, Mosul and Baghdad to keep the Bedouin in check and facilitate regular tax collection.[53] The pasha's proposal was accepted and an initial camel corps was established the following year as the situation was worsening with trouble caused by the Hamawand and Shammar.[54] The corps' number increased at regular intervals over the following years and troops were deployed in strategic locations with significant success.[55]

One of their principal tasks was to visit Bedouin camps in spring or early summer,[56] as the latter moved closer to the city outskirts, and to collect the Bedouin taxes by demonstrating a deterrent force in the desert.[57] The camel corps' number varied between 100 and 500 depending on the city and they rarely engaged in any serious conflict while shadowing the Bedouin groups. The aim was evidently to endow the soldiers with the Bedouin's mobility skills[58] and to strengthen the sheikh's hand, by inferring that the government would not tolerate tribes who refused to pay their taxes. Without these additional

---

[52] See, for example, BOA, DH.TMIK-M 153/39, Mosul, 5 Eylül 1319 [18 September 1903].

[53] BOA, İ.MMS 130/5577, 2 Haziran 1303 [15 June 1887].

[54] BOA, DH.ŞFR 135/104, 28 Nisan 1304 [11 May 1888].

[55] For an example from the Djezire region, see: BOA, BEO 342/25592, 1 Kanun-ı Sani 1309 [14 January 1894].

[56] It is described in the Ottoman documents as the accounting season [*ta'dad mevsimi*], although the animals belonging to them had never been counted.

[57] For a description, see: BOA, DH.ŞFR 325/100, 30 Mayıs 1320 [12 June 1904].

[58] Söylemezoğlu notes that the Bedouin sheikhs informed him that the mule corps could travel for 15–20 hours in a day whereas the cavalry on horseback were able to proceed for only 8–10 hours; they could only travel for two to three days, while the mule corps' endurance was much longer: Söylemezoğlu, *Seyahatname*, 61.

resources, the numbers of mule corps could never be sufficient to coerce the tribes to pay their dues.[59] Prior compromise with the nomadic communities became almost a precondition for the successful implementation of the new system, and the sheikhs' role became crucial to arrive at a reconciliation.

Negotiation thus remained the primary method to raise revenue from the desert societies in the system of mule corps-assisted tax collection. As also exemplified in the third quotation at the start of the Introduction, the sheikh was usually the authority who decided the amount to be paid to the government; this was always much lower than the required sum, which opened space for him to manoeuvre and legitimize his collaboration with the government in the eyes of his community. Similarly, the number of their animals was still unknown to the government officials and the amount to be taxed was based on that declaration. The tribes were still able to refuse additional taxes imposed by the government, such as a tax introduced in 1905 to fund the modernization of military technology [*techizat-ı askeriye rüsumu*].[60]

After the regulation of the nomadic taxes and arrival at a compromise with the nomads by the agency of their sheikhs, the excessive behaviour of the officials became disproportionately less frequent and they were lawfully punished when they acted arbitrarily while collecting the nomads' duties. In one instance, also in 1905, the Bedouin around Karbala were attacked, some tribesmen were killed and their property seized when they refused to pay extra taxes. This caused great upset in the district and peace was only restored according to the following conditions: the Bedouin were 'to have all property taken from them restored'; the officer 'responsible for the attack' on the tribes was to be dismissed; there was to be 'a reduction of the amount claimed from the Arabs as taxes'; and there should be 'the prosecution of the officer responsible for the deaths and disgrace of the Arabs'.[61]

The combination of such incidents, the employment of the mule corps and their pursuit of the Bedouin in rural areas and the desert made

---

[59] An Ottoman officer, who was well-informed about Bedouin affairs, pointed out this reality. For details, see: BOA, BEO 611/45757, 11 Nisan 1311 [24 April 1896]; many other reports imply the difficulty of coercing the Bedouin to accept the government decisions using military means.

[60] BOA, BEO 2035/152560, 14 Mart 1319 [27 March 1903].

[61] FO 195/2188, Baghdad, 27 June 1905.

Figure 6.1 The Mobile Mule Corps (*Estersüvar*). İstanbul Üniversitesi Nadir Eserler Kütüphanesi, 90567/19.

compromises with the tribal sheikhs all the more important: all these both persuaded the Bedouin to pay their *wadi* and prevented the imperial officials from 'disingenuous actions', which could exasperate the tribesmen. To increase their motivation, immediately after the introduction of the new method, the tribal sheikhs were rewarded with expensive *robes d'honneur* [*hil'at*] and medals for good service in their collection of the *wadi*.[62] In addition to their salary, they were guaranteed a generous share (a quarter of the total sum) of the tax collected in return for their help.[63] However, when the sheikh failed to collect a sufficient amount, the outstanding sum was debited from the sheikh's salary, which was indeed re-manifestation of the old tax-farming system in a different fashion.[64] In this way, sheikhs were prevented from

[62] For an example, see: BOA, ŞD 2581/24, 23 Teşrin-i Evvel 1308 [5 November 1892].
[63] BOA, DH.TMIK-M 163/39, 17 Mayıs 1320 [30 May 1904].
[64] BOA, BEO 2104/157785, 17 Haziran 1319 [30 June 1903].

abusing the new system. In addition, the new system is an example of how the old practices reproduced themselves in the new forms.

The new situation led to reciprocal benefits: the sheikhship became more attractive to potential candidates and a cooperative attitude to the *wadi* collection became a key factor in the appointment of a sheikh: they pledged to provide better service in the collection of *wadi* if appointed as sheikh[65] and were supported by a small number of the troops, which became more of an issue for the imperial economy regularly damaged by financial crises. Sheikhs were keen to show their subjects their imperial backing by accompanying – or even com-manding – the camel corps.[66] As such, the sheikh boosted his authority and charisma, reinforcing the 'mutual dependence' of the empire and the tribal sheikhs. The longer-term effects of this practice upon tribal solidarity and the position of the sheikh within the tribal society is also worth some consideration. There is no information in the sources about the impact of the sheikhly cooperation with the state on the intra-tribal relations. However, it is a very obvious fact that the tribal social structure was not damaged by the co-optation of their leaders into the imperial system of taxation. As explained previously, the tribal losses which stemmed from relinquishing the collection of *khuwwa* was compensated by other financial benefits like the increase of the regional, imperial and global demand for the tribal livestock. In add-ition, the consolidation of imperial power in the desert frontier made *khuwwa* collection a risky enterprise for the nomads who might have to return the exacted amount. This deterrent reality presumably pre-vented the tribesmen from blaming their sheikhs for the abolition of *khuwwa* and did not cause a dissolution of the nomadic communities in this period. As for the guidance given by the sheiks, the reason was more or less predictable. As explained by Farhan Pasha to his fellow tribesmen presumably to legitimize his collaboration and to forestall the reaction against him, it was 'robbery by the government'.[67]

In spite of the differential between the pledged revenue and the reality, and annual variation in the collected amount, it is evident from Ottoman reports that the regularization of the tax collection

---

[65] BOA, DH.TMIK-M 163/39, 24 Kanun-ı Evvel 1319 [6 January 1904].
[66] For an example, see: BOA, DH.MKT 2049/30, 25 Kanun-ı Sani 1308 [7 February 1893].
[67] Khidr, *Tarikh al-Muhammad al-Jarba*, 220 quoted in Dolbee, 'The Locust and the Starling', 122.

Figure 6.2 Hacı Arif Bey, a cavalry officer on horseback and the tents of the soldiers in the background (perhaps they encamped in the desert for the *wadi* collection). Gertrude Bell Archives, Newcastle University, Y_064.

multiplied imperial revenues from the nomads. The *wadi* of the Deir Shammar, for instance, usually amounted to 50–60,000 gurush[68] although it increased to 89,000 gurush in exceptional seasons.[69] However, even then their sheikhs had promised to pay 150,000 gurush:[70] the difference between the expected and collected amounts was largely due to the misrepresentation by sheikhs as they attempted to secure imperial favour during the appointment process.[71] Variation in the collected amounts was mainly due to the tribes' preference to remain in the desert some years, their migration to neighbouring provinces and their resistance to counting their livestock, choosing rather to estimate their number.[72] However, the regular collection of taxes certainly increased the tribal contribution to the imperial treasury. As noted in an Ottoman report of 1894, the abandonment of the new method and the sporadic use of other regular troops resulted in the

[68] BOA, DH.TMIK-M. 162/29, 27 Kanun-ı Evvel 1319 [9 January 1904].
[69] BOA, DH.ŞFR. 325/100, 30 Mayıs 1320 [12 June 1904].
[70] BOA, DH.MKT. 208/61, 12 Mart 1310 [25 March 1894].
[71] For an example, see: BOA, DH.TMIK-M 102/45, 29 Mart 1317 [10 April 1901].
[72] BOA, DH.TMIK-M 64/54, 11 Eylül 1315 [24 September 1899].

collapse of the *wadi* collection system and the failure to successfully collect taxes.[73]

The Bedouin groups thus grew accustomed to paying their taxes regularly, which consequently reduced state control and further improved the tax-farming practices. As was the very same in the tax-farming practice of the eighteenth century, some sheikhs bought the tax collection rights for their tribes, became imperial tax-contractors [*mukataacı*] and delivered a set amount to the government, as in the example of Hajim, the sheikh of the Fid'an, whose fellow tribespeople moved between Baghdad and Aleppo.[74] The government preferred this method as it was less costly and enabled the government to use the troops in other tasks. Other sheikhs such as Mazwud bin Qa'shish of the Anizah were dismissed by provincial rulers for his refusal to settle with the government on a fixed amount of tax.[75] When sheikhs were unable to collect duties from their fellow tribesmen – or when they wanted to punish the disloyal branches and increase their own authority within the tribal society using the government troops – they requested governmental help, like Faris Pasha of Deir al-Zor, who ordered in 1902 the despatch of the camel corps to collect the *wadi*.[76] Tax collection was so systematized in certain locations like Baghdad that, by 1908, several Bedouin groups taxed in this province brought the *wadi* share voluntarily to the provincial centre.[77] If, for some reason, they did not pay their taxes, a provincial official was sent to the relevant camps and simply collected the agreed sum: in 1907, Turki al-Mahmud, a member of Deir al-Zor's administrative council and a local elite, visited the Al-Sabit, Fida'a and 'Abwa[?] branches of the Shammar, who had failed to pay their taxes the previous year and collected their duties with no resistance.[78] In other instances, the camel corps was instructed by the Bedouin sheikhs, themselves, to collect the *wadi*. In 1914, Abd al-Razzak of the Shammar commanded

---

[73] BOA, DH.MKT 276/16, 14 Ağustos 1310 [27 August 1894].
[74] He promised to pay 230,000 gurush each year: BOA, İ.ML 74/35, 14 Teşrin-i Evvel 1322 [27 October 1906].
[75] BOA, DH.TMIK-M 249/5, 7 Temmuz 1323 [20 July 1907].
[76] BOA, DH.ŞFR 283/131, 29 Nisan 1318 [11 May 1902].
[77] BOA, DH.TMIK-M 249/5, 15 Mayıs 1324 [28 May 1908]; for a similar example from Mosul in 1912, see: BOA, DH.SYS 26/2-8, 20 Eylül 1328 [3 October 1912].
[78] He collected 62,490 gurush in total: BOA, DH.TMIK-M 254/50, 6 Eylül 1323 [19 September 1907].

the corps of Deir al-Zor for this purpose and advanced as far as the boundaries of Basra province.[79]

Dialogues between the Bedouin sheikhs and the officials imply that the tribal groups were aware of the meaning of modern citizenship, as the partial fulfilment of its requirements they paid the *wadi* to the imperial treasury. The tax exactions were imposed on them as they were under Ottoman sovereignty. However, from the nomads' viewpoint, this loaded the government with a charge of protecting the basic rights of their subjects such as the property rights. In this regard, the Bedouin sheikhs sometimes used the *wadi* to remind the government the reciprocity of the responsibilities with reference to the meaning of tax-paying in modern societies. Faris Pasha of Deir al-Zor, for instance, notified the *mutasarrıf* of Deir al-Zor that he could not assist the government to collect the Shammar's *wadi* without their help to recover his animals stolen by the Milli tribe as the government did not fulfil its task of protection of the tribal subjects' property, which was quite a modern interpretation with regard to the government's responsibilities vis-à-vis their citizens.[80] In this example, the Shammar declined its responsibility of tax payment as the government did not secure their property against the Milli attacks.

Inter-provincial Competition for the Bedouin Taxes

The systematization of tax collection and the increase in revenues obtained from the Bedouin created competition between the various provinces for the right to collect the *wadi* from the many tribes. Provincial rulers fostered closer relations with sheikhs to improve their chances of taking over another province's tax-collecting privileges. The Aleppo and Zor administrations vied for the right to collect the *wadi* from the Anizah branches, while Mosul, Baghdad and Zor wrestled over the Shammar and Anizah branches, the result of which was a significant contribution to the Shammar's provincialization.

The disputes and rivalry emerged soon after the reorganization of the tax collection process: immediately after the adoption of the new method and the beginning of the regular flow of tribal revenues, the rights to the Anizah's tax collection were transferred from Deir to

---

[79] BOA, DH.ŞFR 434/57, 10 Temmuz 1330 [23 July 1914].
[80] BOA, DH.ŞFR 283/131, 29 Nisan 1318 [11 May 1902].

Aleppo, presumably in response to the latter's lobbying of the central government. However, given that the Anizah spent the spring and summer around Deir, and the close relations between the authorities of its *mutasarrıfate* and the Anizah chiefs, the Deir officials' cooperation was still required: according to the central government's decision, duties were to be collected by Deir al-Zor's *mutasarrıf* and handed over to the Aleppo administration; since the Anizah revenues constituted a major income for the Zor treasury, its authorities argued persistently for their right to the Anizah's taxes. In late 1889, according to reports from Aleppo, the Deir authorities firstly detained the Anizah sheikhs, Turki and Farhan, for an extended period in Deir and compelled them to send requests to the Porte requesting the transfer of the tribes' *wadi* collection rights. When this failed, they proposed the abolition of the sheikhs' role in the process and instead the collection of taxes directly by government troops. This would make the imperial tax collection dependent on Deir al-Zor officials and would oblige the central government to transfer Anizah's tax collection rights to the *mutasarrıfate*. Such a move was designed allegedly to prevent the sheikhs from 'imposing heavy duties on the Bedouin subjects' and put an end to 'their atrocities'.[81] Soon after, presumably with the backing of the affronted Aleppo authorities, Tevfik Pasha, the *mutasarrıf* of Deir al-Zor, was accused by his accountant [*muhasebeci*] of plotting the failure of the Anizah's tax-collection business.[82] Deir's authorities refused to relent: they offered several excuses and deliberately did not collect the Anizah taxes in 1893 so as to compel the central authorities to restore their privilege.[83] Upon that, it was decided that the tribal taxes would be collected at one centre: Deir al-Zor. The *wadi* of Mosul and Aleppo would also be collected by the Deir authorities. But these administrations would help the latter with the mule corps under their command. The resistance by the provinces to this decision was so great that the tax collection process seriously halted, and complaints were reciprocally raised by all sides. Finally, upon the proposal of the Deir al-Zor's *mutasarrıf* the project was abandoned.[84]

Another outcome was impinging on the tax collection rights of a governorate by another, to which the tribes were not annexed. The

[81] BOA, DH.MKT 1696/81, 28 Kanun-ı Sani 1305 [10 February 1890].
[82] BOA, DH.MKT 1710/121, 12 Mart 1306 [25 March 1890].
[83] BOA, DH.MKT 2041/31, 26 Kanun-ı Evvel 1308 [8 January 1893].
[84] BOA, BEO 365/27370, 9 Kanun-ı Sani 1309 [21 January 1894].

nomadic groups frequently crossed from one province to another, and sheikhs annexed to different provinces claimed sovereignty over the same groups. In addition, the great majority of the Shammar and Anizah in Syria, Iraq and Arabia were all related and their loyalty often shifted from one sheikh to another. In 1898, for instance, while the mule corps accompanied by Faris Pasha, the sheikh of the Deir Shammar, was collecting the taxes from subjects in the Mosul region, the *wadi* official of the province accompanied by 'Asi, the sheikh of the Mosul Shammar, arrived on the scene, prevented the mule corps from collecting duties, and instead demanded 50,200 gurush from the tribesmen.[85] In response to the subsequent enquiry by central government authorities, the Mosul authorities responded that their officials were already back in the city on the date that the incident supposedly took place, but did not refute the allegations.[86] It appears that central government authorities believed the Mosulis' statement and instructed the Zor officials to continue the tax collection of the contested groups.[87] In another example, a dispute broke out when the al-Sayigh tribe of the Shammar's al-Mujish and al-Siraja branches migrated to Baghdad from Mosul. Both sides claimed they had the right to collect tax. The minister of the interior, unable to decide which party to support, delegated the issue to the Grand Vizier.[88]

The occurrence of such instances after the creation of the mobile corps indicates that their incorporation remarkably increased efficient taxation of the nomads. It seems that the competition between the neighbouring administrations for the taxes of the nomads was not only to add more money to their treasury, but to establish strong relations with the tribes and have further influence in regional politics. It also demonstrates the importance of sheikhs' guidance during the tax-collection process due to the nomads' ability to move easily from the boundaries of one administration to another and claim that they already paid their duties. Therefore, the politics of negotiation still determined the practice of taxation after the creation of the mobile corps, whose service could usually be made more efficient by the help of sheikhs.

[85] BOA, DH.TMIK-M 58/37, 9 Temmuz 1314 [22 July 1898].
[86] BOA, DH.TMIK-M 57/46, 1 Ağustos 1314 [14 August 1898].
[87] BOA, DH.TMIK-M 57/46, 5 Kanun-ı Sani 1314 [18 January 1900].
[88] BOA, DH.TMIK.M 175/67, 8 Ağustos 1320 [21 August 1904].

Conclusion

Taxation of the nomads was directly influenced by the progress of state-tribe relations in the period analysed. As in the other sectors of governance, coercive methods could not become effective in collecting the nomads' taxes. What the imperial authorities initially called tax collection during the 1840s was to raid the tribal encampments and plunder their animal property employing the irregular troops. When this method failed due to the tribal response by counter raids, the tribesmen were forced to deliver by themselves a certain amount decided by the government authorities to the provincial treasuries. But this also did not work as the sheikhs complained about the high rates. Finally, towards 1860, the imperial authorities came to understand that the collection of the tribal taxes could only be possible via negotiation and sat around the table with the sheikhs. Although we do not have sufficient documentation, it seems that during the 1860s, 1870s and 1880s the powerful sheikhs like Farhan and Jed'an played a part and supported the officials in the collection of the *wadi*. The incorporation of the mobile camel and mule corps from the late 1880s in the tax-collection process remarkably augmented the imperial revenues from the nomads. The sheikhly cooperation, however, remained essential for the success of the new method. The effective taxation of the Shammar and the Anizah represented a fundamental component of their 'provincialization'.

Following the reconciliation with the tribes from the 1860s to early 1870s, the concept of negotiated compromise as the basis of Ottoman governance of the Bedouin was evident in the imperial practice of tax collection just as it was in other aspects of imperial policy in the desert. The evolution of the imperial *wadi* collection through the modern era is also an account of the nomadic Arabs' integration into the modern Ottoman system. As such, neither state nor tribes could completely realize their original agenda, as both sides had to make significant concessions: imperial authorities accepted the number of the animals that Bedouin sheikhs declared as taxable property, and could tax the commensurate amount; in addition, they supported the sheikhs to reinforce their authority over the tribes. Furthermore, they granted the sheikhs handsome salaries and a quarter share of the *wadi* tax. In return, the sheikhs consented to pay taxes to the Ottoman government and assisted government troops in the collection of nomadic taxes.

7 | Justice
The Imperial Legal System and the Bedouin Disputes

Thus speaks Farhud in the prison fettered:

> Alas, woe is me for the bondage into which I have fallen!
> Most surely the she-camels will leave with us on the day
> In order to reach Hit before the tenth night.
> An air-filled skin have ready for each on the eleventh day,
> For on the skin we shall cross the clear stream of the Euphrates.
> On the twelfth with the first daybreak to them will appear
> The caravansaray either of al-Mesare or of Alub al-Sidr [High Sidr Tree].
> Oh, how sweet if they may fly to al-Shaikh Ma'ruf
> And Zobaida whose monument rises on high,
> And reach the men from al-Qasim, among who are famed
> Ali's descendants, who find cheap all that is costly.
> Their arms are a double pistol secured to the hip,
> Made in Europe, shining like stars;
> Their dress fine cloth made of the best wool.
> Their warriors are like pack camels;
> They protect the stranger if only at first sight he has asked their help.
> Their riders on camels are ready and by deeds they prove their noble minds.
> I would not say this, if I were not fettered in a narrow cell:
> The youths will come to us at the desired time.
> Their hard task they will accomplish, for they are not fickle men;
> I shall not be otherwise –in a month from this day
> Surely they will be with me.[1]

Presumably in the late-1880s,[2] Farhud, a chief of the Amarat branch of the Anizah, thus expressed his elation in his famous poem recounting

---

[1] Musil, *The Manners and Customs*, 315.
[2] Reference to the European double pistol guns from al-Qasim may demonstrate that the incident took place in the late 1880s when al-Qasim transformed into a region where European guns could be found.

how his friends, who escorted commercial caravans from Baghdad to Syria, sent word to him that they would liberate and bring him back to Baghdad on a certain day. The sheikh had been captured by the governor of Syria in the marketplace of Hama and imprisoned there proving the spatial stretch of the nomads widely analysed in previous chapters. In spite of the increase in security measures along the desert frontier in the preceding decades, the poem describes how, once he had been broken out of the jail, he would be delivered from Hama to Baghdad, safely away from the pasha of Syria, proving the vulnerability of the Ottoman governance in the districts where the Bedouin frequented and strength of the nomads in the Arab countryside.

As well as offering a good example of the Bedouins' freedom of movement in the desert, these lines also demonstrate how their migrant and warrior lifestyle made things difficult for the imperial governors and enabled the tribesmen to escape imperial control even if they were imprisoned. It also proves the complicated relations between the government and the nomads as they were also in the service of the Ottoman government, an almost compulsory relationship to be maintained for both sides that also shaped the legal relations between the nomads and the state: the sheikhs' fellow tribesmen protected caravans from Baghdad to Syria presumably in return for some money and most likely as a result of their contract with the empire. But such engagements did not bring about their *complete* obedience to imperial rules and restrictions. They still acted according to the requirements of tribal solidarity and violated the imperial limits for the sake of tribal fellowship when they had to make a preference. The poem further emphasizes how ambiguous the Bedouins' position was within the Ottoman legal system and demonstrates the practice of imperial justice among the desert societies. The modern Ottoman law could not penetrate into the desert and regulate Bedouin affairs until the end of the Ottoman era in spite of the extensive reforms to modernize the imperial legal practices from the Tanzimat era onwards.[3]

The Ottomans would, indeed, want to assert a legal authority over the tribes if they owned sufficient tools and it would be worth it as the control of the nomads would mean the complete subordination of the nomadic peoples and would pave the way for the effective exploitation

---

[3] For a study on the modernization of the Ottoman law, see: Rubin, *Ottoman Nizamiye Courts*, 55–81; Kenanoğlu, 'Nizamiye Mahkemeleri', 185–188.

of the nomads' human and material resources. As part of the Tanzimat reforms, the Ottoman government adopted an attitude towards legal practices that aimed at maximizing the imperial interference with the issues of individuals which would increase the state's efficiency throughout the empire.[4] Although Abdulhamid adopted a more flexible stance emphasizing the importance of loyalty to the sultan and caliph and paved the way to develop friendly relations with the local power-holders respecting their areas of influence,[5] this did not mean that state control was less crucial for him. The greatest expansion of the Ottoman state occurred during the Hamidian era with the railroad and telegraph lines projects as well as the enormous increase in the number of state schools.[6] The Young Turks ideology was similarly based on the idea of a monolithic state which targeted the local, secondary and autonomous structures of the empire.[7] For those reasons, the imperial officials wanted in principle to extend the influence of the Ottoman law into the tribal society, too, during the modern era. However, as explained in the previous chapters, both the inadequate financial, political and military means which prevented the localization of the nomads, and the stiff resistance by the tribes prevented the realization of these thoughts and Ottoman law could not penetrate tribal society.

That status quo convinced scholars that there was a fundamental distinction in how the legislation impacted on the lives of townspeople versus the tribes. Batatu, for instance, argues that 'the life of urban Arabs was on the whole governed by Islamic and Ottoman laws, that of the tribal Arabs by islamically tinged ancient Arab customs'.[8] Such remarks, however, do not always reflect the reality and they do not mean that the Bedouin enjoyed unrestricted freedom and were entirely immune to the decisions of Ottoman justice. Contrary to common belief, particularly in the period of reconciliation, the Bedouin adopted the Ottoman legal and administrative mechanisms, particularly the Islamic ones, to resolve their own disputes, other than in cases among members of the same tribe, although the imperial system did not always

---

[4] For analyses on the Tanzimat ideology, see: İnalcık and Seyitdanlıoğlu, *Tanzimat*.
[5] For a study highlighting these features of the Hamidian policies, see: Klein, *The Margins of Empire*.
[6] See, for example, Kırmızı, *Abdülhamid'in Valileri*; Fortna, *Imperial Classroom* and 'The Reign of Abdülhamid II'.
[7] See, for example, Hanioğlu, *Preparation*; Mardin, *Jön Türklerin Siyasi Fikirleri*.
[8] Batatu, *The Old Social Classes*, 13–14.

offer successful outcomes. As such, this chapter addresses the efficiency of imperial legal and administrative institutions for the Bedouin in terms of delivering justice, concluding tribal disputes and punishing the crimes committed by tribesmen.

The present chapter first analyses how members of the same tribe resolved the disputes among them and highlights the autonomous character of intra-tribal trials. It goes on to examine individual nomadic cases in the Sharia court records to understand how the Bedouin used the Ottoman courts. The Sharia courts were still the state courts and symbolize the Ottoman sovereignty – and thus are useful for the purpose of this study – although they had to transfer the commercial and criminal cases to the modern Nizamiye courts particularly after the early 1870s. As demonstrated in recent studies – and partly in this study as well – this transfer was not regular everywhere in the empire as the distinction between the Sharia and Nizamiye did not work as planned everywhere and the former was maintained to a certain extent to perform some of its old functions.[9] The lack of criminal cases belonging to the later periods was made up for with examples inferred from the Ottoman archives and, benefiting from them, this chapter subsequently examines crime and punishment processes with a particular focus on the Bedouin's negotiating and factional character. Finally, it explores the role that imperial authorities played in the conclusion – or aggravating – of the inter-tribal conflicts, demonstrating how imperial intervention made the disputes more widespread and intractable.

Making inferences from these processes, the present study argues that the running of the imperial justice mechanism was convenient to the spirit of the principle of 'reconciliation', on which state-tribe relations were based. As the protection of the nomadic structure was crucial for the Bedouin, any intervention by the government in the intra-tribal judicial processes was not possible. In the pre-compromise period, intervention became impossible for the imperial authorities as they could not prevail over the tribes. After setting up the state-tribe agreement, as detailed in the previous chapters, the tribes preconditioned the maintenance of good relations to the assurances by the empire for their autonomy. Proving the tribal autonomy, all the disputes, crimes and their punishments among the members of the same

---

[9] See, for example, Barakat, 'An Empty Land?'; Amara, 'Governing Property'.

tribe were tried by the tribal judicial system. However, the Ottoman government played a part in the solution of imperial disputes and the punishment of the tribal guilty parties when they committed a crime against the settled people, especially after the 'provincialization' of the Shammar and Anizah from the 1870s to the 1890s. Similarly, after the regularization of tribal movements in the 1860s and 1870s, officials assumed an increasing role in inter-tribal disputes and hostilities to protect their partners against the designs of the other provinces. Finally, it is difficult to claim from the available sources the individualization of the nomadic crimes as many of the crimes committed by them represented a communal character.

The Issue of Autonomy: Intra- and Inter-Tribal Cases

The intra-tribal cases are the most exemplary to understand how the tribal structure was protected and how it came to be. It also draws the line where interaction with the settled societies and the Ottoman rule ended. The Bedouin groups resolved internal problems through their intra-tribal procedures. Their justice system differed from that of settled communities inasmuch as they had no written law or recorded code that regulated the resolution of their disputes. Tribal tradition and custom constituted the law ordering their actions. As Islamic law developed 'in a milieu familiar with Bedouin life and firmly bonded to it', however, it is argued that Sharia 'confirmed many of nomadism's institutions and customs'.[10] Under any circumstances, the lack of written law, however, could not be interpreted as a proof of 'inferiority' and 'arbitrariness' as they had very established rules and traditions that every tribesman from all levels of the tribal hierarchy knew and accepted. They had their own multi-staged judicial processes and judges knew the unwritten tribal laws very well.

The imperial government accepted the particularity of the Bedouin system and never attempted to control the intra-tribal processes as it could not reach to such a level of authority in the desert space nor could it force the nomads to abandon the mobile desert life. Similarly, there was no imperial tool – or desire – which would detain the various tribes from resolving inter-tribal disputes according to their laws and customs. As will be explained below, it was also the imperial method to

---

[10] Jabbur, *The Bedouin and the Desert*, 298–299.

observe the tribal traditions and use them as – usually the only – measure in the inter-tribal disputes when the officials were involved in the conflict resolution process as mediators.

Ottoman and consular documents do not provide any detail of how the Shammar and Anizah tribesmen resolved disputes among themselves or how those convicted of a crime against other tribespeople were punished since these were unrecorded intra-tribal processes. Similarly, Sharia court archives do not contain even a single record to suggest that the imperial authorities asserted control over the internal social life of Bedouin nomads. The sedentary tribes such as Bani Khalid, Hadidin, Bashakim and al-Nu'aym brought many intra-tribal disputes to the imperial courts and accepted the decision made there. There are no instances of Sharia courts issuing marriage certificates or registering their inheritance to the nomads.[11] The secondary sources, memoires and travelogues do, however, mention the subject of intra-tribal legal procedures which suggests that there were established methods among the various tribes to settle conflicts between their members. It should finally be noted that the available sources present limited information regarding the intra-tribal judicial processes.

Tribes differed in terms of practices in the solution of their intra-tribal controversies. The authority and charisma of the sheikh among his subjects, and the structure of tribe, it would appear, influenced the intra-tribal legal practices: in communities like the Ruwalla, the sheikh kept his tribe under a strict regime and certainly under Nuri al-Sha'lan's sheikhship, the tribespeople could not act independently. His decisions were so absolute that, when he determined to execute a tribesman, even the man's parents could not raise their appeal against the sheikh. According to Günay, an Ottoman gendarmerie officer served in Hawran, however, Nuri al-Sha'lan respected the government's authority and did not impose such severe punishments in those areas closer to the government centres, thereby avoiding an impression that he created a 'government within the government [*hükümet içinde hükümet*]'. Günay

---

[11] For some examples, from the Hama Sharia court records containing intra- and inter-tribal disputes, marriage registrations and selling and inheritance procedures of the sedentary tribes such as the Hadidin, Bani Khalid, Bashakim and al-Nu'aym, see: SCR-Hama 53, 1267 [1851], pages 44, 45, 46, 48, 56, 77, 80, 81, 104, 135, 145, 161, 194, 202, 206, 210, 214, 216, 222, 231, 239, 247, 250.

Figure 7.1 The Ruwalla women. İstanbul Üniversitesi Nadir Eserler Kütüphanesi, 90567/15.

argues that all such determinations could really be considered government decisions as al-Sha'lan was also the *kaymakam* of Jawf district and
sealed all his judgments as 'the *sheikh* of the Ruwalla and the *kaymakam*
of Jawf [*kaymakam-ı Cevf ve şeyhulmeşayih-i Ruvale*]' 'to declare that
he governs on behalf of the government'. Although Günay's reasoning
was somewhat problematic as the government officials did not have
judicial authority over the people they governed, following the compromise with the Ottoman government, al-Sha'lan's undisputed authority among the fellow tribesmen had been recognized by the officials.
Similarly, when a dispute came about between the two sub-tribes, the
complaint was brought to Nuri and both sides recognized the decision of
the court under the presidency of the sheikh without request for an
appeal. When, according to their customs, he banged his stick on the
ground and announced the verdict, both sides had no choice but to
accept the decision and make peace with one other.[12]

---

[12] Günay, *Suriye ve Filistin Anıları*, 19.

The position of the sheikh was rather different in Iraqi tribes. Wellsted notes that, in most instances, the authority of the sheikh 'scarcely rises higher than that which is exercised by the father of a family over his children'. The sheikh enjoyed an unusual authority over the tribe in war and in extraordinary circumstances by possessing 'the power of life and death'. In ordinary times, however, the sheikh was accompanied by the elders of the tribe and shared his authority with them. The customs of the country or the 'laws' of the Qur'an formed the basis of their law.[13]

These two examples, the Ruwalla and the Iraqi nomads, represent two patterns for the Arab nomadic society. The judicial differences between these tribes originated in the organization of the tribal society. Contrary to the Ruwalla, nomadic tribes described by Wellsted consisted of loose confederations which reduced the authority of the paramount sheikh and required constant collaboration with the tribal elders, most of whom were the sheikhs of the sub-tribes. Therefore, the paramount sheikh shared his authority with the other prominent figures to maintain peace and order within the tribal community.

There was a judicial mechanism to resolve disputes among the various sub-tribes of the same confederation as well as problems between the different tribal groups so they could enjoy peaceful relations rather than fight. Such disputes were very commonly referred to arbitration by an equal number of hereditary magistrates, *'arifa* (pl. *'awarif*) for each side of the dispute. If one of the parties refuses to abide by their decisions, a fifth *'arifa* was recruited, whose decision determined the final judgment. Before making an appeal to the fifth person, both sides signed a contract pledging to abide by the decision and showed it to him before the trial. The punishment for murder might be *hashem*, marrying a girl or more from the family of the guilty man to the relative/s of the victims. This was a conditional marriage as women had the right to return to the house of their fathers after giving birth to a boy and raising him until he turned seven years old. Less severe crimes were compensated for with camels, horses and money depending on the nature of crime. The verdict was binding for all members of the tribes rather than solely the guilty party irrespective of their involvement with the crime.[14]

---

[13] Wellsted, *Travels*, 197.
[14] For details, see: Musil, *The Manners and Customs*, chapter XVI; although the book is called 'Rwala' it includes information about the other branches of the Anizah and Shammar; See, also: Günday, *İki Devir Bir İnsan*, 200.

It should be emphasized that the grand sheikh and the elders' council did not deal with all the disputes among the tribesmen. They resolved the most serious issues and made important decisions such as the declaration of war on other tribes – or, in rare instances, on the government. The sheikh presumably did not know many slight disputes and quarrels were settled by amicable intercession. In such instances, a respectful tribal elder came with one or two companions to the tent of the more powerful party and persuaded him to make peace with the other side. More serious cases such as murder, however, were settled by the hereditary magistrates, in trials held in tent-courts called *salfa* or *tlaba*. The tribesmen paid a certain sum of money to appeal to these courts. The testimony of eyewitnesses and oaths played a crucial role in the verdicts of these trials. In some tribes such as the Ruwalla, if one of the parties did not accept the decision, he/she could appeal to another judge. However, the first decision might have been upheld irrespective of the second. In other examples, the decision of the *'arifa* was irrefutable. The great tribes developed a two-stage *'arifa* system, one of which functioned as a court of the first instance [*bidayet mahkemesi*] while the other was appealed to as the Supreme Court [*temyiz mahkemesi*]. The

Figure 7.2 Woman and child of the Shammar tribe of Bedouins on camel, man and horses in background. Gertrude Bell Archives, Newcastle University, R_065.

'arifas gave a verdict in accordance with tribal customs and many of them were illiterate. Unlike the imperial courts, the trials were informal as no record was kept regarding the content or decision.[15]

The Shammar and Anizah Bedouin petitioned the Ottoman courts and appealed to Ottoman authorities when a controversy arose among and between them and the townspeople and sedentary tribes and rival tribal groups. The following sections will analyse the role of the Ottoman judicial and administrative institutions in resolving Bedouin disagreements and as an agency of punishment and mediation.

Ottoman Law and the Bedouin

The cases that involved Bedouin in the Sharia court records are relatively few in number as they resolved many trials internally in the tribal courts, as detailed in the previous section. In addition, lack of knowledge of nomadic appeals to the modern courts such as the Nizamiye created after 1870 for criminal and commercial reasons debarred us from entirely uncovering the position of the nomads vis-à-vis the Ottoman justice system during the period under scrutiny. However, as will be expressed below, some cases found in the Ottoman archives help us to fill this gap to an extent. Furthermore, many disputes between and among the officials, sedentary society and the Bedouin were settled through negotiation, bypassing imperial legal procedures. This is largely because the nature of the disputes was at the community rather than the individual level. It was almost impossible to *individualize* crimes, locate the suspects and force them to attend the court. However, especially after the increase of the tribal incorporation into the imperial system and their 'provincialization', examples can be found that demonstrate that a Bedouin sheikh petitioned the court to complain of plunder by another tribe. A second Farhan Pasha, not the paramount sheikh of the Shammar but of the Seb'a tribe, for instance, reported the Shammar tribe annexed to Deir al-Zor for having stolen 95 camels and 314 sheep belonging to his tribe. The incident was investigated by the Zor government and the investigating officials claimed that the animals had been found

---

[15] For details, see: Musil, *The Manners and Customs*, chapter XVI; see, also: Günday, *İki Devir Bir İnsan*, 200.

abandoned in the desert and had been sold in the market. The sheikh was told to appeal to Zor's Sharia court for a refund.[16]

The tribesmen also applied to the Ottoman justice system to complain about the acts of the officials. When two merchants from the Seb'a tribe bought animals from Najd and returned to their tribes, they were stopped by the Ottoman soldiers and the animals they bought were captured by the soldiers with the consideration that they were obtained by raid [*gazve*] as it was forbidden. Then the tribesmen went to Deir al-Zor and raised complaints against the soldiers. Although the result is not clear from the available documentation, the *mutasarrıf* understood that the captured animals belonged to the merchants and had not been stolen by them, and acted on their behalf.[17] Proving the changing Ottoman perception regarding the nomads, they were not treated as 'inferior' people, stealing of whose property was legitimate for the soldiers. As exemplified previously, in the early years of the Ottoman modernization, neither the tribes would consider an application to the Ottoman justice nor the authorities would strive to recover the stolen property of the nomads.

Collective crimes notwithstanding, there are sufficient episodes to prove that individual disputes between the nomads and the townspeople or sedentary tribes were brought to the Ottoman courts. Furthermore, the nomads were called as witnesses in disputes among sedentary people, especially cases of stolen livestock. Because the Bedouin developed strong trade relations with the sedentary societies and sold their animals in the markets set up on the outskirts of towns, the cases were mostly commercial disputes and livestock theft by both sides. Even in 1850, for instance, Ujail ibn Eid of the Anizah's Seb'a tribe came to the Hama court to denounce Dandal ibn Hamad of the Bashakim Arabs, a sedentary tax-paying tribe settled in the town's neighbourhood. The plaintiff claimed that his yellow camel had been stolen by the defendant forty-five days earlier and ask that the judge order its return. Ujail ibn Eid brought two witnesses from al-Seb'a with him to court and, as was standard procedure, their credibility was confirmed by two other townspeople. The judge upheld the claim and passed judgment requiring the defendant to return the camel to Ibn

---

[16]   BOA, BEO 442/33126, 2 Ağustos 1310 [15 August 1894]. It is not expressed in the document whether or not he pursued the case at Deir al-Zor's court.

[17]   ŞD 2273/28, 1 Nisan 1298 [14 April 1882].

Eid.[18] In another case of 1852, Khalaf ibn Hamuq of al-Seb'a appealed to the same judge for his yellow donkey that he claimed to have been stolen by Al-Haj Omar ibn Sawwa, a resident of Hama. As in the previous case, he brought two witnesses from his tribe to the court and their credibility was approved by others. On this occasion too, the judge delivered a verdict in favour of the tribesman.[19]

The Shammar's situation was not different from the Anizah. In a case of 1870, a certain Shammari, Bin Zaid appealed to the Urfa court alleging that Ahmed Muhtar Bey, the official accountant of the town, had appropriated his camel that the settled tribes around Urfa had stolen. The judge endorsed his claim as Bin Zaid's account was verified by two other Shammar.[20] It seems that the good relations between the government and the tribes had an influence over the tribal appeals to the government courts. The government and Seb'a had friendly relations in 1850 and as detailed previously, 1852 was when the Anizah groups and the government authorities made a truce due to Jed'an's appointment to the sheikhship of the Fid'an as the Shammar did in Urfa under Abd al-Qarim's and Faris Pasha's sheikhships in the 1860s and 1870s except for a short period of rebellion. The tribesmen felt themselves sufficiently confident about the judges, which convinced them that they would be equally treated in court and the right decision would be made. These occasional instances, however, do not contradict our argument that a peaceful co-existence between the Ottoman administration and the tribal authority could be established after 1870 based on the politics of negotiation.

The relationship between the sides was systematized after making a 'social contract' in which the nomads themselves used the imperial mechanisms to strengthen their position against the government. In this regard, Bedouin groups sometimes wanted the Ottoman courts (Nizamiye) to mediate between them and the government, particularly when they considered that they were in a legitimate position. They demanded court decisions to address government when they appraised that government practices and demands were unlawful. In 1902, for instance, the government authorities in Aleppo asked the Fid'an and Seb'a groups to pay a pasture tax [*otlak rusumu*] in several instalments,

---

[18] SCR-Hama 53, Doc. 30, 7 Şevval 1266 [16 August 1850].
[19] SCR-Hama 53, Doc. 37, 20 Şaban 1268 [9 June 1852].
[20] SCR-Urfa 204, Doc. 100, 24 Rebiulevvel 1287 [24 June 1870], 51.

and to return the animals they had plundered in Homs, Hama and Aleppo. The tribes responded that they had neither avoided taxation nor considered the disputed animals to be their property and insisted repeatedly that they 'would not pay even a piaster without trial and verdict' [*mebaliğ-i matlubeyi zimmet addetmeyerek muhakemesiz ve hükümsüz bir akçe vermeyeceklerini musırran beyan etmekte*]. The governor reported months later that no resolution could be reached due to the difficulty in issuing such a court decision and coercively forcing them to pay the amount, which implies that the tribal position was rightful.[21]

Cases where the Bedouin were denounced by sedentary groups can also be found in the court records. The Bedouin were mostly accused of animal stealing and, in the majority of cases, they were present in court during the trials. In 1854, when Omar bin Halabi from Aleppo found a sheep among the flocks of a certain Fid'an member Ahmad bin Ammar that resembled one he had lost, he applied to the Hama court for its restitution. However, the defendant proved that the sheep had been given to him for grazing by Mashuh al-Hamdan from the Al-Murshid nomads of the Anizah and brought two witnesses to the court where his claim was upheld.[22] In another example, a certain Ahmad Agha al-Rahwan petitioned the court, claiming that Ali bin al-Kallizi from the Anizah had stolen his camel. The defendant refuted the charge, responding that he had stolen the camel from the Shammar two years earlier, an interesting defence to legitimize his position. This case demonstrates the limits of the Ottoman justice very well as 'simple' inter-tribal crimes like animal stealing were not within the scope of the government courts' responsibility as long as they remain within the tribal space since an Anizah tribesman could easily announce in the court that he stole an animal from the Shammar.[23]

In addition to these, particularly after arriving at a certain compromise with the Anizah and Shammar, the nomads testified in court as witnesses, especially in disputes relating to animal trading. In some cases, the nomads confirmed that they had sold the animals to one of

[21] BOA, DH.MKT 467/17, 25 Şubat 1317 [10 March 1902] and 31 Ağustos 1318 [13 September 1902].
[22] SCR-Hama 63, Doc 133, 15 Rebiulahir 1271 [5 January 1855].
[23] SCR-Hama 58, Doc 75/789, 12 Muharrem 1280 [19 June 1863].

the parties in court[24] while, in other instances, they confirmed the plaintiff's charges.[25] Interestingly enough, in at least one example, the plaintiff used the Anizah individuals' testimony to prove that his camel had been stolen by the witness's own tribe.[26] For the nomads, that may be interpreted as the cruciality of maintaining commercial interests with city dwellers, which sometimes prevailed over tribal solidarity. Another possibility, which also supports the strong relationships between the tribes and tradesmen, is that the tribesman testified false witness in the court to help the merchant to be saved from government duties.

Reading between the lines of these cases also reveals the socio-spatial reach of Ottoman rule in the desert. When a witness confirmed that the animal property was stolen by the Shammar or Anizah, the possibility of confirming its authenticity disappears as the nomadic community and space were inaccessible and unreachable for the government. There was no option for the court but to accept such witnesses. 'Stolen' by the nomads meant legally 'lost' due to the difficulty of recovering. This may prove the importance of negotiation for the judicial issues between the empire and the nomads.

Notary services became an important function of the Sharia courts after the establishment of the modern courts and it performed this to approve sales agreements between members of the sedentary society and the nomads as it did between the members of the urban society. They brought their animals to the court together with witnesses to have the purchase approved by the judge.[27] This practice was presumably introduced in response to the increase in animal theft in the region. An unregistered animal bought from the nomads, who would migrate to another region in a short time, could easily be condemned as stolen by others. Most likely to avoid such an incident, both seller and buyer wanted the purchase to be registered at the court. Payment disputes were also resolved through the mediation of the Sharia court: when a certain Hussein from the Ruwalla tribe did not receive the payment of

---

[24] See, for example, SCR-Hama 59, Doc 87/910, 3 Rebiulevvel 1283 [16 July 1866]; SCR-Hama 59, Doc 88/915, 4 Rebiulevvel 1283 [17 July 1866].

[25] See, for example, SCR-Hama 59, Doc 85/548, 5 Safer 1281 [10 Temmuz 1864]; SCR-Hama 59, Doc 86/833, 5 Muharrem 1283 [20 May 1866].

[26] SCR-Hama 60, Doc 153/483, 3 Receb 1283 [11 November 1866].

[27] For a sales agreement of a mare between Sultan al-Sarby (from Anizah) and Hussein al-Madhoun al-Sukhni, see: SCR-Hama 53, Doc 36, 22 Receb 1268 [12 May 1852].

800 piasters, the price for two female camels, from Rahmoun Muhammad ibn Yasin, the court reconciled the sides, stipulating that Hussein should be paid 500 piasters by ibn Yasin.[28]

The cases found in the Sharia court records and the available examples in the Ottoman documents may enable us to make the following inferences: first, the nomads were so acquainted with sedentary society and so knowledgeable about the imperial legal procedures that they individually applied to the local courts when they disputed with the people in their dealings; second, the Sharia courts played an important part in the peaceful solution of desert-city disputes; third, given that they were usually found right by judges, it can also be inferred that their perception by the officials and sedentary communities as 'savages' at an 'inferior level of civilization' did not impact the court verdicts, or they were not exposed to any mistreatment in the court due to their 'inferiority'. The process of punishment of the nomadic crimes may demonstrate further integration of the tribes into the imperial mechanisms of justice and its limits vis-à-vis the desert societies.

Crime and Punishment

When the Ottoman modern state reinstated itself in Syria and Iraq, Bedouin crimes and their punishment presented an important issue for the Ottoman government, as they posed a serious challenge to imperial judicial system. As previously illustrated, the government had to recognize and accept the autonomy of Bedouin justice to address their internal crimes and disputes. The challenge was to deal with the crimes they committed against the sedentary communities since their migrant character and the impenetrability of the desert made it always difficult to capture the suspects and bring them to justice. Given this, as was reported by Ottoman officials, even in 1911, most of the Bedouin crimes could not be properly punished.[29]

During the Tanzimat period when hostilities between the government and tribes continued, crimes were not dealt with on an individual basis: numerous cases can be found of punishing an entire tribe when a tribesman committed crime. Once suspects were caught, the process

---

[28] SCR-Hama 56, Doc 48/132, 11 Zilhicce 1270 [4 September 1854].
[29] See, for example, BOA, DH. SYS 26/2–8, 30 Mayıs 1327 [12 June 1911].

was different to other Ottoman judicial procedure. But the reconciliation also changed the character of the tribal punishment when they committed a crime. As is noted several times, although there are limited sources regarding Bedouin trials in the 'secular' Ottoman courts due to an absence of records, the available archival documents still enable us to evaluate the degree of punishment and demonstrate the negotiating and flexible character of imperial justice when it came to the nomads. The communal and individual crimes committed by the nomadic groups will be examined in the following pages to further clarify the present chapter's argument.

Plundering

Plundering of villages, river boats, other tribal groups and caravans were among the crimes most often committed by the Bedouin nomads. Some Ottoman officials commented on the rarity of other individual crimes among the nomads.[30] Plundering was a communal crime, and it was thus difficult to individualize it and punish the criminal.[31] The Bedouin organized plunder for several reasons, the most common of which was the *gazwah*, a declaration of war on a rival tribe, the government or villages. Given this was a kind of war, as was standard in the pre-modern era for states and other political entities, the Bedouin considered the plundering of their enemies as part of the fighting. Therefore, such plundering could easily be rationalized as Bedouin – or even the early imperial – custom and tradition.[32] The second type – basic robbery – could not be so easily justified as tribal custom. The third type was 'plundering as politics' and aimed at 'bringing the government authorities into trouble' in order to compel them to abandon unpopular policies.[33] According to Ottoman law, however, all these types of plunder were classified as crimes that had to be dealt with.

In the early years of Ottoman modernization, many instances of plunder were carried out by the nomads for the reasons summarized above. The principal Ottoman policy was to ensure the return of the

---

[30] See, for example, Günday, *İki Devir Bir İnsan*, 163.
[31] The names of tribesmen who were engaged in plundering were identified in some examples. See, for example, MW 5/10, 18 Haziran 1314 [1 July 1898].
[32] See, for example, Çarıklı, *Babam Hacim Muhittin Çarıklı*, 34.
[33] See, for example, FO 195/1309, Baghdad, 7 July 1880.

plundered property – or payment of its value – to the owners. Military operations were organized to recover the plundered property although very few cases could be brought to Ottoman courts through this coercive method. Government operations resembled closely the Bedouin plunder when they employed irregulars to recover the plunder: troops attacked a tribe and plundered its property without establishing whether their targeted group had actually been engaged in the original act of plunder. When the Ottoman soldiers confiscated the property of the tribes, it was shared out among the victims.[34] That was not an effective method, however, as the operations caused further unrest in the countryside and usually failed to return the plundered property.[35] This inefficiency constituted another reason on the part of the empire which persuaded the officials to end the coercive policies and find a way of reconciling with the nomads. With the consequent decrease of hostilities in the 1860s and 1870s, in many cases, negotiation was used as the principal method to restore plundered property, involving tribal sheikhs as imperial collaborators. As such, sheikhs played a crucial role in the implementation of imperial justice. Through their mediation, the plundered property – or money and animals equal to its value – was returned to the injured party although a number of such cases could not be thus resolved. The process was smooth if the sheikh wielded sufficient authority over his subjects and enjoyed good relations with the government.[36] If not, it proved almost impossible to regain the plundered property.[37]

The provincialization of the tribes also increased tribal applications to the government for the restitution of the nomadic property raided by

[34] See, for example, BOA, A.MKT.MHM. 80/31, 19 Rebiulevvel 1272 [29 November 1855]; FO 195/727, Damascus, 31 December 1862; BOA, A.MKT. MVL. 54/20, 23 Ramazan 1268 [11 July 1852].

[35] See, for example, FO 195/204, Baghdad, 24 April 1842; FO 195/1047, Damascus, 8 December 1874.

[36] See, for example, FO 195/416, Aleppo, 3 February 1857; FO 195/803, Baghdad, 28 November 1866 and 12 December 1866; BOA, DH.MKT 1478/100, 5 Kanun-ı Evvel 1303 [18 December 1887]; FO 195/1647, Baghdad, 23 February 1889; FO 195/2024, Damascus, 30 June 1898; for an example from Hawran where all the property belonged to the Najdi tribes plundered by the Bani Sakhr were returned by the mediation of the latter's prominent sheikhs, see: Rogan, *Frontiers*, 68.

[37] See, for example, FO 195/394, Mosul, 3 January 1853; FO 195/416, Aleppo, 5 January 1857; FO 195/1647, Baghdad, 4 March 1889; FO 195/2055, Mosul, 11 January 1899.

the rival groups, which would normally be returned by the attacked party through organizing a counter-raid. In 1882, for instance, the most powerful Anizah sheikh Turki of Fid'an applied to the Aleppo government to file a complaint against the Shammar sheikhs, Faris Pasha and 'Asi, who raided the Anizah animals and killed two of his fellow tribesmen. He noted that his tribe would have to arrange a counter *gazve* to revenge and save the plundered animals if the government did not punish the suspects and compensate them for their losses. The Baghdad and Deir al-Zor governments, to which 'Asi and Faris, respectively, were annexed, were warned by the central government about the return of the Anizah's animals with the fear that the plundered party would attack the plunderers, leading to hostility between the two greatest tribes of the region that would almost completely destroy the regional order.[38]

The political aspect of such appeals, however, should be taken into account. Tribes sometimes complained about their rivals to the government prior to organizing a raid against them so as not to be on bad terms with the state. They tried to abdicate responsibility to the rival side and make them guilty in the eyes of the government.

Individual Crimes

As the introductory poem suggests, capturing the tribal individual suspects and keeping the guilty tribesmen imprisoned posed another major problem for the Ottoman government in the modern period, and seriously damaged its prestige. In one way or another, tribes could liberate their members from the government's clutches. It was relatively easy for the tribes to do that in the early years of the modernization when the Ottoman reinforcement in the desert and countryside was very sparse and the nomads were the absolute masters of the countryside. A clear instance of this was when Necib Pasha of Baghdad's *Mutesellim* arrested Sheikh Hawar of the Shammar's Sayigh tribes in 1845 and brought him to the city centre in irons as if the settlers of the Americas had captured a 'native red-Indian'. The Sayigh tribesmen attacked the convoy on the road and rescued their sheikh. Hawar was subsequently recaptured by an Anizah sheikh, the Shammar's archenemy, and delivered to

[38] BOA, Y.PRK.DH 2/53, 26 Temmuz 1299 [8 August 1882].

government officials.[39] Similarly, in 1848, Mahmud al-Nasr of the Anizah [Wuld 'Ali] escaped from Damascus where he was imprisoned. The troops in pursuit of him failed to capture the sheikh.[40] In yet another instance, in 1854, the Bedouin tribes of the Anizah besieged the towns of Homs and Hama, their chiefs having been imprisoned for the plunder of a caravan. The Bedouin seized some policemen as collateral for their chief. The British consul in Damascus reported that 'the government will be compelled to liberate him to prevent the destruction of the crops and the sacking of the villages'.[41] Although such incidents were rare in the Hamidian period due to the increase in regular troops and arrival at a compromise with the nomads, an effective judicial system was yet to be established: a famous Shammar bandit, Saw'an, who regularly attacked the villages of Mosul, was only caught and delivered to the court in 1902, a full seven years after his first crime.[42] The deteriorating relations between the Shammar and the government in Mosul which are explained in Chapter 5 definitely made an impact on the enforcement of the law and capture of the tribal suspects. The nomads of Mosul began again to act communally against the government and it became impossible for the officials to move towards the individualization of the crimes in the tribal community.[43]

It seems, on the other hand, that the reconciliation and augmentation of military power in the desert increased the imperial ability to carry out justice among the tribal communities and determine individual crimes, although punishment still remained an issue of negotiation. The capture of Farhan Pasha's cousin offers a good example of this: during the fighting between the Anizah and Shammar in 1884 near Baghdad, Farhan Pasha's cousin Naif killed one man with his bare hands. He was reported to the government and the Ottoman authorities sent gendarmes to summon Naif to come at once to Mosul in order to answer the charges brought against him.[44] Shortly afterwards, he was thrown into prison in Mosul awaiting trial for murder.[45] Such an

---

[39] FO 195/228, Mosul, 29 November 1845.
[40] The document does not detail how he took flight from the prison: BOA, A.MKT 118/69, 4 Rebiulahir 1264 [10 March 1848].
[41] FO 195/458, Damascus, 27 July 1854.
[42] BOA, DH.TMIK-M 138/19, 3 Kanun-ı Evvel 1318 [16 December 1902].
[43] For details on the state-Shammar conflict in Mosul, see: Chapter 5.
[44] FO 195/1479, Bagdad, 8 September 1884.
[45] FO 195/1509, Mosul, 31 December 1884.

operation would have caused great disturbance among the tribesmen in the early years of modernization and ruined the regional order. By 1884, however, the Ottomans had recruited sufficient troops to capture a Shammar sheikh as suspect while keeping his fellow tribesmen tranquil and respecting the imperial authority. Naif was most likely delivered to Ottoman justice by Farhan Pasha, the paramount sheikh, and released later from prison as a result of his negotiations in Baghdad. But the incident itself was sufficiently instructive to understand the changing influence of Ottoman justice among the tribesmen.

Another example from the Shammar demonstrates more clearly the increasing operational skills of the Ottoman justice system in the nomadic society: Humaidi Bey, the paramount sheikh, had been arrested by the Mosuli authorities on various charges in 1914. His trial, however, was postponed by the intervention of the central government due to opposition from Baghdad where it was argued that the sheikh's arrest would cause great unrest in the region.[46] The correspondence implies that Humaidi's arrest originated in a dispute between the government of Mosul and Baghdad rather than a real crime that required action. Although it is still a valuable case that the Shammar's paramount sheikh could be arrested by a local government, this, however, should not be exaggerated. Humaidi's special position must also be highlighted here for a more balanced picture of the official penetration among the Shammar: he was a graduate of the Tribal School [*Aşiret Mektebi*] in Istanbul and appointed by the government as the Shammar sheikh rather than having naturally gained legitimacy among the tribespeople, which largely made him dependent on the Ottoman government. This conferred an unusual authority to the government on Humaidi and constituted a primary reason for the incident. The official insistence on the arrest could still have caused reaction by the Shammar as highlighted by Baghdad's governor due to the tribal solidarity ties. A similar humiliation of Sheikh 'Asi, for instance, would incomparably cause greater disturbance as he enjoyed a widespread authority among the Shammar. His imprisonment in Mosul in 1904 had caused widespread disturbance among the Shammar.[47]

In spite of the increasing efficiency of imperial justice, there was still remarkable room for negotiations about the tribal suspects which may

---

[46] BOA, MV 191/1, 16 Temmuz 1330 [29 July 1914].
[47] CADN, Serie D, 166PO/D54/10, Damascus, 28 February 1905.

be unimaginable for a fully functioning modern state. Other cases demonstrate more clearly the negotiated character of Ottoman justice. During the negotiations between the Shammar of Deir al-Zor and Milli tribe to arrive at a peace in the late 1890s, the Shammar's sheikh Faris Pasha introduced a condition of the release of his cousin Ali Abd al-Razzaq, imprisoned in Diarbekir for an individual crime.[48] Although it had previously been decided by central government to try him according to usual court procedure,[49] the cabinet had to issue a subsequent decision of amnesty to release him to facilitate negotiations between the two parties.[50]

Justice as an Instrument and Excuse

The improvement of the operational capabilities of the Ottoman government was not the only concern of the Ottoman officials. Local government authorities at times instrumentalized the judicial mechanisms and used justice as a weapon to persuade the tribes to conform to their desired line of action. To that end, they were quite willing to punish an entire tribe for the crimes of one individual when they felt that the nomads were 'out of control'. Ottoman local officials would exaggerate crimes committed by the tribespeople if they wanted to influence the direction of imperial policies and to enforce a total punishment of entire tribes. Between 1911 and 1913, for instance, the Diarbekir and Deir al-Zor administrations regularly dispatched telegraphs to the central government in an attempt to enact a tribe-wide punishment of all the Shammar with the excuse that there had been a sharp increase in the number of crimes.[51] Similarly, the governor of Zor requested the start of military operations against the Shammar justifying it with the Shammar's robbing of a soldier. Proving the plurality of approaches to the tribes among government circles and representing a smoother negotiating attitude, the Mosul governor falsified the other statement and reported that the soldier had not in fact been robbed by the Shammar, but had rather lost a rucksack [*bohça*] in a hostelry [*han*] that had later been found by the innkeeper. Furthermore, the governor

---

[48] BOA, BEO 759/56899, 12 Mart 1312 [25 March 1896].
[49] BOA, DH.MKT 2053/18, 6 Şubat 1308 [19 February 1893].
[50] BOA, MV 89, 21 Cemaziyelevvel 1314 [29 October 1896].
[51] BOA, DH.SYS 26/2–8, 30 Mayıs 1327 [12 June 1911] and 15 Eylül 1328 [28 September 1912].

of Mosul supported the Shammar on the grounds that their loyalty to the government had improved with the establishment of the constitutional regime and any totalizing military action would cause them to rebel.[52] In spite of the high number of criminals among the Shammar,[53] he felt it would be more appropriate to punish Bedouin crimes individually.[54]

Such proposals might stem from a perspective aiming at indicating the government's strength to the tribes to increase tribal loyalty to the local governments as the nomads gained substantial independence from the state during the Shammar-Milli conflict and hostilities between the rival factions of the Shammar and the government in Mosul for the sheikhship. Another possibility might be the changing ideological directions of the Ottoman Empire with the 1908 Revolution. The method of the Diarbekir and Zor governors was inspired by the unionist ideology of the ruling CUP (Committee for Union and Progress) which aimed at establishing a monolithic and unitarian state, and destroying all local particularisms. Mosul's governor, however, advocated the politics of negotiation which was the norm between the state and the tribes from the 1870s. Central government did not change the traditional policy of tribes at all, which worked effectively to regulate state-tribes relations and followed the advice from Mosul.

Mediating Tribal Disputes

In a number of cases, imperial authorities played a key role in the solution of inter-tribal disputes although, in many other instances, their intervention only aggravated the situation mainly due to the provincialization of the nomads from the 1870s and complexification of the state-tribe relations. Although it solved the major questions between the state and the nomads and established a mutual understanding, as explained particularly in Chapter 5, the adoption of the politics of negotiation did not smoothen everything in all the places where the nomads migrated. The disputes between the neighbouring provinces with regard to the official treatment of the nomads continued

[52] BOA, DH.SYS 26/2–8, 29 Mayıs 1327 [11 June 1911] and 20 Eylül 1328 [3 October 1912].
[53] BOA, DH.SYS 26/2–8, 29 Mayıs 1327 [11 June 1911].
[54] BOA, DH.SYS 26/2–8, 24 Şubat 1328 [9 March 1913].

to exist and occasionally determine government actions. To put it differently, the interest relations of the various localities with the different tribal communities echoed themselves in their administrative and political decisions about them.

Such instances of the conflicting interests between the neighbouring provinces became visible when they interfered with the inter-tribal disputes to find a solution. Tribes regularly came into conflict with one another over issues such as blood feuds and pasture disputes. These posed a serious threat to the regional order as their hostilities did not take place in remote parts of the desert but rather spilled over into settled areas especially in the summer. In response to pressure from central government the local authorities had to arrange meetings to halt prolonged tribal conflicts. Their involvement as mediators, however, often made the problem more complicated and difficult to revolve since they were far from disinterested parties in the outcome. On many occasions, they took one party's side rather than 'objectively' trying to reach a solution. Although it served well for the termination of the state-tribe conflict and incorporation of the nomads into the imperial system, the provincialization of the tribal administration prevented any coherent imperial conflict resolution system to address inter-tribal disputes. As a result, a dispute might continue for several years and develop into an inter-provincial problem as in the case of the Shammar-Milli conflict. In such situations, peace between the two sides could only be achieved by the reconciliation of the two different factions, each of which made up of bureaucrats, elites and sheikhs.

The interest relations between the nomads and local governments worked positively and resulted in different outcomes when intra- or inter-tribal disputes took place among those who were provincialized in the same administrative unit: Deir al-Zor's government, for example, mediated between Faris Pasha's loyal subjects and the Anizah of Deir al-Zor to end their feud. They were reconciled several times by the Deir al-Zor government and written promises [*sened*] were obtained from their sheikhs to respect provincial peace and order. Both parties trusted the Zor officials and the mediation process progressed smoothly.[55] In another conflict between the Druze and the Bedouin in

---

[55] BOA, DH.ŞFR 214/78, 2 Eylül 1313 [15 September 1897]; BOA, DH.TMIK-M 39/39, 10 Eylül 1313 [23 September 1897] and 10 Şubat 1313 [23 February 1898].

Hawran, government troops were ordered to forcibly prevent the Druze from attacking the Bedouin territory, if the Druze did not engage fully with the mediating efforts of officials. The governor of Syria warned the local officers that the Druze had to recognize the government as the sole authority that could apply coercive methods leaving reconciliation under the government's arbitration as the only option for them.[56] Similar attitudes were adopted when Wuld 'Ali and Ruwalla tribes attacked other tribes and sedentary communities.[57] As Rogan observes, 'much emphasis on negotiation' and 'development of relations of trust' between the government and these communities contributed to these conflicts' resolution.[58]

Good relations with sheikhs did not always guarantee 'good solutions' to the inter-tribal disputes under the arbitration of the imperial institutions, however. Justice could easily be sacrificed by the 'official partisans' of the nomads in the provinces to satisfy their favourite sheikh on the pretext of maintaining good relations with them. An incident between the Mawali and Anizah Bedouin following the appointment of Jed'an as the Anizah's paramount sheikh in 1871 and the consolidation of good relations demonstrates how the Ottoman 'conflict resolvers' at times adopted partisan attitudes. During the conflict with the Anizah, four horsemen of the Mawali were apprehended and pursued by thirty horsemen who were Jed'an's fellow tribesmen, the Fid'an's pro-government paramount sheikh who prevailed, as detailed in Chapter 1, over Dahham as a result of long-lasting inter-tribal hostility. Two of the Mawali horsemen arrived at the camp of a local sedentary tribe, the Fardun, from where they were forcefully taken by the Ottoman regular troops to Aleppo and imprisoned there.[59] They were tried by the Ottoman court and acquitted of the charges brought against them. They were then sent to the local government with the recommendation that they should be released immediately. However, instead, they were shackled together with tight iron collars round their necks, and 'were sent under escort to their enemy, Jed'an' in spite of opposition from Hikmet Bey, the secretary general of the province.[60]

[56] MW 5/2, 18 Teşrin-i Sani 1311 [30 November 1895].
[57] See, for example, MW 5/9, 18 Nisan 1313 [1 May 1897]; 5/4, 5 Haziran 1313 [18 June 1897]; 5/5 17 Haziran 1314 [30 June 1898].
[58] Rogan, *Frontiers*, 68.   [59] FO 195/976, Aleppo, 31 May 1871.
[60] FO 195/976, Aleppo, 8 July 1871.

The most difficult cases to settle with regard to inter-tribal conflicts were those in which neighbouring provinces supported rival groups and tried to find solutions that would favour their tribal allies. Governors and sub-governors exploited imperial power to punish the rival party. The Tay-Shammar conflicts and the Shammar-Milli conflicts in the late 1890s and early 1900s indicate how various local administrations created obstacles to resolution and indeed contributed to the increase of the regional chaos. Hostilities commenced in the late 1890s between the Shammar of Deir al-Zor and Tay tribe of Diarbekir near Nusaybin. To stop the fighting between the two parties, the Shammar were driven back into their districts by the mule corps dispatched from Deir al-Zor.[61] It appears that the authorities did not actively intervene that year. The hostilities were halted the following year by means of coercive mediation by Diarbekir officials, and the Shammar were again forced to leave the pastures around Nusaybin.[62] This did not mark the end of aggression, however, as the Shammar attacked the Tay and plundered their property around the town in 1899.[63] In addition, Deir al-Zor's mule corps, charged with the collection of Shammar taxes in the Nusaybin district, tried to capture Abdurrahman Bey, the sheikh of the Tay, who escaped arrest by fleeing to the town centre. It was obviously an act of 'official partisanship' aimed at favouring the Shammar against the Tay as the former were annexed to the Deir and paid their tax to this *mutasarrıfate*.[64] Hostilities also continued into the following year: Faris Pasha, the sheikh of the Shammar, went to Nusaybin accompanied by the Deir al-Zor's mule corps with the excuse of collecting taxes from the Shammar around the town. Earlier, the Diarbekir authorities had warned the Zor government that the taxes ought to be collected within the boundaries of Deir al-Zor so as not to cause any conflict between the two sides. The authorities also alerted the Zor government that the Shammar were preparing an attack on the Tay, and advised that a battle could be prevented by the intervention of regular troops from

---

[61] BOA, DH.ŞFR 208/128, 30 Nisan 1313 [13 May 1897].
[62] BOA, DH.TMIK-M 53/39, 15 May 1314 [28 May 1898].
[63] BOA, DH.MKT 2219/8, 23 Haziran 1315 [6 July 1899].
[64] The incident was investigated and some of the local officials from Nusaybin were found responsible for the humiliation of Abdurrahman Bey's honour: BOA, DH.MKT 2220/13, 26 Haziran 1315 [9 July 1899].

Diarbekir.[65] Deir al-Zor's *mutasarrıf*, however, argued that their troops would stop any conflict between the tribes, while certain Nusaybin officials and elites who were ill-disposed towards the Tay sheikh incited the Shammar to attack the Tay.[66] A mediation committee was established, headed by Ali Muhsin Pasha, a general from Adana province. The two sides, accompanied by Diarbekir and Deir al-Zor officials, came together[67] and were reconciled in 1901 on specific instruction of the central government.[68]

As detailed in Chapter 5, the Shammar-Milli conflict spread from Diarbekir to Aleppo and Deir al-Zor, and continued from 1896 to 1908. As such, it is the longest case in the analysed period, and demonstrates clearly how Ottoman local authorities collaborated with tribal leaders and how they attempted to use conflict resolution to benefit their allies. Several commissions were established, made up of local elites, bureaucrats, army officers and tribal leaders from both Deir al-Zor and Diarbekir, to end the hostilities between the Shammar and the Milli tribes that had almost totally destroyed peace in the region.[69] However, the intervention of local authorities on behalf of their allies and, simultaneously, the tribal sheikhs' refusal to compromise, made resolution more difficult as the authorities' aim was always to have their allies emerge supreme.[70] Hostilities were only finally halted when the Ottoman government completely abandoned Ibrahim Pasha – Abdulhamid's favourite – and declared him an outlaw following the proclamation of the constitutional regime in 1908.

The obvious inference from these long-lasting hostilities and the involvement of the provincial administrations was that the Ottoman bureaucracy played a central part in the tribal conflict resolution processes following the reconciliation with the nomads around 1870. The Ottoman documents do not prove the availability of such instances in the early years of the Tanzimat when the nomads usually conflicted with the state, frequently refused it as the supreme authority and preferred to apply to the tribal customs. Provincialization of the

[65] BOA, DH.ŞFR 248/22, 26 May 1316 [8 June 1900].
[66] BOA, DH.ŞFR 248/45, 31 Mayıs 1316 [13 May 1900].
[67] BOA, DH.TMIK-M 90/52, 21 Haziran 1316 [5 July 1900].
[68] BOA, DH.TMIK-M 84/27, 29 Kanun-ı Sani 1316 [10 February 1901].
[69] See, for example, BOA, DH.ŞFR 178/80, 12 Ağustos 1311 [25 August 1895]; BOA, DH.TMIK-M 28/53, 27 Kanun-ı Sani 1313 [9 February 1898].
[70] For details, see: Chapter 1.

nomads and improvement in the interdependence of the parties on each other paved the way for the 'Ottomanization' of the dispute resolution processes among the nomads presumably to the detriment of the inter-tribal mechanisms explained in the previous sections.

Conclusion

Judicial process among the desert societies demonstrates both the autonomous and mutually dependent aspects of the Ottoman-Bedouin relations as well as the level of interaction between the sedentary and migrant societies. Contrary to the claims in the existing scholarship, the Ottoman government was closely involved in inter-tribal conflicts and the disputes between and among the sedentary and nomadic societies, although the Bedouin enjoyed complete freedom in the settlement of intra-tribal issues through their own judicial system. The imperial intervention in the tribal disputes, however, did not always mean 'an objective stance'. As the local officials who interfered with the disagreements or hostilities on behalf of the empire also had close relations with the tribal sheikhs annexed to their administrative units, they favoured their collaborators in the solution process and further exacerbated the situation. Finally, similar to other official decisions, justice was evidently a matter of negotiation between the government and the tribes as the initial verdicts and attitudes of the Ottoman courts were often revised during the subsequent discussions.

Conclusions

Until recently, the role of the nomads in world history had not been adequately assessed by the majority of historians who put 'civilization' or activities of sedentary and urban societies at the centre of their analyses and thus subtly sidelined migrant societies as if they lived in a lesser period of history. The nomads' significance to history was often considered only in terms of the devastating impact they had on the progress of civilizations such as China, India, Islam and Christianity. Many historians of previous generations exclude the nomads entirely as active agents of history. Even the empires they established were only deemed 'successful' inasmuch as they 'created fluid environments, suitable for travel and trade that allowed the peripheral civilizations to come into contact with one another'.[1] In such approaches, the nomads could not be regarded as the key players in laying the foundations for the likes of Venetian merchants, Arab mariners, Chinese inventors and European missionaries, all of whom took the limelight rather than the nomads. All such attitudes may be characterized as a version of 'subtle orientalism', preventing the nomads from occupying an important place in history.

These attitudes, however, have gradually changed with the new approach to studying the histories of world communities and this book has contributed to balancing the picture in favour of the nomads. In this study, I have adopted a different approach to the Ottoman-Arab nomadic societies, which I call 'equalized perspectives' to highlight the nomadic agency in the order of things during late Ottoman history. I deliberately abstain from calling my perspective 'bottom-up' or 'history from below' as it assumes a 'top' and 'bottom' – or a 'below' and an 'up' – which subtly situates the nomads in a lower position in a hierarchized classification. I do not think either nomads or the empire fit any of these positions: through the chapters, I explored the

---

[1] Di Cosmo, 'State Formation and Periodization', 4.

techniques and strategies used by the Ottomans to integrate the Bedouin nomads into the imperial system of governance and offered the hypothesis that what differentiated these techniques was the 'politics of negotiation' in an attempt to 'Ottomanize' the nomads. The preceding chapters have examined various aspects of Ottoman governance in the different regions of the Syrian, Iraqi and West Arabian deserts and along their frontier over a period spanning the Tanzimat state, the Hamidian regime and the Young Turk era together with the response of the nomads which made a considerable impact on the ultimate outcome and transformed the imperial policies according to the nomadic conditions. Therefore, it will not be an exaggeration to conclude that the politics of negotiation was successful in integrating the nomads into the Ottoman structure, while the coercive strategies served to alienate them from the empire. Although the Tanzimat state used coercive techniques and initially tried to subjugate the nomads to imperial authority, by the early 1870s such policies had been completely abandoned and a new conciliatory approach had been adopted.

The increase in Ottoman power in the Arab countryside and the desert frontier where the nomads had dominated at least since the end of the eighteenth century compelled the Anizah and Shammar groups to negotiate with the government and not to destroy the new governance strategy by raids and plunder. On the part of the empire, however, the inability of the Ottoman state to expand into and colonize the desert and the failure to subjugate the nomadic tribes were the principal reasons to adopt and maintain a politics of negotiation as well as the changes in imperial policies from 'idealism' to 'pragmatism', along with the inter-imperial global conditions which have been analysed through the chapters of this book.

This book has also demonstrated how difficult it is to construct a 'state-society', 'nomads-settlers' or 'sedentary-nomadic' dichotomy. As stated at the start of this chapter, such divisions put the sedentary communities and their political organization in a central position and introduce a 'subtle orientalism' to the view of the nomadic tribes by marginalizing their roles in history. Yet, the comparisons between the 'desert' and the 'sown' were primarily about determining the patterns of socio-politico-spatial interactions which included the contradictions and infirmities of local society and government, as well as the hierarchical problems of the imperial bureaucracy and cannot be fully grasped by a state-centric approach or with a view from the desert. State-centric or 'tribe-centric' perspectives have either evaluated the tribes as a 'headache' or described the empire as an 'oppressor', both of which prevent any light being shed on the interactions, and extent of integration, of the nomadic and settled societies.

Focusing on the agency of 'both sides' in this book when examining government policies has indicated how the behaviour and actions of Ottoman officials and their collaborators contributed to Bedouin unrest which was described in all the contemporaneous reports as the principal issue originating in the desert. Chapters 5 and 7 particularly have demonstrated how sporadic tribal attacks on and plunder of the sedentary communities cannot only be considered exclusively a consequence of nomadic lifestyle that made them difficult to control, but a rather more far-reaching question involving the entire imperial system, shaped by the factional struggles of various interest groups whose members included bureaucrats, local elites and sheikhs of the nomadic tribes.

Peaceful empire-tribe relations could be ensured by mutual respect for each other's interests and mutual concessions from their so-called initial positions. The empire had to recognize the tribal privileges in the imperial lands they used as pastures and allow them to contact the sedentary populations to sell their animals and their products, and buy what they needed such as clothes. On the other hand, the nomads had to accept imperial authority, abandon the practice of *khuwwa* and pay a certain tax to the government. They were, however, not transformed into ordinary Ottomans as they remained 'nomadic', were almost completely autonomous in their internal affairs and were immune from many services requested by the state such as compulsory military service.

Findings of this study also challenge the research into the nature of modernization of the Middle East in the nineteenth century. The dominant paradigm assumes social and administrative transformation took place through top-down methods at the initiative of idealist imperial officials during the Tanzimat, Hamidian and Young Turk eras. According to scholars, centralization of bureaucracy and expansion of the Ottoman rule over the local society with a *mission civilisatrice* remained the most noteworthy achievement and basic character of the modernization and 'Ottomanization' enterprise. In the case of the nomads, this book has instead highlighted the participation of local society in the reform processes and demonstrated how the initial projects of central government have undergone significant change with the 'intervention' of the target groups, that is, the nomads. This does not mean, however, that they ubiquitously rejected state projects that concerned them, but that their involvement enabled them to shape and adapt them in line with their interests. The warrior and migrant character of the Bedouin increased their influence and, as explained in Chapters 1 and 2, enabled them to resist Ottoman reformers when the latter's projects threatened tribal interests and lifestyle. Therefore, it will not be an exaggeration to conclude that the politics of negotiation was successful to integrate the nomads into the Ottoman socio-politico-spatial whole while the coercive strategies served its failure.

Reinstatement of the Ottoman administration in Deir al-Zor and the southern regions of the Damascus/Syria province took place in such a way that tribal consent and cooperation had to be secured by the imperial authorities for a successful end. Although some branches of the Anizah resisted these extensions of imperial power towards the desert, viewing it as a threat to their way of life and interests, others chose to cooperate with the government authorities. The Shammar offered no resistance to the establishment of the *mutasarrıfate*. When it became clear that the imperial expansion would be confined to providing security to the desert routes and the settlement of the small tribes around the Zor on the agricultural lands around the town, all of which had no deleterious impact on their migrant lifestyle, all the nomadic groups accepted the legitimacy of the *mutasarrıfate*, and their sheikhs cooperated with the Zor authorities to increase the government's efficacy in the desert. A similar process of cooperation took place between the imperial authority and the Ruwalla and Wuld 'Ali branches of the Anizah in southern Syria while the Ottoman expansion gained momentum in the 1870s. They both accepted the Ottoman expansionism and cooperated with the authorities to further extend imperial bureaucracy towards the south such as Ma'an and Kerak. Open resistance by the nomads would have made consolidation of the Ottoman state in these regions either impossible or very costly. As was the case in the Mosul and Jazira regions after the 1890s, disputes with the nomadic groups caused great regional disturbances in the countryside.

A negotiation process also took place regarding the obligations of nomads as imperial subjects and the privileges of the nomads acknowledged by the empire which constituted important aspects of the state-tribe conciliation. Taxes to be paid by nomadic groups were the thorniest issue negotiated by the government and tribal leaders. This book has demonstrated that the process differed starkly from the unidirectional forms of coercive taxation established by state modernization in the nineteenth century: it was not solely the government who decided what taxes to exact from tribal properties; instead, the tribesmen also wielded influence over the final amount and significantly moderated the amount to be paid. In addition, the sheikhs played an important role in the regular collection of the taxes of the tribes, escorting imperial officials among their fellow tribesmen in the desert. In return for this, sheikhs were rewarded with handsome salaries and a quarter share of the collected amount which constituted a sizeable amount for the provincial treasuries.

The tribes were also a major tax-collecting authority for the villages on the desert frontier, caravans crossing their territory and river boats navigating on the Euphrates and Tigris from 1840 onwards, when modern Ottoman bureaucracy started to function in the Arab lands with the Tanzimat reforms. Although the Bedouin continued to collect *khuwwa* until the 1860s, thereafter, a sophisticated deterrent process was introduced to prevent them from acting as a second taxation authority, with significant success. When the tribes disputed with the government as in case of the Mosuli Shammars in late 1890s, their sheikhs immediately restarted extracting *khuwwa* from the villages under imperial authority.

Last, but not least, justice was also negotiated between the authorities and the nomads: the imperial government never intervened in intra-tribal trials and gave full autonomy to the tribal courts. As the modernizer bureaucrats of a modernizing state, the Ottoman officials would definitely be willing to make Ottoman justice effective among the nomadic groups to enhance the imperial capacity of control among the desert communities. The authorities, however, played an important role in concluding inter-tribal disputes although, in many cases, their intervention only ignited the conflict and extended the scope and duration of the problem. The tribal influence, on the other hand, shaped the judicial processes as their sheikhs abstained from cooperation when their fellow tribesmen was arrested by the officials and a possibility of heavy punishment emerged. As the Chapter 7 has revealed, in light of the Sharia court records, tribesmen individually also applied to the imperial courts for justice in their disputes with the peasants, sedentary tribes and townspeople and vice versa.

The persistence of the tribal societies during the Ottoman reform age has had an influence over the later periods and contemporary politics in the Middle East. Although the drawing of borders, efforts by subsequent governments and development of the means of control somewhat limited nomadic migration and slightly changed their mobile lifestyle,[2] they are still among the major actors in contemporary politics. The destruction of the states of Syria and Iraq and civil war have increased the importance of secondary identities such as tribal allegiance, and this has played a major role in the creation of fighting groups. A Shammar sheikh, for instance, was selected as the first president of the newly established autonomous administration in northern Syria and another prominent Shammar figure, Ghazi Mashal Ajil al-Yawar, became the interim president of Iraq during the transition government in the post-Saddam era. The Bedouin also supported other opposition and resistance groups against the government in the regions of Hama and Deir al-Zor. It seems that they will retain their importance in the new structures of the Middle East, which are still evolving. The region is on the eve of a new era and a new process of political reconstruction will begin, sooner or later. Tribal agency will inevitably play a major role in the creation of the new Middle East and the drawing of new borders.

---

[2] For studies on tribal policies during the British and French Mandates in Syria, Transjordan and Iraq, see: Fletcher, *British Imperialism*; Neep, *Occupying Syria*, chapter 7; for a study on the transformation of the migrant lifestyle among the nomads, see: Chatty, *From Camel to Truck*.

Bibliography

Archival Sources

Başbakanlık Osmanlı Arşivi (BOA), Prime Ministry Ottoman Archives, Istanbul

A.AMD	Sadaret Amedi
A.MKT	Sadaret Mektubi
A.MKT.MHM	Sadaret Mektubi Mühimme
A.MKT.MVL	Sadaret Mektubi Meclis-i Vala
A.MKT.UM	Sadaret Mektubi Umumi
Ayniyat Defterleri	169, 172, 173, 174, 175, 176, 177, 178, 180, 181, 182, 187
BEO	Bab-ı Ali Evrak Odası
C.DH	Cevdet Dahiliye
C.ML	Cevdet Maliyet
DH.EUM.EMN	Dahiliye Emniyet-i Umumiye Emniyet Şubesi
DH.İ.UM	Dahiliye İdare-i Umumiye
DH.İD.	Dahiliye İrade Dahiliye
DH.MKT	Dahiliye Mektubi
DH.MUİ	Dahiliye Muhaberat-ı Umumiye
DH.SYS	Dahiliye Siyasi
DH.ŞFR	Dahiliye Şifre
DH.TMIK	Dahiliye Tesri-i Muamelat ve Islahat Komisyonu
HR.TO	Hariciye Tercüme Odası
İ.DH	İrade Dahiliye
İ.ML	İrade Maliye
İ.MMS	İrade Meclis-i Mahsusa
İ.MVL	İrade Meclis-i Vala
İ.ŞD	İrade Şura-yı Devlet
İD	İrade Dahiliye
MF.MKT	Maarif Mektubi
MV	Meclis-i Vükela
MVL	Meclis-i Vala
ŞD	Şura-yı Devlet
Y.MTV	Yıldız Mütenevvi Maruzat
Y.PRK.ASK	Yıldız Perakende Evrakı Askeri Maruzat

Sharia Court Records, ISAM, Istanbul

Hama: 53, 54, 55, 56, 57, 58, 59, 60, 61, 62, 63, 64
Urfa: 204, 205, 214
Mardin: 179, 244

The National Archives, London

FO 195
FO 78

Centre des Archives Diplomatiques, Nantes

Consular de France
Aleppo
Damas
Mosul
Baghad

Constantinople: Correspondence avec les Echelles
Aleppo
Damas
Mosul

Archives du Ministère des Affaires Etrangères, Paris

Correspondance Politique et Commercial

Department of Documentation and National Archives, Amman

Mirza Wasfi Collection

Published Material

Abu-Manneh, B. (1973), 'Sultan Abdülhamid II and the Sharifs of Mecca (1880–1900)', *Asian and African Studies*, 9/1:1–21.

Ali, A. A. (2014), 'Le role politique des tribus kurdes Milli et de la famille d'Ibrahim Pacha à l'ouest du Kurdistan et au nord du Bilad al-Cham (1878–1908)', in Jean-Claude David and Thierry Boissiere eds., *Alep et ses territoires: Fabrique et politique d'une ville, 1868–2011* (Beirut: Presse de l'ifpo): 67–81.

Ahmet Selahaddin Bey (2015), *Kabe Yollarında* (Istanbul: Dergah Yayınları).

Akalın, Ş. (1953), 'Mehmed Namık Paşa', *İÜEF Tarih Dergisi*, 7: 127–145.

Akarlı, E. D. (1986), 'Establishment of the Ma'an-Karak *Mutasarrıfiyya*, 1891–1894', *Dirasat*, 13/1: 27–42.

Akpınar, A. (1997), *Osmanlı Devleti'nde Aşiret Mektebi* (Istanbul: Selçuk Kitabevi).

Akyüz, F. (2015), 'Osmanlı Ordusunun Modernizasyonu: Irak ve Hicaz Ordusu Örneği (1848–1876)', Marmara University, unpublished PhD dissertation.

Al-Amr, S. M. (1974), *The Hijaz under Ottoman Rule, 1869–1914* (Riyadh: Riyadh University Press).

Al-Rasheed, M. (1997), *Politics in an Arabian Oasis: The Rashidis of Saudi Arabia* (London: I. B. Tauris).

Ali Suad (2015), *Seyahatlerim* (Istanbul: Taş Mektep Yayıncılık).

Amara, A. (2016), 'Governing Property: The Politics of Ottoman Land Law and State Making in Southern Palestine, 1850–1917', New York University, unpublished PhD dissertation.

Artuç, N. (2010), 'Osmanlı Devleti'nin Son Dönem Irak Politikası'na Bir Örnek: Nazım Paşa'nın Bağdat Valiliği (25 Kasım 1909–15 Mart 1911)', *Belleten*, 271: 833–870.

Auler Paşa (2017), *Hicaz Demiryolu İnşa Edilirken-I: Şam-Maan Hattı* (Istanbul: İş Bankası Kültür Yayınları).

Babanzade, İ. H. (2002), *Irak Mektupları* (Istanbul: Büke Yayınları).

Barakat, N. (2015), 'An Empty Land? Nomads and Property in Hamidian Syria', University of California-Berkeley, unpublished PhD dissertation.

    (2015) 'Marginal Actors? The Role of Bedouin in the Ottoman Administration of Animals as Property in the District of Salt, 1870–1912', *Journal of the Economic and Social History of the Orient*, 58: 105–134.

Barbir, K. (2014), *Ottoman Rule in Damascus 1708–1758* (Princeton: Princeton University Library).

Barker, J. (2005 [1876]), *Syria and Egypt under the Last Five Sultans of Turkey I* (London: Elibron Classics).

Barout, M. J. (2014), 'La renaissance de la Jéziré: Deir ez-Zor ottomane, de la désertion à la reconstruction', in Jean-Claude David and Thierry Boissiére, eds., *Alep et ses territoires, Fabrique et politique d'une ville, 1868–2011* (Damascus and Beirut: Presses de l'ifpo): 107–115.

Barthorp M. and D. N. Anderson (1996), *The Frontier Ablaze: The North-West Frontier Rising, 1897–98* (London: Windrow & Greene).

Batatu, H. (1978), *The Old Social Classes and the Revolutionary Movement in Iraq* (Princeton: Princeton University Press).

Bell, G. (1924), *Amurath to Amurath* (London: Macmillan).

Blunt, A. (1968[1879]), *Bedouin Tribes of Euphrates I–II* (London: Frank Cass).

Bostan, İ. (1986), 'Zor Sancağı'nın İmar ve İskanıyla İlgili Üç Layiha', *Osmanlı Araştırmaları*, 4: 163–221.

Büssow, J. (2012), 'Bedouin Historiography in the Making: An Indigenous History of the Hasana Tribe in Syria', in Laila Prager, ed., *Nomadismus in der 'Alten Welt': Formen der Reprasentation in Vergangenheit und Gegenwart* (Berlin: Lite Verlag): 160–183.

Ceylan, E. (2014), 'Abdurrahman Nureddin Paşa'nın Osmanlı Irak'ına Dair 1880 Tarihli Bir Layihası Üzerine', *Divan Disiplinlerarası Çalışmalar Dergisi*, 37/2: 85–115.

(2011), *Ottoman Origins of Modern Iraq: Political Reform, Modernization and Development in the Nineteenth-Century Middle East* (London: I. B. Tauris).

Chatty, D. (2010), 'The Bedouin in Contemporary Syria: The Persistence of Tribal Authority and Control', *Middle East Journal*, 64/1: 29–49.

(2013), *From Camel to Truck: The Bedouin in the Middle East* (Cambridge: White Horse Press).

Çakır, C. (2013), 'Bir Tanzimat Bürokrat ve Düşünürü Abdüllatif Suphi Paşa ve Islahat Layihası', in Feridun M. Emecen, İshak Keskin and Ali Ahmetbeyoğlu, eds., *Osmanlı'nın İzinde: Prof. Dr. Mehmet İpşirli Armağanı I* (Istanbul: Timaş Yayınları): 423–449.

Çarıklı, T. (2005), *Babam Hacim Muhittin Çarıklı*, ed. Y. Hakan Erdem (Istanbul: Boğaziçi Üniversitesi Yayınları).

Çetinsaya, G. (2006), *Ottoman Administration of Iraq*, (London: Routledge).

Çiçek, M. T. (2017), 'The Tribal Partners of Empire in Arabia: The Ottomans and the Rashidis of Najd, 1880–1918', *New Perspectives on Turkey*, 56: 105–130.

(2014), *War and State Formation in Syria: Cemal Paşa's Governorate During World War I* (London: Routledge).

Daumas Lieutenant-Colonel (1845), *Le Sahara Algerien* (Paris).

Davenport H. (1909), *My Quest of the Arab Horse* (New York: B. W. Dodge).

Davison, R. (1990), 'The Advent of the Electric Telegraph in the Ottoman Empire', in Roderic Davison, ed., *Essays in Ottoman and Turkish History, 1774–1923* (Austin: University of Texas Press).

Dawn, C. (2013), *From Camel to Truck: The Bedouin in the Middle East* (Cambridge: White Horse Press).

Dean, M. (2010), *Governmentality, Power and Rule in Modern Society* (London: Sage).

De Perthuis, C. (1896), *Le désert de Syrie et l'Euphrate* (Saint-Didier: Editions l'Escalier).

Deringil, S. (2003), '"They Live in a State of Nomadism and Savagery": The Late Ottoman Empire and the Post-Colonial Debate', *Comparative Studies in Society and History*, 45/2: 311–342.

Di Cosmo, N. (1999), 'State Formation and Periodization in Inner Asian History', *Journal of World History* 10/1: 1–40.

Diyarbekir Vilayet Salnamesi, 1882 (H. 1302).

Diyarbekir Vilayet Salnamesi, 1884–1885 (H. 1302).

Dolbee, S. (2017), 'The Locust and the Starling: People, Insects, and Disease in the Late Ottoman Jazira and after, 1860–1940', New York University, unpublished PhD dissertation.

Douwes, D. (2000), *Ottomans in Syria: A History of Justice and Oppression* (London: I. B. Tauris).

Emrence, C. (2012), *Remapping the Ottoman Middle East: Modernity, Imperial Bureaucracy and the Islamic State* (London: I. B. Tauris).

Fattah, H. and C. Badem (2013), 'The Sultan and the Rebel: Sa'dun al-Mansur's Revolt in the Muntafiq, c. 1891–1911', *International Journal of Middle East Studies* 45: 677–693.

Fattah, H. (1997), *The Politics of Regional Trade in Iraq, Arabia and the Gulf 1745–1900* (New York: SUNY Press).

Fletcher, R. (2015), *British Imperialism and 'The Tribal Question': Desert Administration and Nomadic Societies in the Middle East, 1919–1936* (Oxford: Oxford University Press).

Fortna, B. (2002), *Imperial Classroom: Islam, the State and Education in the Late Ottoman Empire* (Oxford: Oxford University Press).

(2008), 'The Reign of Abdülhamid II', in *The Cambridge History of Turkey*, vol. 4, Reşat Kasaba, ed. (Cambridge: Cambridge University Press).

Foucault, M. (2010), *Security, Territory, Population* (London: Palgrave).

Fraser, D. (1909), *The Shortcut to India: The Record of a Journey along the Baghdad Railway* (London: Blackwood & Sons).

Gedikli, F. (1999), 'Midhat Paşa'nın Suriye Layihası', *Divan: İlmi Araştırmalar* 7: 169–189.

Glubb, J. B. (1948), *The Story of the Arab Legion* (London: Hodder and Stoughton).

Gordon, C. (1991), 'Governmental Rationality: An Introduction', in Graham Burchell, Colin Gordon and Peter Miller, eds., *The Foucault Effect: Studies in Governmentality* (Chicago: University of Chicago Press).

Gölbaşı, E. (2011), '19. yüzyıl Osmanlı emperyal siyaseti ve Osmanlı tarihyazımında kolonyal perspektifler', *Tarih ve Toplum. Yeni Yaklaşımlar*, 13: 199–222.

Gülsoy, U. (1994), 'Hicaz Demiryolu', Marmara University, unpublished PhD thesis.

Günay S. (2006), *Bizim Kimlere Bırakıp Gidiyorsun Türk? Suriye ve Filistin Anıları* (Istanbul: İş Bankası Yayınları).

Günday, A. F. (2011), *İki Devir Bir İnsan*, ed. Süleyman Beyoğlu (Istanbul: Bengi Yayınları).

Haj, S. (1991), 'The Problems of Tribalism: The Case of Nineteenth-Century Iraqi History', *Social History*, 16/1: 45–58.

Hanioğlu, M. Ş. (2001), *Preparation for a Revolution: The Young Turks, 1902–1908* (Oxford: Oxford University Press).

Hannoyer, J. (1989–1990), 'Politique des notables en Syrie, la naissance d'une ville (Deir ez-Zor, 1850–1921)', *Bulletin d'Etudes Orientales*, 41–42: 113–142.

Hathaway J. (2008), *The Arab Lands under Ottoman Rule: 1516–1800* (London: Pearson).

Hourani, A. (1993), 'Ottoman Reform and the Politics of Notables', in A. Hourani, P. S. Khoury and M. C. Wilson, eds., *The Modern Middle East: A Reader* (Berkeley: University of California Press): 83–110.

Hut, D. (2006), 'Musul Vilayeti'nin İdari, İktisadi ve Sosyal Yapısı (1864–1909)', Marmara University, unpublished PhD dissertation.

Husain, F. (2018), 'The Tigris-Euphrates Basin under Early Modern Ottoman Rule, c. 1534–1830', Georgetown University, unpublished PhD dissertation.

İnalcık H. and M. Seyitdanlıoğlu (2019), *Tanzimat: Değişim Sürecinde Osmanlı İmparatorluğu* (Istanbul: İş Bankası Yayınları).

Jabbur, J. S. (1995), *The Bedouin and the Desert: Aspects of Nomadic Life in the Arab East* (Albany: SUNY Press).

Kappeler, A. (2001), *The Russian Empire* (London: Longman).

Karal, E. Z. (1940), 'Zarif Paşa'nın Hatıratı, 1816–1862', *Belleten* 4/16: 443–494.

Kahraman Ş. (2016), '214 Nolu Urfa Şer'iyye Sicilinin (H.1287-H.1288/ M.1870–1871) 1–163. Sayfaları Arası Transkripsiyon ve Değerlendirilmesi', Harran University, unpublished MA thesis.

Kenanoğlu, M. M. (2007), 'Nizamiye Mahkemeleri', *Diyanet İslam Ansiklopedisi*, Vol. 33, 185–188.

Khidr, T. H. M. (2002), *Tarikh al-Muhammad al-Jarba wa Qabilat Shammar al-Arabiyya fi Iqlim Najd wa al-Jazira* (Beirut: Dar al-Arabiyya li al-Mawsua'at).

Khoury, P. S. (1983), *Urban Notables and Arab Nationalism: The Politics of Damascus* (Cambridge: Cambridge University Press).

Kırmızı, A. (2012), 'Going Round the Province for Progress and Prosperity: Inspection Tours and Reports by Late Ottoman Governors', *Studies in Travel Writing*, 16/4: 387–401.

(2017), *Abdülhamid'in Valileri: Osmanlı Vilayet İdaresi* (Istanbul: Klasik Yayınları).

Klein, J. (2011), *The Margins of Empire: Kurdish Militias in Ottoman Tribal Zone* (Stanford: Stanford University Press).

Korkmaz, A. (2005), 'Midhat Paşa'nın Bağdat Valiliği, 1869–1872', Istanbul University, unpublished PhD dissertation.

Köksal, Y. (2006), 'Coercion and Mediation: Centralization and Sedentarization of Tribes in the Ottoman Empire', *Middle Eastern Studies* 42/2: 469–491.

Kühn, T. (2011), *Empire, Islam and Politics of Difference* (Leiden: Brill).

Lewis, N. (1987), *Nomads and Settlers in Syria and Jordan, 1800–1980* (Cambridge: Cambridge University Press).

(2000), 'The Syrian Steppe during the Last Century of Ottoman Rule: Hawran and Palmyrena', in Martha Mundy and Basim Musallam, eds., *The Transformation of Nomadic Society in the Arab East* (Cambridge: Cambridge University Press), 33–44.

Ma'oz, M. (1968), *Ottoman Reform in Syria and Palestine* (Oxford: Oxford University Press).

Makdisi, U. (2002), 'Ottoman Orientalism', *The American Historical Review*, 107/3: 768–796.

Mardin, Ş. (2015), *Jön Türklerin Siyasi Fikirleri* (Istanbul:İletişim).

Marufoğlu, S. (1998), *Osmanlı Döneminde Kuzey Irak, 1831–1914* (Istanbul: Eren Yayınları).

McDougall, J. (2017), *A History of Algeria* (Cambridge: Cambridge University Press).

Mehmed Hurşid Paşa (1997), *Seyahatname-i Hudud* (Istanbul: Simurg).

Mills, W. H. (1897), *The Pathan Revolt in North West India* (Lahore: Civil and Military Gazette Press).

Minawi, M. (2015), 'Beyond Rhetoric: Reassessing Bedouin-Ottoman Relations along the Route of the Hijaz Telegraph Line at the End of the Nineteenth Century', *Journal of Economic and Social History of the Orient* 58: 75–104.

(2016), *The Ottoman Scramble for Africa: Empire and Diplomacy in the Sahara and the Hijaz* (Stanford: Stanford University Press).

Musil, A. (1928), *The Manners and Customs of the Rwala Bedouins* (New York: American Geographical Society).

Müller, V. (1931), *En Syrie avec les Bedouins: les Tribus du Desert* (Paris: Libraire Ernest Leroux).

Neep, D. (2012), *Occupying Syria under the French Mandate: Insurgency, Space and State Formation* (Cambridge: Cambridge University Press).

Osterhammel, J. (2014), *The Transformation of the World: A Global History of the Nineteenth Century* (Princeton and Oxford: Princeton University Press).

Öğüt, T. (2002), 'Birecik Sancağı'nda İktisadi ve Sosyal Yapı', Istanbul University, unpublished PhD dissertation.

Özbek, N. (2015), *İmparatorluğun Bedeli: Osmanlı'da Vergi, Siyaset ve Toplumsal Adalet (1839–1908)* (Istanbul: Boğaziçi Üniversitesi Yayınları).

Paton, A. A. (2005 [1844]), *The Modern Syrians or Native Society in Damascus, Aleppo and the Mountains of the Druses* (London, Elibron Classics).

Rogan, E. L. (1996), 'Abdülhamid II's School for Tribes (1892–1907)', *International Journal of Middle East Studies*, 28: 83–107.

(1998), 'Instant Communication: The Impact of the Telegraph in Ottoman Syria', in T. Philipp and B. Schaebler, eds., *The Syrian Lands: The Processes of Integration and Fragmentation-Bilad al-Sham from the 18th to the 20th Century* (Stuttgart: Franz Steiner): 113–128.

(2002), *Frontiers of the State in the Late Ottoman Empire: Transjordan, 1850–1921* (Cambridge: Cambridge University Press).

Rubin, A. (2011), *Ottoman Nizamiye Courts: Law and Modernity* (New York: Palgrave Macmillan).

Saliba, N. A. (1971), 'Wilayat Suriyya, 1876–1909', University of Michigan, unpublished PhD dissertation.

Salman, K. A. (1992), 'The Ottoman and British Policies towards the Iraqi Tribes, 1831–1920', University of Utah, unpublished PhD dissertation.

Saydam A. (2015), 'Tanzimat Devrinde Halep ve Musul Dolaylarında Aşiretlerin Yol Açtıkları Asayiş Problemleri', *Ondokuz Mayıs Üniversitesi Eğitim Fakültesi Dergisi*, 8/1: 243–256.

Sayigh, F. (1991), *Le desert et la gloire : Les Memoires d'un agent syrien de Napoleon*, Joseph Chelhod trans. (Paris: Gallimard).

Shields, S. D. (2000), *Mosul before Iraq: Like Bees Making Five-Sided Cells* (New York: SUNY Press).

Simner, M. (2016), *Pathan Rising-Jihad on the North West Frontier of India, 1897–1898* (London: Fonthill).

Söylemezoğlu, S. Ş. (2012), *Hicaz Seyahatnamesi* (Istanbul: İz Yayıncılık).

Tandoğan, M. (2018), *Büyük Sahra'da Son Osmanlı Tebaası Tevarikler* (Ankara: TTK Basımevi).

Tepeyran, E. H. (1998), *Hatıralar* (Istanbul: Pera Turizm ve Ticaret).

Tozlu, S. (2004), 'Bağdat-Halep İskenderun Yoluyla İstanbul'a Bir Seyahat', in *Birinci Ortadoğu Semineri* (Elazığ: Fırat Üniversitesi Yayınları).

Ussher, J. (1865), *A Journey from London to Persepolis* (London: Hurst and Blackett).

Wallach, J. (1999), *The Desert Queen* (London: Anchor Books).

Wellsted, J. R. (1840), *Travels to the City of the Caliphs, along the Shores of the Persian Gulf and Mediterranean* (London: Henry Colburn).

Winter, S. (2019), 'Alep et l'émirat du désert (*çöl beyliği*) au XVIIe-XVIIIe siècle', in Stefan Winter and Mafalda Ade, eds., *Aleppo and its Hinterland in the Ottoman Period/Alep et sa province à l'époque ottomane* (Leiden: Brill), 86–108.

Zakariyya, A. W. (1983), *Asha'ir al-Sham* (Damascus: Dar al-Fikr).

(2008), *Rihlatu ila al-Furat wa maqalat al-Ukhra* (Damascus: Daru Raslan).

Zurcher, M. (2016), *La pacification et l'organisation de la Kabilie Orientale de 1838 à 1870* (Saint-Denis: Editions Bouchene).

Index

Printed by Printforce, United Kingdom